AF328898

GEOLOGICAL SURVEY OF MICHIGAN.

UPPER PENINSULA

1869-1873

VOL. II.

APPENDICES TO PART I., VOL. I.—IRON-BEARING ROCKS (ECONOMIC)

BY

T. B. BROOKS

PUBLISHED BY AUTHORITY OF THE LEGISLATURE OF MICHIGAN

UNDER THE DIRECTION OF THE

BOARD OF GEOLOGICAL SURVEY

NEW YORK
JULIUS BIEN
1873

TABLE OF CONTENTS.

APPENDIX A.

LITHOLOGY.

BY

ALEXIS A. JULIEN.

T. B. Brooks,

State Geologist in Charge of Survey of Lake Superior Iron Region:

Sir—I hereby submit my preliminary report on the five hundred specimens from the Iron Region, selected by you from your large collection to represent the lithological character of the rocks and ores of the Huronian formation in that district.

The subject of their lithology has already been briefly and popularly treated, for the benefit of the explorer and miner, in Chapter III. of your own report.*

However, you have desired me to make—*first*, a detailed description of the same specimens ; *secondly*, a series of provisional names ; and *finally*, such a lithological examination and classification as time should permit.

The great number of the specimens—the variety and frequently novel character of the rocks they represent—their commonly fine-grained texture—and the short time at my disposal for this investigation, have effectually precluded my report from any claim to being exhaustive. So that although over fifty microscopic sections have been made and hastily examined of all the principal fine-grained varieties, and this essential branch of the work has not been neglected, nor such chemical examinations as seemed absolutely necessary to confirm the most doubtful results ; all these have been only begun, and no mention will be made of them in this report. I make this omission the more readily, on account of the careful microscopic investigation, on another collection, reported in Appendix C, by Mr. Charles E. Wright, in association with Profs. Kreischer and Von Cotta, of Freiburg ; all interested in this subject may refer to that report, in which are given, I believe, the

---

* Vol. I., page 82.

first published results on microscopic sections of Lake Superior rocks. With most of the compact rocks I have been compelled to rely mostly on their coarser transition varieties, observed in the field during a visit to that region in the summer of 1866. Consequently the careful examination of the microscopic texture of the finer-grained crystalline varieties: the identification of the minerals, which I will provisionally class under the names Amphibole, Chlorite, Mica, and Feldspar: the determination of the exact nature and relations of the remarkable processes of alteration to which these minerals have been subjected, and of the interesting series of transition-rocks, which have been the result: and the whole subject of the origin both of the rocks and ores, must be deferred to some other time and channel.

My present aim, therefore, in accordance with your expressed desire, is but a provisional one, viz., to give a somewhat popular description of such characteristics of the common varieties as may be easily discerned (with a very few exceptions) in the field, with the use of such simple means as a pocket lens (loupe), a knife, and a magnet: and also to propose a temporary nomenclature and classification for the present use of your Report.

The descriptions begin with that characteristic of the fresh fracture —color—which is usually most quickly apparent: and then proceed with the general hardness, texture, and structure of the rock: its constituent minerals, their physical characteristics, and their proportion (approximately estimated by the eye in *tenths*): the fracture, streak (in a fine-grained rock), and magnetic character: the joints, seams, and veins: and the nature of the weathered surface. Where the depth of weathering is not stated, a merely superficial stain is meant. I have made no determinations of specific gravity, on account of the full series given in your Report. In regard to nomenclature, although anxious to avoid novelty in the present inchoate state of my work and of American Lithology, I venture to adopt entirely and throughout the changes in mineralogical nomenclature proposed by Prof. J. D. Dana (*e.g.* Amphibole in place of Hornblende, Sphalerite in place of Blende, etc.); and also his suggestion*—the necessity of which, and of its immediate

---

* System of Mineralogy, page xxxiv.

adoption, I believe every lithologist will approve,—that the termination *yte* should be substituted for *ite*, to distinguish rocks from minerals, with the exception of granite and syenite (and, I also understand, dolomite). The result of this last change is the introduction into my report of the unfamiliar terminations of Quartzyte, Novaculyte, Argillyte, Dioryte, Amphibolyte, and Aphanyte. But, as generally happens in working up a new region, I have also been reluctantly compelled, even for my temporary object, to propose some slight modifications of names long accepted (*e.g.* Anthophyllite-Schist, Feldspathic Argillyte, Micaceous Greenstone-Schist, etc.), for the reasons stated in the Introduction. The choice and use of my compound names, chiefly schists, have been founded on the following principles, which I believe to be generally admitted, though not always consistently adhered to. *First*—The generic name of the schistose form of a rock possessing a distinctive name, or of a rock chiefly composed (more than half) of any one mineral, is formed by simply prefixing the name of the rock or of the mineral to the word "schist" (*e.g.* Dioryte-Schist, not Diorytic Schist, and Chlorite-Schist, not Chloritic Schist). *Secondly*—The name of a variety, produced by a large proportion (less than half) of another mineral, is distinguished by an adjective termination (*e.g.* Chloritic Dioryte-Schist); but when the chief constituents of the rock have not been certainly made out, but one mineral imparts a distinctive character, then the name of the latter is prefixed, with an adjective termination (*e.g.* Chloritic Schist, Talcose Schist, etc., where the chief constituent may be Feldspar, Quartz, or an Argillyte).

In regard to classification, I have adopted in the main, as at least best adapted to my present purpose, that system employed in the works on Petrography, etc., by Zirkel and Credner, rather than those of other authors.*

---

* The following are works on Lithology, etc., to which references are made in this report merely by the author's name :

Bischof, G. Chemical and Physical Geology. 3 vols. London, 1858.

Blum, J. R. Handbuch der Lithologie oder Gesteinlehre. Erlangen, 1860.

Cotta, B. Von. Rocks classified and described. Lawrence's edition. London, 1866.

My chief departures from that system have been in grouping Amphibolyte and Serpentine under Dioryte, Hornblende-Schist under Hornblende-Gneiss, the Greenstone-Ashes together with Argillyte, and a series of peculiar rocks (made up of Feldspar and Chlorite) under Dioryte, because, in each of these cases, the first-mentioned is certainly a transition form of the second.

The object of the examination has been purely the lithological character of the Huronian rocks ; but about fifty specimens are also included from a few classes of the Laurentian rocks, especially the Gneisses and Mica-Slates, which happen to be closely allied in composition to the Huronian rocks, and intimately associated with them on the borders of the Marquette region. Specimens are also described which represent a few boulders from unknown beds which may yet be discovered in the course of exploration.

The numbers, from 1 to 100, refer to the series of which many duplicates, almost complete, have been widely distributed, of the specimens of which only brief descriptions were therefore considered necessary, and of which a table is given in Appendix B.

The numbers, 101 to 360, refer to the descriptions given in this report, and are adopted throughout the chapter above mentioned. The specimens were furnished me from your private collection of over 2,000 specimens, which have an independent numbering ; but when any of these, not included in the above 360, shall be referred to, they are distinguished by numbers which commence above 600. About thirty additional full descriptions have been omitted, and a large number of others greatly condensed, in order to abbreviate this Report. To prevent confusion, and also to facilitate reference

---

Credner, H. Elemente der Geologie. Leipzig, 1872.
    "   "   Article.—"Die Vorsilurischen Gebilde der ' Oberen Halbinsel von Michigan'in Nord-Amerika." Zeits. der D. geol. Gesell., XXI. Band, 1869.
Dana, J. D. System of Mineralogy. New York, 1869.
Foster and Whitney. Report on the Geology of the L. S. Land District. Part II. Washington, 1851.
Jukes, J. B. Student's Manual of Geology. Edinburgh, 1862.
Kenngott, A. Elemente der Petrographie. Leipzig, 1868.
Naumann. Lehrbuch der Geognosie. Vol. II. Leipzig, 1862.
Senft, F. Lehrbuch der Mineralien und Felsartenkunde. Jena, 1869.
Zirkel, F. Lehrbuch der Petrographie. 2 vols. Bonn, 1866.

to any desirous to consult your collection, comparative tables of both series of numbers are also appended.

Finally, I would call your attention to the first organic remains yet discovered in the formation—the imperfect fucoidal impressions which I have observed, in the course of this examination, in the Carbonaceous Shale (No. 251) and in Hematite-Ochre (No. 67). They will be hereafter submitted to some competent authority for examination. My acknowledgments are due, for the loan of specimens, to Prof. J. S. Newberry, of the School of Mines, Columbia College, and Prof. M. W. Harrington, of the University of Michigan.

I remain, very respectfully,

Your obedient servant,

ALEXIS A. JULIEN.

SCHOOL OF MINES, COLUMBIA COLLEGE,
NEW YORK, July, 1873.

COMPARATIVE TABLES OF NUMBERS.

I.*

Number.	Specimen.	Name.
101	984	Ferruginous Crystalline Limestone.
102	1231	White Saccharoidal Dolomite-Marble.
103	1233	Grayish Saccharoidal Dolomite-Marble.
104	877	Fine-grained Greenish-white Dolomite.
105	1242	Fine-grained Gray Dolomite-Marble.
106	·795	Coarse Red Dolomite.
107	796	Banded Dolomite-Marble.
108	797	Rosy Siliceous Dolomite.
109	798	Mottled Dolomite-Marble.
110	799	Talco-Siliceous Dolomite.
111	800 } 808	Rosy Talcose Dolomite.
112	809	Mottled Dolomite.
113	811	Rosy Talcose Dolomite.
114	688	Black Quartz-Conglomerate.
115	715	Gray Quartz-Conglomerate.
116	716	Mottled Quartz-Conglomerate.
117	717	Chloritic Quartz-Conglomerate.
118	718 719 720 721 727 }	Greenish Quartz-Conglomerate.

---

* The numbers in the first column are those attached to the descriptions, merely for their arrangement in this report ; those from 1 to 100 are given in Appendix B. The numbers in the second column are those attached to the specimens from the collection of T. B. Brooks ; a few loaned from the collection of the School of Mines, Columbia College, by the kindness of Prof. J. S. Newberry, have been designated by the letter "S", and a few, from my own collection, by the letter "J".

Number.	Specimen.	Name.
119	J.	Kaolinic Hematite-Breccia.
120	875	Red Jasper-Conglomerate.
121	878	Brown Jasper-Conglomerate.
122	1085	Micaceous Conglomerate-Schist.
123	693	Quartzose Feldspar-Breccia.
124	1487	Schistose Jasper-Breccia.
125	1490	Drusy Jasper-Breccia.
126	990	Grayish-white Quartzyte.
127	991	Conglomeritic Feldspathic Quartz:
128	803	Reddish-brown Quartzyte.
129	1251	Light-brown Quartzyte.
130	1471 1472	Flesh-colored Quartzyte.
131	907 909 1243	Smoky-gray Quartzyte.
132	1459	Greenish-gray Quartzyte.
133	812	Rosy-gray Quartzyte.
134	816	Slaty-gray Quartzyte.
135	1473	Brownish-gray Quartzyte.
136	1476	Bluish-gray Quartzyte.
137	901	Manganiferous Smoky Quartzyte.
138	939 977	Feldspathic Quartzyte.
139	1478	Jaspery Quartzyte.
140	1479	Magnetic Jaspery Quartzyte.
141	1477	Chalcedonic Quartzyte.
142	1225	Reddish Hematitic Quartzyte.
143	993	Ochrey Cellular Quartzyte.
144	902	Banded Quartz-Schist.
145	903	Banded Quartz-Schist.
146	1232	Greenish Quartz-Schist.
147	1092	Chloritic Quartz-Schist.
148	801 802	Calcareous Quartz-Schist.
149	891	Opaline Quartz-Schist.
150	J.	Talcose Quartz-Schist.
151	734	Magnetic Quartz-Schist.

Number.	Specimen.	Name.
152	740	Magnetic Quartz-Schist.
153	999	Magnetic Quartz-Schist.
154	1227	Hematitic Quartz-Schist.
155	1236	Hematitic Quartz-Schist.
156	994	Ferruginous Quartz-Schist.
157	883	Limonitic Quartz-Schist.
158	1484, 1493, 1499, 1500	Green Banded Siliceous Schist.
159	1508	Argillaceous Siliceous Slate.
160	806	Greenish Siliceous Schist (Novaculyte).
161	804, 805, 807	Greenish-drab Siliceous Slate (Novaculyte).
162	1509	Banded Talco-Siliceous Slate.
163	1458	Ferruginous Siliceous Slate.
164	1503	Ferruginous Siliceous Slate.
165	747	Hematitic Siliceous Schist.
166	1485	Banded Jasper-Schist.
167	1486	Banded Jasper-Schist.
168	1491, 1492	Banded Jasper-Slate.
169	1510	Banded Jasper-Slate.
170	1506	Green Jasper-Slate.
171	690	Magnetic Jasper-Slate.
172	1480	Hematitic Jasper-Schist.
173	1488	Hematitic Jasper-Schist.
174	1088	Brown Anthophyllitic Quartz-Schist.
175	1090, 1091	Brown Anthophyllite-Schist.
176	1093, 1094, 1095	Brown Anthophyllite-Schist.
177	1098	Brown Anthophyllite-Schist (passing into Magnetite-Schist).
178	1116, 1155	Magnetic Anthophyllite-Slate.

Number.	Specimen.	Name.
179	729	Pseudomorphous Chlorite-Schist.
180	730	Pseudomorphous Chlorite-Schist.
181	731	Pseudomorphous Chlorite-Schist.
182	820	Dark-green Chlorite-Schist.
183	828, 829	Green Calcareous Chloritic Schist.
184	1097	Garnetiferous Chlorite-Schist.
185	1130	Green Chlorite-Schist.
186	1148	Porphyritic Chlorite-Schist.
187	1543, 1544	Chloritic Feldspathic Schist.
188	1545	Green Calcareous Chloritic Schist.
189	692	Micaceous Feldspathic Argillyte.
190	794	Brown Chloritic Argillyte.
191	810	Brown Feldspathic Argillyte.
192	814	Banded Chloritic Argillyte.
193	815	Banded Chloritic Argillyte.
194	881	Micaceous Feldspathic Argillyte.
195	882	Greenish-gray Shale.
196	906	Siliceous Feldspathic Argillyte.
197	908	Greenish-gray Feldspathic Argillyte.
198	917, 918, 919	Banded Feldspathic Argillyte.
199	920, 921, 922	Greenish Feldspathic Argillyte.
200	982	Gray Feldspathic Argillyte.
201	992	Green Speckled Argillyte.
202	998	Brownish-gray Feldspathic Argillyte.
203	1101	Magnetic Feldspathic Slate.
204	1102	Micaceous Feldspathic Slate.
205	1109	Amygdaloidal Amphibole-Schist.
206	1138	Greenish Feldspathic Argillyte.
207	1238	Micaceous Feldspathic Argillyte.
208	1240	Chloritic Argillyte.
209	1249	Chloritic Feldspathic Argillyte.
210	1250	Micaceous Siliceous Slate.

Number.	Specimen.	Name.
211	1368	Iron-gray Argillaceous Mica-Slate.
212	1369	Gray Feldspathic Schist (Siliceous).
213	1379	Banded Magnetic Mica-Slate.
214	1380	Banded Magnetic Siliceous Schist.
215	1390	Greenish Feldspathic Schist (Siliceous).
216	1466	Feldspathic Siliceous Schist (Micaceous).
217	1467	Feldspathic Siliceous Schist (Micaceous).
218	1474 1475	Green Feldspathic Schist (Siliceous).
219	1523	Decomposed Chloritic Schist.
220	1540 1541	Green Feldspathic Schist (Siliceous).
221	968 969 970 971 983	Bluish-gray Argillyte-Slate.
222	974 975	Bluish-gray Argillyte-Slate.
223	976 979	Pyritiferous Argillyte-Slate.
224	1104	Talcose Feldspathic Argillyte.
225	1241	Talcose Feldspathic Argillyte.
226	1081	Magnetic Talc-Schist.
227	S.	Porphyritic Talc-Schist.
228	738	Tabular Magnetite-Schist.
229	728	Fine-grained Magnetite-Schist.
230	1502	Black Magnetite-Slate.
231	737	Chloritic Magnetite-Schist.
232	733	Chloritic Magnetite-Schist.
233	1512	Green Magnetite-Schist.
234	736	Quartzose Magnetite-Schist.
235	1230	Quartzose Magnetite-Schist.
236	735	Ochrey Magnetite-Schist.
237	689	Specular Iron-Schist.
238	1234	Quartzose Hematite-Schist.
239	1235	Quartzose Hematite-Schist.
240	1237	Quartzose Hematite-Schist.

Number.	Specimen.	Name.
241	1429	Ochrey Quartzose Hematite-Schist.
242	872	Calcareous Ochrey Siliceous Schist.
243	995	Ochrey Calcareous Hematite.
244	896	Kaolinic Ochre-Schist.
245	890	Brown Limonite-Schist.
246	879	Carbonaceous Slate.
247	904	Carbonaceous Shale.
248	880	Quartzose Carbonaceous Shale.
249	898	Quartzose Carbonaceous Slate.
250	899	Graphitic Shale.
251	900	Graphitic Shale.
252	S.	Coarse Red Granite.
253	1228	Ferruginous Granite.
254	741	Fine-grained White Granite.
255	746	Fine-grained Black Gneiss.
256	1248, B.	Fine-grained Black Gneiss.
257	1252, 1253	Fine-grained Grayish-Black Gneiss.
258	935, 936, 937	Coarse Reddish Gneiss.
259	947	Grayish-white Gneiss.
260	1548.	Mottled Gneiss.
261	1224, 1226, 1229	Black Hornblende-Gneiss.
262	949	Black Hornblende-Gneiss.
263	742	Coarse Altered Hornblende-Gneiss.
264	744	Altered Hornblende-Gneiss.
265	954	Altered Hornblende-Gneiss.
266	1086	Chloritic Hornblende-Gneiss.
267	1087	Hornblende-Gneiss.
268	1361	Banded Hornblende-Gneiss (Epidotic).
269	1362, 1363	Chloritic Hornblende-Gneiss.
270	1370	Altered Hornblende-Gneiss.
271	1089	Black Hornblende-Schist.
272	946	Chloritic Hornblende-Schist.

Number.	Specimen.	Name.
273	948	Chloritic Hornblende-Schist.
274	950	Chloritic Hornblende-Schist.
275	1393	Greenish Chloritic Gneiss.
276	867	Chloritic Gneiss.
277	870 874	Epidotic Chloritic Gneiss.
278	938	Chloritic Gneiss.
279	941	Red Chloritic Gneiss.
280	942	Red Chloritic Gneiss.
281	951 953	Porphyritic Chloritic Gneiss.
282	952	Greenish Chloritic Gneiss.
283	955	Coarse Chloritic Gneiss.
284	956	Fine-grained Chloritic Gneiss.
285	1128	White Chloritic Gneiss.
286	1367	Fine-grained Chloritic Gneiss.
287	1375	Banded Chloritic Gneiss.
288	1377	Chloritic Gneiss.
289	1378	White Chloritic Gneiss.
290	1381 1383	Banded Chloritic Gneiss.
291	1391	Decomposed Chloritic Gneiss.
292	1392	Decomposed Chloritic Gneiss.
293	1398 1399	Banded Chloritic Gneiss.
294	1400	Red Chloritic Gneiss.
295	1402	Chloritic Gneiss.
296	1546 1547	White Chloritic Gneiss.
297	940	Talcy Chloritic Gneiss.
298	944	Talcy Chloritic Gneiss.
299	945	Talcy Chloritic Gneiss.
300	1389	Brownish-gray Mica-Slate.
301	No. 61.	Staurolitiferous Mica-Schist.
302	743	Altered Porphyritic Dioryte.
303	1103	Black Dioryte.
304	1244	Green Dioryte.
305	1246	Green Altered Dioryte.

Number.	Specimen.	Name.
306	1409	Black Porphyritic Dioryte (Micaceous).
307	1427	Black Dioryte.
308	1432	Altered Porphyritic Dioryte (Magnetic).
309	1454	Fine-grained Gray Dioryte.
310	1498	Fine-grained Blackish-green Dioryte.
311	1501	Fine-grained Black Dioryte.
312	1504, 1505	Greenish Altered Dioryte.
313	1549, 1550, 1551	Fine-grained Black Dioryte.
314	1720, 1721	Quartzose Porphyritic Dioryte.
315	1723	Quartzose Porphyritic Dioryte.
316	1724, 1725	Epidotic Porphyritic Dioryte.
317	1733	Porphyritic Dioryte.
318	1734	Quartzose Porphyritic Dioryte.
319	J.	Coarse Green Amphibolyte.
320	745	Coarse Green Amphibolyte.
321	876	Black Serpentine.
322	1245	Green Magnesian Dioryte (Serpentine).
323	1247	Black Magnesian Dioryte (Serpentine).
324	1530 to 1539	Chloritic Dioryte.
325	1428	Chloritic Dioryte-Wacké.
326	818, 823	Chloritic Dioryte-Schist.
327	1099	Blackish-green Dioryte-Schist.
328	1384	Greenish Dioryte-Schist.
329	1385	Greenish Dioryte-Schist.
330	1401	Greenish Dioryte-Schist.
331	821	Calcareous Dioryte-Greenstone.
332	1527, 1528, 1529	Fine-grained Dioryte-Greenstone.
333	819	Epidotic Dioryte-Greenstone.

Number.	Specimen.	Name.
334	S.	Dioryte-Greenstone.
335	826	Micaceous Greenstone-Schist.
336	827	Micaceous Greenstone-Schist.
337	1096	Micaceous Greenstone-Schist.
338	1100	Schalstone.
339	824 825	Green Aphanyte-Schist.
340	817	Greenish-gray Chlorite-Potstone.
341	1494 to 1497	Green Chlorite-Potstone.
342	884 885	Black Trappean Dioryte.
343	886	Black Trappean Dioryte.
344	888	Trappean Dioryte.
345	889	Altered Trappean Dioryte.
346	905	Speckled Trappean Dioryte.
347	912	Black Trappean Dioryte.
348	913	Brown Trappean Dioryte.
349	915	Brown Trappean Dioryte.
350	996 997	Compact Green Trappean Dioryte.
351	911	Green Porphyry.
352	887	Brown Wacké.
353	914	Speckled Wacké.
354	1110	Black Dioryte-Aphanyte.
355	1382	Black Dioryte-Aphanyte.
356	S.	Black Dioryte-Aphanyte.
357	S.	Green Dioryte-Aphanyte.
358	732	Arenaceous Sandstone-Schist.
359	739	Magnetic Arenaceous Sandstone-Schist.
360	923	Chloritic Sandstone-Schist.

II.

This Table is inserted to facilitate reference to the numbers of my descriptions, given on the right hand of each pair of parallel columns, from the numbers of the specimens in Brooks's Collection, given consecutively in the left-hand column.

Specimen.	Number.	Specimen.	Number.	Specimen.	Number.	Specimen.	Number.
688	114	799	110	880	248	936	258
689	237	800	111	881	194	937	258
690	171	801	148	882	195	938	278
692	189	802	148	883	157	939	138
693	123	803	128	884	342	940	297
715	115	804	161	885	342	941	279
716	116	805	161	886	343	942	280
717	117	806	160	887	352	944	298
718	118	807	161	888	344	945	299
719	118	808	111	889	345	946	272
720	118	809	112	890	245	947	259
721	118	810	191	891	149	948	273
727	118	811	113	896	244	949	262
728	229	812	133	898	249	950	274
729	179	814	192	899	250	951	281
730	180	815	193	900	251	952	282
731	181	816	134	901	137	953	281
732	358	817	340	902	144	954	265
733	232	818	326	903	145	955	283
734	151	819	333	904	247	956	284
735	236	820	182	905	346	968	221
736	234	821	331	906	196	969	221
737	231	823	326	907	131	970	221
738	228	824	339	908	197	971	221
739	359	825	339	909	131	974	222
740	152	826	335	911	351	975	222
741	254	827	336	912	347	976	223
742	263	828	183	913	348	977	138
743	302	829	183	914	353	979	223
744	264	867	276	915	349	982	200
745	320	870	277	917	198	983	221
746	255	872	242	918	198	984	101
747	165	874	277	919	198	990	126
794	190	875	120	920	199	991	127
795	106	876	321	921	199	992	201
796	107	877	104	922	199	993	143
797	108	878	121	923	360	994	156
798	109	879	246	935	258	995	243

Specimen.	Number.	Specimen.	Number.	Specimen.	Number.	Specimen.	Number.
996	350	1233	103	1398	293	1502	230
997	350	1234	238	1399	293	1503	164
998	202	1235	239	1400	294	1504	312
999	153	1236	155	1401	330	1505	312
1081	226	1237	240	1402	295	1506	170
1085	122	1238	207	1409	306	1508	159
1086	266	1240	208	1427	307	1509	162
1087	267	1241	225	1428	325	1510	169
1088	174	1242	105	1429	241	1512	233
1089	271	1243	131	1432	308	1523	219
1090	175	1244	304	1454	309	1527	332
1091	175	1245	322	1458	163	1528	332
1092	147	1246	305	1459	132	1529	332
1093	176	1247	323	1466	216	1530	324
1094	176	1248(B)	256	1467	217	1531	324
1095	176	1249	209	1471	130	1532	324
1096	337	1250	210	1472	130	1533	324
1097	184	1251	129	1473	135	1534	324
1098	177	1252	257	1474	218	1535	324
1099	327	1253	257	1475	218	1536	324
1100	338	1361	268	1476	136	1537	324
1101	203	1362	269	1477	141	1538	324
1102	204	1363	269	1478	139	1539	324
1103	303	1367	286	1479	140	1540	220
1104	224	1368	211	1480	172	1541	220
1109	205	1369	212	1484	158	1543	187
1110	354	1370	270	1485	166	1544	187
1116	178	1375	287	1486	167	1545	188
1128	285	1377	288	1487	124	1546	296
1130	185	1378	289	1488	173	1547	296
1138	206	1379	213	1490	125	1548	260
1148	186	1380	214	1491	168	1549	313
1155	178	1381	290	1492	168	1550	313
1224	261	1382	355	1493	158	1551	313
1225	142	1383	290	1494	341	1720	314
1226	261	1384	328	1495	341	1721	314
1227	154	1385	329	1496	341	1723	315
1228	253	1389	300	1497	341	1724	316
1229	261	1390	215	1498	310	1725	316
1230	235	1391	291	1499	158	1733	317
1231	102	1392	292	1500	158	1734	318
1232	146	1393	275	1501	311		

INTRODUCTION.

(NOTE.—The numbers from 1 to 100 are found in Appendix B.)

A. SIMPLE ROCKS.

I. Calcareous Rocks.

(See Vol. I., page 109.)

Granular Limestone.—Only one specimen occurs (No. 101), which is a grayish-white, coarsely-granular limestone, containing very little magnesia, but intermingled with much Siderite. The concretionary arrangement of the latter within the grains of Calcite will be further studied. Weathers with a brownish-red, roughly-pitted surface.

Granular Dolomite.—The specimens from one locality represent a fine-grained white saccharoidal Marble (No. 102), sometimes abounding in crystals of Tremolite (No. 103). Weathers rather evenly to a yellowish-brown. A Silurian variety, from Presqu'isle, is of a grayish-white color, and is rich in particles of Serpentine (No. 104).

Talco-Siliceous Dolomite.—The purest form is a rare variety, made up of coarse, cleavable, red masses of the pure mineral (No. 11). After solution in heated hydrochloric acid, the coloring matter of the rock remains as an insoluble red powder of very small amount, whose composition has not yet been determined. More common varieties consist of alternations of reddish-white and brownish-red Dolomite (No. 107), generally rich either in films and bunches of Quartz (Nos. 9, 66, and 105), or in flakes of Talc (No. 106), or in both (Nos. 111 and 113), and pass into a still commoner form, in which the two minerals are disseminated in thicker films and layers (Nos. 110 and 112), finally predominating so as to pass into a fine-grained schistose Quartzyte, with peculiar cleavage, of feldspathic appearance (No. 148). The association in the same rock of two minerals of such different hardness as Dolomite and Quartz of course produces a remarkably-ribbed, weathered surface, the siliceous layers sometimes projecting an inch or more, and which is very beautiful where the Quartz laminations are very thin, parallel, closely aggregated, and bent into zigzag forms (No. 108). The color of the weathered surface is usually mottled with brown and cream color. A rare variety occurs, mottled with hard brownish-red rhombs of Dolomite, ¼ to ½ inch across, and resembling a Feldspar in appearance, abundantly disseminated throughout both the Dolomitic and Quartzose layers, making a fine contrast when the general color is light, and often projecting above the weathered surface (No. 109). All the limestones were examined before the spectroscope for Barium, Strontium, Lithium, etc., without finding any trace.

II. Quartzose Rocks.

Quartz-Conglomerate.—The ordinary varieties of this rock, which is a coarse conglomeritic form of Quartzyte, often of a schistose structure, consist chiefly of pebbles of all sizes, up to several inches in diameter (1 to 2 feet at the Keystone Company's mine), chiefly of smoky and milky Quartz, and more rarely of Chalcedony and Jasper (Nos. 114 and 119). The pebbles often consist mostly (No. 116) of soft white arenaceous Quartz, exactly like that of No. 7, sometimes intermingled with fragments of Chlorite-Schist (No. 115), or embedded in a fine-grained aggregate of Quartz and Chlorite (Nos. 117 and 118). A little Pyrite is almost always disseminated. In some cases the matrix abounds in Mica (No. 51) or in Mica and Micaceous-Iron (No. 122). The weathered surface is unchanged in color, but always greatly roughened, where a softer constituent, like Chlorite, has been worn away. In a Silurian variety from Presqu'isle, the pebbles consist chiefly of brownish-red Jasper (Nos. 120 and 121) ; weathered surface uneven.

Quartz-Breccia.—This is a common rock, which in general consists chiefly of angular flat fragments of brownish-red or of greenish Jasper (No. 125), often having a schistose structure (No.

124), more or less intermingled with similar fragments of smoky Quartz and Hematite and passing into a Hematite-Breccia sufficiently rich for an ore (No. 119). An interesting variety, from a boulder, is a Quartzose Feldspar-Breccia (No. 123). Most of these Conglomerates and Breccias pass through their finer-grained varieties directly into the ordinary Quartzytes.

*Quartzyte.**—This rock occurs in great variety, both as to color, texture, and composition. The color is generally light shades of white, ranging through greenish (Nos. 21 and 132), brownish (Nos. 8, 129, and 135), slaty (No. 134), grayish (No. 126), reddish (Nos. 128 and 130), bluish (No. 136), rosy (No. 133), smoky (Nos. 131 and 137), and purplish (No. 128); but sometimes still darker, even black (No. 127). The texture is rarely so compact as to disguise its granules (No. 136), but the latter are generally plainly revealed on a fresh fracture (Nos. 130 and 134), and especially on the weathered surface (Nos. 126 and 128). Though nearly always composed of grayish-white and glassy Quartz, often milky and smoky (No. 135), some varieties consist chiefly of Jasper and Chalcedony, with enough Magnetite to render them magnetic (Nos. 139, 140, and 141). It is sometimes mixed with a few fragments of Feldspar (Nos. 127, 131, and 138), Argillyte (Nos. 133 and 138), Pyrolusite (No. 137), Calcite (Nos. 131 and 136), Talc (No. 133), Magnetite and Micaceous-Iron (Nos. 50 and 142), Ochre (Nos. 8, 128, 135, and 143), and rarely Hornblende (No. 127), Garnet, Actinolite, and Mica (Nos. 129 and 142), and perhaps Kaolin (No. 126). A little Pyrite is also commonly disseminated. A sub-schistose structure is often more or less apparent (Nos. 130, 132, and 133), passing into that of the next rock.

When Talc is present in some quantity, the rock sometimes graduates into Talcose Schists—as on the Lake shore east of the Chocolate River. Weathers usually with only a superficial loss of lustre and a little lighter color, the constituent grains being sometimes brought out prettily by the glacial polish. See also Nos. 1027, 1029, 1041, 1042, and 1056 of Appendix C.

Quartz-Schist.†—A very common rock, of finer grain than most

---

* See Vol. I., page 106. † See Vol. I., page 97.

of the Quartzytes, and with less variations in color. Some varieties
are banded and contain a little Ochre and Pyrolusite (Nos. 144 and
145), while others contain a green mineral, as yet undetermined
(No. 146), Semi-Opal and Pyrolusite (No. 149), Dolomite, as stated
in connection with the calcareous rocks (No. 148), Talc (Nos. 74
and 150), and Garnets (No. 23). A peculiar variety (No. 147)
seems to be a pseudomorphous aggregate of arenaceous Quartz,
Chlorite, and Mica, with a brown mineral. Most commonly, however, the schistose structure is produced by a greater or less intermixture of Magnetite (Nos. 15, 19, 23, and 52), or of Micaceous-
Iron, often in triangular scales (Nos. 32, 33, 36, and 37), or of Magnetite and Micaceous-Iron, in which either the former predominates
(Nos. 151, 152, and 153), or the latter (Nos. 16, 154, and 155), associated with a little Mica or Chlorite : and in other cases of Limonite
(No. 26), of Limonite-Ochre (No. 157), or of Calcite, Hematite, and
Limonite-Ochre (Nos. 57 and 156), or Talc (No. 74). By the predominance of such minerals, all these varieties pass into the Iron
ores. Compare Nos. 1040 and 1069, and Nos. 1045, 1064, 1066,
1075, and 1076, of Appendix C. No. 16 is a Micaceous-Iron Quartz-
Schist, which passes into a Mica-Schist containing Feldspar, and is
therefore allied to Itabirite ; but it differs from that rock in the concentration of the Micaceous-Iron in somewhat parallel films or seams,
in the predominance of the Quartz, and in the absence of the various
minerals which are necessary (Specular-Iron and Magnetite) or accessory (Talc, Chlorite, Actinolite, etc.) constituents of Itabirite.
An Ochrey Quartz-Schist, of very cellular structure, also occurs at
the Foster mine, in which the chief constituent—Quartz—is almost
entirely stalactitic, and the cavities are lined or filled with more or
less Ochre of coppery color and lustre. When chiefly Quartzose,
weathers like Quartzyte, the laminæ being rendered more distinct
by the glacial polish ; when partially made up of laminæ of other
minerals, weathers unevenly and often to darker or ochrey shades
of color. See also Nos. 1035 and 1078 of Appendix C.

Siliceous Schist.—Many varieties of this rock occur, whose colors
vary from white, drab (No. 164), green (Nos. 158, 160, 161), brown
(No. 159), and iron-gray (No. 165), to black (No. 163). The
structure is sometimes slaty (Nos. 163 and 164), often banded (Nos.
158, 159, 161, 162, and 165), and sometimes characterized by a

peculiarly sharp rhombohedral cleavage (No. 163). Its composition and physical properties are varied by the presence of Limonite (No. 163), Mica and Chlorite (Nos. 158 and 164), or Talc, and in the last case becomes a Novaculyte (Nos. 13, 160, and 161), or passes, by alternating layers, through No. 162 into Talcose Schist, through No. 139 into Argillyte, and through No. 165 into Hematite-Schist. Weathers smoothly (except when a softer mineral is present) to a rather darker brownish shade ; the chloritic variety (*e.g.* that which occurs near Lake Fairbanks) weathers, to the depth of several inches from the surface, and along the fissures, to a deep reddish-brown. A peculiar variety occurs at Presqu'isle (No. 242), which is intermingled and colored with Ochre, and traversed by an abundance of thin reticulating seams of Calcite.

Jasper-Schist.—This, the finest-grained form of the Quartzose rocks, is a common and abundant accompaniment of the ores, and varies in texture from the coarse Conglomerates (Nos. 120 and 121) and Breccias (No. 125) already mentioned, to the crypto-crystalline schists described below. A rare form is a thinly laminated green slate (No. 170) ; but the structure is generally banded, and the colors consist of alternating stripes of brownish-red, gray, green, brown, yellow, and black (Nos. 166, 167, 168, 169, 171, 172, and 173). It sometimes contains a little Mica (Nos. 170 and 172), Göthite (No. 168), Chlorite (No. 169), and Magnetite (No. 171) ; but the most common form consists of alternations of bluish-black crystalline Hematite (Martite) and brownish-red Jasper, associated sometimes with a little Ochre and Kaolin (Nos. 172 and 173). Weathers smoothly and unchanged in color, but layers containing a ferruginous mineral become darkened in color and sometimes more deeply worn.

III. Silicate Rocks.

Amphibolyte.—(See under Dioryte.)

Amphibole-Schist.—(See under Dioryte.)

Hornblende-Schist.—(See after Hornblende-Gneiss.)

*Anthophyllite-Schist.**—This is a form of Quartz-Schist, through which is disseminated an abundance of a brownish-gray hydrous mineral, in tiny silvery scales or fibrous blades, first identified by Prof. G. J. Brush as Anthophyllite, and of which I have made no examination. The Quartz sometimes predominates (No. 174), but usually the Anthophyllite (Nos. 175 and 176). Magnetite is almost always present, either generally dispersed in minute granules (No. 174), or especially gathered into certain laminæ (Nos. 27, 175, and 176), or into thicker alternating layers (No. 177), so that the rock becomes strongly magnetic (Nos. 177 and 178), and passes into an ore of Magnetite, associated with much Pyrolusite, which imparts to the rock a metallic streak (No. 59). A little Hematite-Ochre is also disseminated through these latter varieties (No. 58). Weathers unevenly to a reddish-brown, or, when rich in Pyrolusite, to a blackish-brown, slightly shining. See also Nos. 1027, 1032, 1033, and 1037, of Appendix C.

Chloritic Schist.†—This rock is developed in great abundance and with several interesting varieties. Its color is usually olive- to blackish-green ; its texture is very fine-grained ; and its schistose structure sometimes approaches that of a slate, and is sometimes distinct only on a large scale. Five marked varieties occur, which may be distinguished by their apparent origin.

First.—Chlorite-Schist, derived from Hornblende- or Actinolite-Schist by alteration (Nos. 179, 180, 181, and perhaps 184 and 185). Streak light-green to greenish-gray. Consists chiefly of minute scales of Chlorite ; is sometimes filled with Garnets (Nos. 179 and 184), has generally much Magnetite disseminated in octahedra, which are often altered into Chlorite (No. 179. See Bischof's *Chem. and Phys. Geology*, London, 1855, Vol. II., p. 409) or Martite (No. 185)§, and sometimes still retains the blades of Amphibole, more or less altered (No. 180). A highly quartzose variety (No. 76) may fall within this division. Its deep green color, feeble lamination, and granular structure (produced by the tiny scales of Chlorite, inclined in all directions, of which it chiefly consists) sufficiently distinguish this from the succeeding varieties.

---

* See Vol. I., page 114.   † See Vol. I., page 104.
§ See also Credner, Article, page 545.

Secondly.—Chloritic Schist, derived from Chloritic Dioryte-Schist, through Aphanyte-Schist, by the increased proportion of Chlorite (Nos. 182 and 183). Streak greenish-white. Consists chiefly of Feldspar, with rather less Chlorite, and is always traversed by Calcite in more or less abundant films and seams. It may generally be distinguished by its geological association, by its light color and streak (due to the predominance of Feldspar), and by its aphanitic texture and somewhat irregular scaly cleavage. See also Nos. 1015 and 1026 of Appendix C.

Thirdly.—Chloritic Schist, produced in Greenstone-Ash or Argillyte, by the increased proportion of Chlorite (No. 188). Streak generally greenish-white. Consists chiefly of Feldspar, and generally contains Calcite. It can generally be distinguished from the other kinds by the transition varieties (Nos. 28, 208, and 219), which pass into the Greenstone-Ashes, by its parallel lamination, dark color, and the frequent isolation but parallel arrangement of its scales of Chlorite.

Fourthly.—Chloritic Schist, produced in Chloritic Gneiss by the increased proportion of Chlorite (Nos. 186 and 187). Streak greenish-gray. Consists of about equal quantities of Feldspar, Chlorite, and Quartz. The Quartz may generally be distinguished by the lens, but the chief difference between this kind and the three foregoing consists in the isolation and greater size of the individuals of Feldspar, so as to frequently produce a porphyritic structure (No. 186).

Fifthly.—Chloritic Schist, produced in Argillyte by the presence of a small quantity of Chlorite (see Nos. 10, 190, 191, 192, 193, etc., under Feldspathic Argillyte, with which they are most nearly connected). This class may very possibly consist only of aphanitic varieties of the First and Third. One form, which occurs in great abundance North of Teal Lake and elsewhere, seems to be an indurated rock derived from Chloritic Schist by alteration, exhibiting a coarsely schistose structure on a large scale, containing a little Talc (in tiny shining scales) and filled with the irregular cracks due to contraction (largely occupied by Calcite).

By the decomposition of all these varieties of the Fifth class, and the further oxidation of the Ferrous Oxide, the color partially or entirely passes into reddish-brown, and the rock graduates into a mottled Chloritic Argillyte, an Ochrey Argillyte, and ochrey schists, in which the more compact and softer portions sometimes consist of Red Chalk. All these varieties may be best studied at Kimball's Cut, on the Peninsular Railroad.

Weathers unevenly to shades of reddish-brown, often mottled with greenish. See also Nos. 1028, 1030, 1038, and 1052, of Appendix C.

Argillyte * (Greenstone-Ash, etc.).—The fine-grained schistose rocks or slates, evidently metamorphic forms of mechanical deposits (Argillaceous, Chloritic, Talcose, Feldspathic, and Siliceous schists), are very largely developed and with many varieties. They are naturally divided into two great groups, Huronian and Laurentian, including many similar varieties. The latter are evidently deposits derived from the erosion of the Laurentian Gneisses, etc., and their discussion will be taken up further on under the heading of Mica-Slates, although their descriptions (Nos. 187, 188, and 211 to 220) are mostly arranged in association with the others.

The former group, or Huronian, will be alone discussed here. They are evidently derived from the erosion of diorytic rocks, and are apparently identical with the fine-grained forms of Greenstone-Ash (Jukes, pages 68, 81, and 323), or Greenstone-Tuff (Cotta, page 310, and Zirkel, II., page 535, the latter including only the European form, derived from Diabase-Greenstone).

The less alterable constituent of the Diorytes, Feldspar, of course predominates in most of the rocks, revealing itself in chemical analysis by the presence of a notable quantity of the alkalies, and on microscopic examination of a section, in exceedingly abundant, irregular, and somewhat angular particles ; but it has often subsequently been decomposed in a greater or less degree into Kaolin. The other constituent, Amphibole, seems to be of such a character as very rarely to resist decomposition, and its fragments have almost always passed into Chlorite or Mica, or have been resolved into its elements, Silica, Ferric Oxide, etc. The accessory minerals of the Diorytes, Quartz, Mica, Chlorite, and Talc, seem to have generally passed unchanged into these deposits ; the Magnetite has been gathered, through its greater Specific Gravity, into an iron-sand, and has thus been concentrated into certain beds,

---

* See Vol. I., page 111.

layers, or laminæ ; while the Pyrite has probably been generally decomposed and diffused in the form of ochre.

The result has been a series of rocks, whose exact constitution can of course be only determined by a thorough microscopic and chemical investigation, which I have as yet only begun. These I will now divide into three classes, in which the material is made up respectively of Feldspar, of Amphibole or Chlorite, or of amorphous substances derived from the decomposition of these minerals.

First, a schistose rock, mainly composed of particles of Feldspar, but little altered, with varying quantities of Mica, Chlorite, Talc, Quartz, etc. This is very abundant, and has generally been called Clay-Slate or Argillyte ; but as its chief component seems to have been a feldspathic rather than ordinary clay, I have called it *Feldspathic Argillyte*. Its chief characteristics are its peculiar fusibility, light color, and, I presume, its content of the alkalies. (Nos. 197, 198, 199, etc.)

The following varieties are produced by the decomposition of the Feldspar, and by the presence of one of the accessory minerals in such proportion or method of concentration or arrangement as to render it conspicuous.

Argillyte, or *Shale*, a slaty or shaly form of the preceding, in which the Feldspar seems to have been mostly converted into Kaolin ; so that the fresh fracture yields an argillaceous odor, when moistened, and clings to the tongue. It is distinguished by these clayey characteristics, and, I presume, by containing but little of the alkalies, and therefore seems to be a normal Clay-Slate or Argillyte.

Siliceous Feldspathic Argillyte, a schist to which the particles of Quartz impart a peculiar hardness and the streak partly consists of a metallic abrasion from the knife ; it sometimes passes into a kind of *Siliceous Slate*, in which the Quartz seems to predominate above the Feldspar, while the slaty structure is produced by the Mica. The presence of the latter mineral, and a slight fusibility, distinguish this Siliceous Schist from that associated with the Quartzytes.

Micaceous Feldspathic Argillyte (or, as above, *Micaceous Siliceous Slate*), passing into *Feldspathic* or *Argillaceous Mica-Slate*, with the increased proportion of Mica. It is distinguished from the Laurentian Mica-Slates, described further on, by the much smaller content of Mica, in this rock, and its distribution in minute isolated scales, and by the siliceous character of the Laurentian variety.

Chloritic Feldspathic Argillyte, or *Chloritic Argillyte* (see Zirkel, II., p. 599 ; Blum, pp. 77 and 227 ; Kenngott, p. 205 ; and Naumann, p. 544). This includes the fifth variety of *Chloritic Schist*, already described under that heading, and passes into the *Chlorite-Schist* of the Second Class. It differs from the other varieties in its greenish color, and sometimes the scales of Chlorite are distinct. Its color is of a darker green than that of the similar Laurentian rock.

Talcose Feldspathic Argillyte (see Zirkel, I., p. 318 ; Kenngott, p. 205 ; and Naumann, p. 544), a rare variety, distinguished by its soapy feel, but in which the Talc never predominates.

Magnetic Feldspathic Slate, sufficiently distinguished by its magnetic character, and which closely approaches a Laurentian variety.

Secondly, a schistose, often slaty rock, derived from the erosion of Diorytes rich in Amphibole—but which rarely retains any large quantity of particles preserving the form of that mineral—which may be called an *Amphibole-Schist* (No. 205).

Generally the Amphibole survives only in the form of Chlorite, associated with an abundance of particles of Quartz, and so this class includes the first and third varieties of *Chlorite-Schist*, already described under that heading (Nos. 179, 180, 208, 219, etc.).

Thirdly, *Argillyte-Slate* (Nos. 221, 222, and 223), the typical "roofing-slate," whose constitution appears to be generally amorphous, even under the microscope, and which in most cases is probably made up of the ruins of the minerals of the preceding two classes. However, it often retains a sufficient quantity of these minerals unaltered as to be divided into Actinolitic, Feldspathic (light-colored), or Chloritic (greenish) varieties. The name " Argillyte" is ordinarily taken to imply a schistose structure, but for its slate lithologists employ either an additional name, " Clay

Slate" (Thonschiefer), which however seems to be used in English very loosely, or the popular term "roofing-slate," whose objectionable character is apparent. In the hope to simplify the matter, I propose, with the approval of Prof. Dana, the latinized translation of Thonschiefer—*Argillyte-Slate*—as a slight but sufficient distinction, for the purposes of this Report.

Feldspathic Argillyte and *Chlorite-Schist.*—On account of the greenish color of the Feldspar, as well as of the Chlorite, of which the schists of the first two classes are composed, their color is in most cases a shade of greenish-gray; but in others, the color is grayish-white, grayish-green (Nos. 201, 206, and 209), brown and yellow (Nos. 190, 191, 192, and 193), cast-iron gray (No. 200), blackish-gray (Nos. 203 and 204), and grayish-black (No. 205). The texture is almost always crypto-crystalline, but the materials can often be distinguished by means of a lens, and are occasionally so coarse as to reveal the striated facets of Feldspar (No. 196), or the scales of Mica (No. 207, etc.) distinctly to the eye. The structure is in almost all cases imperfectly schistose. It is also often minutely streaked or banded (No. 189, etc.), in consequence of a fibrous cleavage (Cotta, page 255). Occasionally an amygdaloidal structure occurs (No. 205). The composition seems generally to consist chiefly of Feldspar (No. 206, etc.), which sometimes may be partly decomposed into Kaolin (No. 195). With the Feldspar a brownish-gray Mica is generally associated, sometimes white, silvery-gray, and black, usually in minute disseminated scales (No. 210), which sometimes are very abundant (No. 207). Granules of Quartz are sometimes associated with the Feldspar (Nos. 204, 208, 209, and 210), or are gathered into separate layers alternating with Argillyte, and making a transition form (No. 159). Chlorite often replaces the Mica, either partially (No. 208) or entirely (Nos. 28, 190, 192, 193, and 199), being sometimes present in such quantity as to produce a Chloritic Schist. (Compare Nos. 1039, 1068, and 1072 of Appendix C.) When the Chlorite is decomposed, another brown variety results, which strongly resembles a coarse Clay-Slate in odor when moistened, etc., but which contains in place of Alumina a considerable proportion of Hematite-Ochre (Nos. 190, 191, 192, 193, and 199). A very little Talc also occurs in a few rare varieties (No. 201)—one of which contains a sufficient quantity

to be called a Talcose Schist (No. 225)—and also in association with
Chlorite (Nos. 190 and 192). A common transition variety, near
the mouth of the Chocolate River, is a Talco-Argillaceous Slate,
with siliceous bunches, which passes by the predominance of any
one of its constituents into a Talcose, an Argillaceous, or a Siliceous
Schist. Magnetite is disseminated through a few varieties (Nos.
55, 203, and 204). Micaceous-Iron sometimes replaces the scales
of Mica, either partially or wholly (No. 206). Pyrite and Calcite
(No. 194) are also very generally disseminated, in minute particles
and films, and one variety (from a boulder) contains many small
bunches of Siderite (No. 189). Weathers evenly and without
change of color, but, in the common chloritic varieties, more or
less unevenly to brownish shades.

Argillyte-Slate.—Its color is the usual blackish-gray, inclining to
bluish and to greenish (Nos. 221 and 222); seems to be chiefly
composed of Quartz, Feldspar, and Mica ; and is sometimes filled
with particles and films of Pyrite (No. 223). It is connected through
the imperfectly schistose varieties (Nos. 221 and 222) with the
Feldspathic Argillytes. Weathers rather evenly to a lighter color.

Talcose Schist.—The scarcity of Talc in the rocks of this region,
and especially of its concentration in beds, makes this rock of rare
occurrence. Two kinds occur, the Feldspathic (already described)
and Quartzose. In addition to the usual greenish-gray variety of
the first (No. 225), mentioned under Feldspathic Argillyte, the color
is sometimes grayish-green (No. 53), or brownish-gray (No. 54).
Other varieties occur, which differ chiefly in the dissemination of
Magnetite (Nos. 54 and 226), or Hematite-Ochre (No. 227) : in the
last case porphyritic with Feldspar crystals. All these consist chiefly
of triclinic Feldspar * and Talc, in various proportions, the Talc
rarely amounting to half. The most common form of the Quartzose
variety is a Siliceous Schist permeated with Talc in minute scales—
Novaculyte (Nos. 13, 160, and 161). A transition form is made up
of alternating talcose and siliceous layers (No. 162). A rarer and

---

* Credner (Article, pages 529 and 553) considers it Orthoclase, in a Menominee
variety, and indeed finds that feldspar also in a Huronian Chlorite-Schist (page 539)—
both which cases seem to me doubtful.

coarser variety is a thinly laminated white Quartzose Slate, made up of laminæ and scales of Quartz and white Talc (No. 74), or of Jasper and Talc (near E. Section line in S. E. ¼ of N. E. ¼ of Section 23, T. 47, R. 26) : sometimes passing into a talcy Quartzyte (N. W. ¼ of N. W. ¼ of S. 24, T. 47, R. 26, and near mouth of Chocolate River, etc.), or into a Talcy Quartz-Schist (No. 150) ; and sometimes, by an intermixture of Quartz pebbles, into a Conglomeritic Talc-Schist or a Talcose Conglomerate (N. side of Lake Palmer) ; or, by an intermixture of pebbles of Dioryte-Greenstone, into a Talcose (perhaps Chloritic ?) Greenstone-Conglomerate (S. W. ¼ of S. W. ¼ of S. 1, T. 47, R. 27).—See Vol. I., page 99 : also Cotta, page 310.

By an intermixture of Feldspar with the Talcose Quartz-Conglomerate above mentioned (N. side of Lake Palmer), a Talcy Conglomeritic Gneiss is produced, or, with the Talcy Quartz-Schist, a Talcose-Gneiss (" Protogine Gneiss "), or Talcy Chloritic Gneiss, in considerable beds ; but this is merely a local development, and the rounded grains or pebbles generally distinguish these Huronian varieties from the allied Laurentian gneisses described further on.

Steatite is said to occur at a locality north of Teal Lake, but there is no specimen in this collection.

The Talc-Schists weather rather unevenly to darker shades of brown.

IV. Iron-Ore Rocks.

(See also Vol. I., page 85.)

The collection does not include any great variety of these rocks, most of which are lithologically identical with the similar ores from other regions ; but the specimens have apparently been selected rather from those which represent the local characteristics, and to these only the following remarks will be specially devoted.

Magnetite-Schist.—The color of these rocks is usually bluish-black (No. 738), sometimes grayish-black (No. 39), or brownish-black (Nos. 40, 41, and 42), often having a greenish shade by the presence of Chlorite (No. 233), or mottled by grayish-white Quartz (No. 234). The lustre is generally much less, and the texture of a much finer grain, than in the ores from the Adirondack region of New York, Northern New Jersey, etc., but the granules are more perfectly octahedral, even in the ores of steely compactness.

A crypto-crystalline, dull variety also occurs (No. 230). A schistose structure is in consequence strongly defined in most cases, and sometimes becomes tabular or slaty (No. 228). Films of Chlorite are often disseminated (Nos. 42, 43, 231, and 232): a Mica, allied to Chlorite, more rarely (Nos. 15, 233, and 235): in one case, Garnet (No. 23): and very commonly, Quartz, in bunches or alternating laminæ, and thus passing into Quartzyte (Nos. 234 and 235), or Quartz-Schist (Nos. 19, 23, and 52). But the greatest peculiarity depends upon the extensive process of alteration to which most of the original magnetic ores have been subjected, and the result is shown in a series of transition varieties between Magnetite and Hematite. The present beds of compact Magnetite have been thus affected only in a small degree, though many varieties of Hematite show evidences of this method of origin (Nos. 2, 5, 43, 46, and 49)—as in the " red ore " of the Washington mine (a mixture of the two ores), and in the iridescent seams and in the chloritic films which traverse the Magnetite beds at the same mine. The chief alteration has taken place in the more common schists, made up of thin alternations of fine-grained Magnetite with Quartz (Nos. 151, 152, and 153), or Jasper (No. 171): the ferruginous layers being chiefly (Nos. 238, 239, and 240), or wholly (Nos. 172 and 173) composed of Martite (Dana's System of Mineralogy, No. 180, *A*) when associated with Jasper, and of Micaceous-Iron (Nos. 16, 33, 38, 50, and 142), when associated with Quartz (see also under Quartz-Schist). Hematite-Ochre is sometimes dispersed in small quantity (No. 236); and a rare variety is made up of thin alternating laminæ of Actinolite and Magnetite (No. 17. See also Nos. 1032, 1033, 1034, 1037, 1057, 1058, and 1061, of Appendix C). The association with Anthophyllite has already been referred to, under the Anthophyllite-Schists (Nos. 174, 175, 177, and 59); and also the association with Feldspathic Argillyte, under that head; in both cases only lean, worthless ores being produced. Weathers rather evenly to lighter, usually brownish shades. (See also Nos. 1044, 1054, and 1059 of Appendix C.)

Hematite-Schist.—This ore presents the characteristics and varieties usual in other regions of America. They may be arranged as follows, in reference to crystalline condition.

First. An Ochrey Hematite-Schist (Nos. 35 and 67), sometimes containing much Pyrolusite, Quartz, and Kaolin (Nos. 24 and 25), and often disintegrated into gravel (No. 34). Peculiar varieties occur (Nos. 25 and 34), sometimes rich in Quartz and Calcite (Nos. 242 and 243), or in Kaolin (No. 244). Compare No. 1074 of Appendix C.

Secondly. A Compact Hematite-Schist, having a feeble lustre (Nos. 5 and 68), and sometimes containing Kaolin (No. 44). In other cases it contains many octahedra of Martite (No. 5), or Magnetite, being a transition variety (No. 43) from a Magnetite-Schist.

Thirdly. A Specular-Iron Schist, with decided lustre (Nos. 6, 38, 45, 47, and 237), made up of thin scales and laminæ of shining Specular-Iron and of minute granules of Quartz. Dispersed crystals of Martite (No. 48), or decomposed Garnets (No. 6), sometimes produce the so-called " Birdseye ore."

Fourthly. A Micaceous-Iron Schist, with high lustre (No. 46). This also sometimes contains octahedra of Martite or Magnetite (No. 49).

Fifthly. A fine-grained Martite-Schist, made up almost entirely of that mineral with a little Quartz and Kaolin (No. 2). See also No. 1060 of Appendix C.

With these are associated two common transition varieties of Quartz and Jasper-Schist, called " lean ores." The one is produced by the alternation of layers of Micaceous-Iron and Quartz, the latter usually predominating largely, so as to produce a Quartz-Schist (Nos. 16, 32, 33, 36, and 37). Magnetite is generally associated with the Micaceous-Iron, and sometimes the former predominates (Nos. 151, 152, and 153), and sometimes the latter (Nos. 16, 154, and 155), together with a little Mica. The other transition variety is made up of layers of crystalline bluish-black Martite, alternating with others of brownish-red Jasper (Nos. 172 and 173), or of grayish-white Quartz (Nos. 238, 239, and 240), which passes through a transition variety (No. 241) into the ochrey schists. A rather infrequent variety, by which this rock is connected with the Quartz-Breccias, is a Hematite-Breccia, sometimes abounding in Kaolin (No. 119) and generally schistose, as at the Jackson mine and on the north side of Moss Mountain. Weathers unevenly to reddish-,

3

yellowish-, and blackish-brown.　See also Nos. 1046, 1050, 1067, 1070, 1071, and 1073, of Appendix C.

Limonite-Schist.—This ore (No. 245) is not usually developed to any great extent, and its varieties and mammillary concretions resemble those from the other Iron regions.　A little Göthite and Turgite are associated with it in a few localities.　It is connected with Quartzyte and the Quartz-Schists through the banded transition varieties (Nos. 26, 57, and 157), made up of alternations of Limonite and Quartz.　Weathers smoothly, with a surface covered with Ochre.

V. Carbonaceous Rocks.

(See Vol. I., page 115.)

These slates and shales (Nos. 246 and 247), which are of rare occurrence and little variety, have usually a grayish or brownish-black color, dull lustre, and fine-grained texture ;　are usually so soft as to soil paper ;　receive a high polish by friction ;　and sometimes contain much Quartz and Ochre, and a little Mica, in veins and seams (Nos. 248 and 249).　The Carbon seems to constitute only a small part of the rock, and more rarely some of it occurs in bright films of Graphite, so as to produce a Graphitic Shale (Nos. 250 and 251).　Weathers smoothly and without change of color, graphitic laminæ assuming a polish.　See also No. 1036 of Appendix C.

B. MIXED CRYSTALLINE ROCKS.
OLDER FELDSPATHIC ROCKS.
ORTHOCLASE ROCKS.

VI. Granite.

This abundant rock in the Laurentian region is barely represented in the collection, and the only typical variety (No. 252) is a very coarse aggregate of Orthoclase and Quartz, with a very little Mica ; by the disappearance of the latter, varieties of Pegmatite and Graphic Granite are produced, in considerable abundance.　Two

Huronian specimens are included in this group, merely for temporary convenience. The one (No. 253) is from a dyke through a bed of Iron-ore, and consists of Feldspar (perhaps Orthoclase), Quartz, and Micaceous-Iron in place of Mica ; thus corresponding to the " Eisen Granit " of German Lithology. The other (No. 254) is a fine-grained rock, which is chiefly made up of a triclinic Feldspar, and may very probably turn out to be a variety of the Gneiss of similar composition described below.

PLAGIOCLASE ROCKS.

Under this name, adopted by Breithaupt for the group of triclinic Feldspars, it seems best at present to follow Credner in classifying the Gneisses and Greenstones of this region.

VII. Gneiss.

Common Gneiss.—This is a very abundant Laurentian rock, and is here represented by a very few varieties. Its color generally inclines to black, when its Mica is prominent (Nos. 255, 256, and 257) ; and sometimes to reddish (No. 258) or grayish-white (No. 259), by the predominance of its Feldspar. Its texture is rather fine-grained, the grains rarely exceeding ⅛ inch in diameter, and its structure sometimes approaches a slate (No. 257). The Feldspar has almost always a good cleavage and lustre ; many of its facets are minutely striated ; its general color is grayish-white, becoming reddish-brown by incipient decomposition (No. 258) ; occurs sometimes in small crystals (Nos. 258 and 259) ; and it amounts to from 4 to 7 parts (tenths) of the rock. The Quartz is generally grayish-white and smoky, in still smaller grains, and amounts to from 2 to 5 parts. The Mica is generally black or blackish-brown, but is rendered soft and yields a greenish-gray streak by incipient decomposition (No. 258), and amounts to from 1 to 4 parts. Pyrite is universally disseminated in small quantity (No. 256). Epidote occurs in one specimen (No. 259), and Chlorite (No. 257). A peculiar and very coarse variety (No. 7) seems to be rich in Orthoclase. Weathers evenly to a lighter color, usually reddish-gray.

Hornblende-Gneiss.—This abundant Laurentian rock is represented by only 2 specimens from a Huronian locality (Nos. 266 and 267). It is composed of the same minerals as the Gneiss just described, with the substitution, in the unaltered specimens, of greenish-black Amphibole in place of Mica. Its general color is blackish-green,—dull, in the Huronian variety, or sparkling, in the Laurentian,—more or less speckled (especially in the Laurentian) with grayish-white, according to the amount of Feldspar. Its texture is usually rather fine-grained—few of the granules, scales, etc., exceeding $\frac{1}{16}$ inch; but coarser layers are common, in which the diameter of the grains reaches $\frac{1}{8}$ to $\frac{1}{4}$ inch. The structure is always decidedly schistose, often banded by the lighter-colored coarser layers (Nos. 263, 264, and 270), and becomes fissile by the presence and increase of scales of Mica and Chlorite. The Feldspar is exactly like that of the common Gneiss just described, very rarely greenish-white in color, does not often assume the reddish tinge by incipient decomposition (Nos. 264 and 270), and makes up from 1 (No. 266) to 6 parts of the rock (No. 265); it especially predominates in the Laurentian variety, and is at once distinguishable on a fresh fracture, while, in the Huronian, it is obscured by the Amphibole. The Quartz makes up from 2 to 6 parts of the rock, and is often arranged in parallel flakes (No. 266). The Amphibole makes up from 2 to 5 parts, and has been subjected to a process of alteration, whose several stages are well illustrated in this Collection (see especially Nos. 261 and 269), and show that the micaceous gneisses have been, at least sometimes, and the chloritic gneisses perhaps always, derived from this rock. It very rarely, especially in the Huronian variety, retains its normal hardness, structure, color, and streak (Nos. 261, 262, and 267); but the blades become soft to the knife, with a greenish-gray streak (Nos. 265 and 268), assume a blackish-green color, yellowish-green translucency, and scaly structure (No. 269), pass into blackish-green scales of Chlorite, which often still retain the fibrous structure (No. 266), and finally into scales of a harder Mica, which sometimes are greenish-black (No. 265), brownish-black (No. 263), black (No. 264), and grayish-white (Nos. 264 and 266): a Mica of two of these colors being often intermingled in the same specimen (No. 264). A little Pyrite is disseminated throughout this rock in minute particles (Nos. 262, 267, etc.). Epidote abounds in the more altered varieties (Nos. 263, 264, and 268), often in grains ⅛ inch across ; and sometimes the presence of Calcite is shown by the effervescence of the rock when immersed in acid (No. 268). The weathered surface is generally even though rough, and, in the Laurentian variety, of a lighter color, reddish or brownish (Feldspar), while in the Huronian it is often mottled with blackish-green (Amphibole). This rock may possibly be related to some of the Specimens, Nos. 1019, 1020, 1021, 1022, 1023, and 1029, of Appendix C.

Hornblende-Schist.—A less common variety of the preceding rock, represented by specimens from both a Huronian and a Laurentian locality. It is generally fine-grained (Nos. 271, 272, and 273), sometimes coarse (No. 274), is chiefly composed of Hornblende, almost always effervesces slightly in acid, and contains a little Chlorite, especially in the Laurentian variety. Only one variety occurs in this collection which has been derived from or is related to any other rock—a Greenstone-Ash (No. 205)—but I shall refer, under Dioryte, to a variety I have frequently observed in the field, derived from that rock. Weathers unevenly, with a surface mottled with brown and green.

Chloritic Gneiss.—This exclusively Laurentian rock has evidently resulted by the complete disappearance of the Hornblende from the preceding. Its color is generally greenish-gray (Nos. 276, 278, 282, etc.), or grayish-white (Nos. 285, 288, 289, etc.), often brownish-red, by the decomposition of its Feldspar (Nos. 279, 280, 294, etc.), and sometimes reddish-white (Nos. 80 and 291), olive-green (No. 269, Sp. 1362), or greenish-black (No. 287). Its texture varies from very fine-grained (Nos. 284, 287, 290, etc.), to coarse (Nos. 280, 283, etc.). Its structure is decidedly schistose when the Micas are abundant (Nos. 278, 295, etc.), and also when, in other varieties, the Quartz occurs in parallel flakes, but quite massive in their absence (Nos. 280, 285, and 289), and is sometimes banded (Nos. 290 and 293) or porphyritic (No. 281).

The Feldspar is the chief constituent, being generally greenish-white (Nos. 279 and 280), reddish (Nos. 8 and 282), or grayish-white (No. 281), sometimes light-brown (No. 3) ; has almost always good cleavage, lustre, and distinct striation, but is sometimes milky-white and amorphous (No. 288) ; and occurs generally in minute granules, often $\frac{1}{16}$ to $\frac{1}{8}$ inch in diameter, but sometimes $\frac{1}{4}$ to $\frac{1}{2}$ inch or even 1 inch (Nos. 280, 281, 283, and 288). The Quartz varies in amount from 1 part, when it can be distinguished with difficulty (No. 279), to 2 or 3 parts, sometimes occurring in bunches $\frac{1}{2}$ inch across (No. 280), but more commonly in thin parallel equidistant flakes, which appear on the section as abundant lines, about $\frac{1}{4}$ to $\frac{1}{2}$ inch long, $\frac{1}{32}$ inch thick, and about $\frac{1}{8}$ to $\frac{1}{4}$ inch apart. The micaceous constituent is either a greenish-black or brown (No. 284), or grayish-white Mica (Nos. 276 and 279), generally softened, so as to cut with nearly the softness of Chlorite, or it consists of the latter mineral in scales, sometimes fibrous (No. 279), or in films (Nos. 276 and 282), amounting to nearly 3 parts (No. 281), or almost disappearing from the rock. Epidote generally replaces the Chlorite in the last case, sometimes being present to the extent of 2 or 3 parts (Nos. 277 and 290, Specimen 1383), and very commonly disseminated in small quantity (Nos. 281, 288, etc.), sometimes in transparent crystals (No. 296). A peculiar fine-grained Greenstone occurs as a broad vein in this rock, which consists of Feldspar, Chlorite, and about 3 parts of Epidote (No. 277, note). The Chlorite is sometimes partly decomposed into a brownish-yellow Ochre (No. 291), or is entirely replaced by it (No. 292). Seams of Calcite often traverse the rock (Nos. 278, 279, and 284); and a little Pyrite is commonly disseminated (No. 287, etc.). Weathers to the depth of $\frac{1}{8}$ to $\frac{1}{2}$ inch, with an even surface, generally roughened by the greater erosion of the Chlorite, with a lighter and duller shade of the same color as the fresh fracture, or inclining to brownish.

Talcose Gneiss.—In a rare variety of the preceding Laurentian rock, a greenish form of Talc seems to replace a part (Nos. 297, 298, and 299), or all (No. 65), of the Chlorite in the green films, being distinguished by its lighter-colored silvery scales, greenish-white streak, and more greasy feel. It is possible that future exploration may show that this variety is far more abundant than would appear from its representation in this collection and from my own limited examinations of the borders of the Huronian region, where the Chloritic Gneiss abounds.

The greasy feel of many varieties, classed under Chloritic Gneiss, also suggests a magnesian constituent—perhaps Talc, in many or possibly in all cases. But at present it seems an accidental and rare form, and for that reason alone it seems unwise to adopt the name " Protogine-Gneiss," which has sometimes been applied to this rock as well as to the preceding. It is further to be considered that the name Protogine is etymologically objectionable, especially if used beyond the region in which it originated; and that although its micaceous constituent, like that of the rock under discussion, is either a decomposed Mica, Talc, Chlorite, or related mineral, the Talc seems to be its most characteristic feature. I have therefore adopted for the preceding rock the name Chloritic Gneiss—used by Zirkel, Blum, Credner, and Roth,—and for this variety the names of Talcose Gneiss and Talcy Chloritic Gneiss.*

By the disappearance of the Chlorite and Talc in the preceding two rocks, a variety of Pegmatite is sometimes produced (*e.g.* near Collinsville), but which is generally easily distinguished from the Granitic Pegmatite, already referred to, by its gneissoid structure, and often by the presence of the parallel lenticular flakes of Quartz.

In the vicinity of Lake Palmer there occur several forms of a Huronian Talcose Schist, which graduate into a Talcose and Talcy Chloritic Gneiss, entirely distinct from the above Laurentian rocks.

VIII. Mica Schist.

(See Vol. I., page 113.)

This abundant Huronian rock, of which Formation XIX. chiefly consists (No. 301), is entirely made up of small scales of brownish or brownish-black Mica, and tiny granules of grayish-white Quartz ; the former inclining to bend round the tiny bunches of Quartz and crystals of Staurolite, etc., and so producing a decidedly bunchy structure ; the Quartz generally predominating, sometimes to such a degree as to produce almost a micaceous Quartzyte. The Quartz is also often isolated in seams and bunches ; sometimes an abundance of small Garnets, of scales of Chlorite, or blades of black Hornblende, occurs in seams or distributed through certain layers ; and elsewhere the rock is remarkable for the small crystals of blackish-brown Staurolite, the larger but imperfect crystals or crystalline

---

* Credner in his Article (loc. cit., pages 520–524) mentions similar varieties as occurring on the Menominee.

masses of fibrous, pink Andalusite, or both, disseminated in considerable abundance throughout. See also Nos. 1030 and 1031 of Appendix C. Weathered surface lighter in color, by the bleaching of the Mica. Again, one variety of the micaceous Greenstone-Schist, derived from the alteration of a Huronian Dioryte, seems to be so rich in black and brown Mica as to have been sometimes styled a Mica-Schist (at Republic Mountain).

Mica-Slate.—A large and important group of Laurentian Schists, temporarily styled "Gogebic Schists" by Messrs. Brooks and Pumpelly in the course of their survey (on account of their abundance in the vicinity of the lake of that name), are intimately allied to the Huronian Argillytes, Chloritic Schists, etc., but have apparently been derived from the mechanical erosion of the Laurentian Gneisses. Feldspar is never so prominent a constituent as in their Huronian allies, and often disappears; but, on the other hand, Mica and Quartz generally predominate, frequently attended with a slaty structure. The texture of the rocks is generally rather coarser than in the Huronian, so that even the lustre and cleavage of the Feldspar may be generally distinguished by means of a loupe. The ordinary varieties are as follows :

Feldspathic Argillyte; coarser than the Huronian ; sometimes Chloritic (No. 187) and always Siliceous (Nos. 187 and 218), and so passing into

Siliceous Schist ; generally Feldspathic (Nos. 212, 215, and 220), and also decidedly Micaceous (Nos. 216 and 217), and rarely Magnetic (No. 214).

Mica-Slate ; a micaceous variety of the Feldspathic Argillyte (No. 300). In regard to this as well as its Huronian ally, as the scales of Mica are small, and as it is "a shining slaty rock, smooth in surface, intermediate between Mica-Schist and Clay-Slate," I prefer this name, "Mica-Slate," recently proposed for a similar rock by Prof. J. D. Dana (*Am. Jour. Sci.*, 2, iv., Nov., 1872). An argillaceous form of the same rock occurs (No. 211), and also a siliceous form, rich in Magnetite (No. 213).

Chloritic Schist (No. 219); sometimes rich in Calcite (No. 188).

Finally, although the Hornblende-Schists already described (after the Hornblende-Gneisses), are probably in most cases produced only by a predominance of Hornblende in the latter rock, others may hereafter be found which are fragmentary deposits, and belong to the present group (No. 215).

The rocks of this Laurentian group of Schists can be generally distinguished from the Huronian by the following characteristics : A slightly coarser texture, with distinguishable particles of Feldspar : the abundance of Mica, and its concentration in continuous films, with the consequent inclination to a slaty structure (although the Huronian varieties, Nos. 204 and 210, are similar) : the almost universal presence of particles of Quartz, making the fresh surface slightly harder to the knife, with a partially metallic streak by abrasion (although the Huronian varieties, Nos. 196 and 210, are similar) : and the method of weathering, which in the Huronian Argillytes generally produces a surface which is smooth, darker than the fresh fracture, and colored by brownish Ochre, from the decomposition of Chlorite, while in the Laurentian the surface is generally lighter colored (except in the rare chloritic varieties), and slightly roughened, by the weathering out of the Mica and projection of minute particles of Feldspar or of flakes of Quartz.

IX. Greenstones.

(See also Vol. I., page 99, and Appendix E in this Volume.)

This is one of the largest and most varied classes of rocks in the Huronian region ; but the commonly fine-grained and often crypto-crystalline texture demands a careful microscopic investigation, which I have had as yet only enough time to begin. For the same reason no analyses have yet been made of the constituent minerals —the Feldspar and Amphibole—although a few varieties are sufficiently coarse for their mechanical separation and determination in this way. Their descriptions, therefore, and the following classification, are offered only as a provisional attempt.

Certain Greenstones occur throughout this region, interstratified with the ore-beds in great abundance (as in the vicinity of Negaunee)—whose texture is fine-grained, often nearly compact—which are of indistinct constitution, but contain a notable quantity of Magnetite and Chlorite, and are thereby colored a dark greenish-gray, and which effervesce slightly in acids. For these reasons, and perhaps also because the dichromatic power of their Amphibole crystals is often very feeble, in a microscopic section they greatly resemble the Diabase of Europe, and have been called by that name. From my observations in the field and the extensive collection I have had the opportunity to examine, I can hardly believe that any other rock but this can occur in the Iron region to which Credner has applied the name (Elemente der Geologie, pages 276 and 282–285). This would be applicable if used, as by Dana, for "a fine-grained, compact hornblende-rock, tough and heavy," but most authors (Credner, Zirkel, etc.) define it to consist of Labradorite and Augite as the chief constituents. As will be explained below, I consider all these Greenstones to have been derived from the alteration of Diorytes, and, although compelled at present to rely more on ordinary observations in the field than on microscopic investigation, I am decidedly of opinion that no Augite occurs in these rocks (not even perhaps as an accessory mineral), and that there is no Diabase whatever in this region. See also, in this connection, Nos. 1012 and 1025 of Appendix C.

The massive varieties of Dioryte will first be given, and then the schistose—which are usually the more altered. In regard to the Huronian Diorytes, even when massive, there is as yet no method of determining (though the study of microscopic sections may possibly reveal it) whether any given Dioryte belongs to the original source of the *present* Greenstone-Ashes (*i.e.* the present Argillytes, Chloritic Schists, etc.) or is an indurated form of these more recent fragmentary rocks. There is reason to suspect that No. 210 may belong to the latter class, from its characteristics and from its association with certain Huronian Chloritic Schists ; but, on the other hand, all the schistose forms of the Huronian Diorytes, which are of course more open to this suspicion (see Jukes, pages 82 and 323), seem to have derived their schistose structure from the scales of Mica and films of Chlorite produced by the process of alteration. Furthermore, there are Laurentian varieties, sometimes massive (No. 324) and sometimes schistose (No. 329), which *may* owe their origin to the induration of the Ashes of the Laurentian Gneisses, etc.

Dioryte.—This occurs both as a Laurentian and as a Huronian rock, but in the latter case in great abundance and in several varieties. The most typical and beautiful is that represented by Nos. 314 to 318, while several are of doubtful character and may *possibly* contain Pyroxene in place of Amphibole (Nos. 306, 308, and 313). The color varies from black (Nos. 306, 307, etc.), to greenish-black (Nos. 302, 303, etc.), blackish-green (Nos. 308, 314, etc.), to greenish-gray (Nos. 304 and 308). Its texture varies from a coarse aggregate of grains, $\frac{1}{4}$ inch or more across (Nos. 30, 303, 306, 314, etc.), to a fine-grained rock, with granules less than $\frac{1}{32}$ inch across (Nos. 307, 310, 311, etc. See also Nos. 1011, 1024, and 1017, of Appendix C), and more rarely to a Jasper-like mass, which occurs in seams of small quantity (Nos. 315 and 318) ; the rock is characterized by a remarkable toughness under the hammer, often powdering before fracture. Its structure is generally compact, often traversed by joints and fissures, and frequently rendered minutely porphyritic by tiny Amphibole crystals (Nos. 69, 302, 305, 307, etc). On a hill near Negaunee, west of the Pioneer Furnace, the weathered surface of the Dioryte abounds in large crystals of Feldspar, implying an unusual porphyritic structure. Among the Diorytes, porphyritic with Amphibole, observed on a section from Teal Lake northward to the Holyoke mine, a rock resembling a Dioryte-Porphyry was observed, consisting of tiny black crystals of Amphibole through a hard gray aphanitic paste.

The Amphibole generally predominates, amounting to 5 or 6 parts (Nos. 302, 304, 310, etc.), or sometimes to only 3 parts (No. 315). Its fibrous blades average $\frac{1}{16}$ to $\frac{1}{8}$ inch in length, but sometimes amount to $\frac{1}{4}$ and even to $\frac{5}{8}$ inch (Nos. 302 and 315). Its color when unaltered is black or greenish-black, sometimes brownish-green (No. 69), and gives a grayish or greenish-white streak (Nos. 305, 311, and 314); but when altered, it is blackish-green (Nos. 310, 318, etc.), cuts soft like Chlorite, and gives a greenish-gray streak (Nos. 303, 306, 312, etc.). In the latter cases it sometimes loses its lustre and fibrous structure, and becomes smooth (No. 302), or assumes a micaceous structure (No. 303), or passes into a Chlorite whose scales still retain the fibrous markings (No. 313). The Feldspar* resembles that of the

---

* Probably Oligoclase.

Gneisses, and generally amounts to about 4 parts of the rock, but sometimes increases up to 6 or 7 (Nos. 308, 313, and 315). Its granules range in size from $\frac{1}{32}$ to $\frac{1}{4}$ inch (No. 315), averaging $\frac{1}{16}$ to $\frac{1}{8}$ inch across, and are less commonly striated than in the Gneisses (No. 313). Its color is generally greenish-gray (No. 312), grayish-white (Nos. 306, 307, and 310), or yellowish-white (No. 309), sometimes white (No. 69), and, when partially decomposed, brownish-red (No. 314), or brown (No. 305); two of these colors being often intermingled in the same specimen (Nos. 302, 308, etc.). It has generally good cleavage and lustre (Nos. 308 and 309), but loses both in altered specimens (Nos. 302 and 304). Seams or bunches of Feldspar and Quartz sometimes occur (No. 315), or of pure brownish-red Feldspar, containing small drusy geodes (No. 316). Chlorite seems to be almost always disseminated, generally in quantity sufficient to brighten the greenish color of the rock (No. 303, etc. See also Nos. 1001 and 1023 of Appendix C), sometimes retaining somewhat of the fibrous bladed form of the crystals of Amphibole, from which it has been derived (No. 313), and sometimes occurring as a crypto-crystalline green paste (No. 305). A brown magnesian Mica often occurs in small scales: see Nos. 18 and 22 of Appendix B, and Nos. 1018, 1019, 1020, 1021, 1022, and 1023, of Appendix C: also the variety from a boulder (No. 306), which may be a quartz-less form of a Laurentian Hornblende-Gneiss. Quartz occurs in small quantity in several varieties (Nos. 308, 309, etc.), sometimes in large bunches easily observed (Nos. 314 to 318), so as to resemble a Conglomerate (No. 71) or even in a hand specimen, amounting to nearly one part (No. 303). Magnetite is universally distributed in minute crystalline granules, especially remarkable on a weathered surface, and in one case seems to amount to nearly 3 parts (No. 308). On finely pulverizing the rock, the magnet separates * from 2.8 (No. 309) to 8.5 (No. 308) per cent. by weight, of a powder whose color generally shows it to consist chiefly of Magnetite, with more or less of the rock-powder adhering. The rock usually affects the magnetic needle, and decidedly so when over 5 per cent. can be thus separated from its powder by a magnet.

---

* See Appendix H.

Pyrite is also distributed in small quantity, associated with the blades of Amphibole, sometimes in abundant granules $\frac{1}{16}$ inch in diameter (Nos. 305, 306, 308, and 318), or even amounting to nearly one part (No. 304).

Epidote is also sometimes attached to the blades of Amphibole (No. 318) in masses $\frac{1}{8}$ to $\frac{1}{4}$ inch across (No. 316), or occurs in thin seams (No. 75); but the Diorytes differ from the Gneisses in the comparatively rare occurrence of this mineral. Calcite can sometimes be distinguished in films (No. 305), but its presence is very commonly shown only by the effervescence of the rock when immersed in acid.

The weathered surface is generally even or rounded, but, especially in the coarser varieties, roughened by the projection of the harder crystals of Amphibole, sometimes larger crystals of the Feldspar, little bunches of Quartz, Magnetite, etc.; its color is usually some shade of brown, mottled by blackish-green if the Amphibole projects; an exceptional and beautiful weathering is described under No. 317; the weathering is generally deep, sometimes an inch or more, and the Dioryte-Wacké probably represents its last stage. See also Nos. 1002, 1003, 1004, 1007, 1008, 1009, 1010, 1012, 1013, 1014, 1016, 1024, 1025, 1043, 1047, and 1049, of Appendix C.

Amphibolyte.—By the predominance of the Amphibole in Dioryte to about 7 parts, a common Amphibolyte is produced, very tough under the hammer, which appears to the eye to be made up entirely of coarse facets, $\frac{1}{8}$ to $\frac{3}{4}$ inch in diameter, of blackish-green and almost unaltered Amphibole, inclined irregularly in all directions; but on closer examination of a fresh fracture, a greenish-gray paste is revealed, amounting to about 3 parts, which is made up of minute granules of greenish-gray, grayish-white, and yellowish-green Feldspar (No. 319). In a similar rock from a boulder (No. 320), the paste amounts to about 5 parts, and is made up of Feldspar, tiny needles of Amphibole, scales of white Mica, and granules of Quartz. It is peculiar to the weathering of this rock and of many Diorytes, that the Feldspar resists decomposition better than the Amphibole, and becomes whiter and more prominent; so that the conclusion might be obtained—exactly contrary to that derived from the fresh fracture—that the Feldspar was the predominant constituent.   A transition form is a Chloritic Amphibolyte, in which a softened Amphibole occurs, in broad curving films or flakes inclined in all directions, and passing into Chlorite.   Chlorite, green Quartz, and a purplish Feldspar were found in a vein through the Amphibolyte first mentioned above. See also Nos. 1003, 1004, 1018, and 1020, of Appendix C.   The schistose form of Amphibolyte, Amphibole-Schist, is considered further on.

Magnesian Dioryte (Serpentine).—No true Serpentine* occurs in this collection or was observed by me in the field ; but a few rare varieties of Dioryte occur (Nos. 321, 322, and 323), first noticed by Foster and Whitney in their Report (Part II., pages 17 and 25), which have been altered apparently by the introduction of Magnesia, and approach impure Serpentine (especially No. 322) in physical character, though imperfectly in chemical composition (Foster and Whitney's Report, Part II., page 92).   They are rather hard, compact, with a dull iron-black color, mottled by greenish-gray, and a texture which is fine-grained and almost crypto-crystalline, but in one case coarse (No. 323).   They are made up of about 7 parts of dull, black, angular masses, with a slightly columnar structure, apparently altered Amphibole (No. 78), in a greenish-gray, or yellowish-green Feldspathic or Magnesian paste. A brown Mica, brownish-white Calcite, Pyrite, and Ochre also occur in small quantity.   Weathers unevenly to mottled shades of reddish- and blackish-brown.

Chloritic Dioryte.—A rather common form of Dioryte (No. 324), which contains sufficient Chlorite not only to cause the color to incline to green, but to be distinguishable in minute scales and films, and to render the other constituents rather indistinct ; more or less of a brown Mica is also associated with it, together with Calcite, Quartz (No. 71), and sometimes reddish Ochre derived from its decomposition.   By the gradual alteration and disappearance of the crystals of Amphibole, transition varieties are produced, which finally pass into Dioryte-Greenstone.   Weathers evenly to brown-

---

* Credner (Article, pages 534, 535, 544, 545, 553) identifies a rock as Serpentine at the Michigamme Iron Mt., and at the Jackson Mine, but I have never seen it.

ish and greenish shades.　　See also Nos. 1001, 1005, 1006, and 1023, of Appendix C.

Dioryte-Wacké.—A rather rare form (No. 325) of a Chloritic Dioryte, decomposed by weathering or other agency ; the Feldspar becoming reddish-brown ; the Amphibole, soft, blackish-green, and indistinct ; and the Chlorite almost entirely decomposed into a brick-red or reddish-brown Ochre, which imparts its color to the rock.　　The weathered surface is uneven and mottled with reddish- and yellowish-brown.

Dioryte-Schist.—A greenish-black and rather fine-grained form of Dioryte (represented by both Huronian and Laurentian varieties), having a more or less schistose, sometimes flaky, structure, so as to break up into layers which are often less than an inch thick.　　There are two varieties.

First. A Dioryte-Schist produced by the parallel arrangement of the blades of Amphibole (No. 29).　　Sometimes the Feldspar occurs as a granular paste through which the Amphibole crystals are uniformly disseminated.　　Again, the Feldspar may occur gathered and intercalated in thin parallel white lenses, 1 to 5 inches long, which assist in producing the schistose structure ($3\frac{2}{3}$ miles from Holyoke mine, on road to Marquette).　　In still another case (Forestville) the Amphibole occurs in dull, dark-green, flaky lenses, distributed with a parallel arrangement through a paste of finely-granular white Feldspar.

I believe the Laurentian Dioryte-Schists to belong chiefly, perhaps entirely, to this class, but are easily distinguished from the Huronian by the bright crystalline character and black color of their Hornblende.

Secondly. A Dioryte-Schist (Huronian) produced in general by the alteration of the tiny blades of Amphibole, which first become iridescent and soft and assume a micaceous structure, and then pass into scales of blackish-green Chlorite, which retains more or less of the form of the blades (Nos. 327, 328, 329, and 330), and has somewhat of a parallel arrangement.

Other forms occur, which display the changes mentioned under Chloritic Dioryte and Dioryte-Wacké (No. 326), and the same accessory minerals occur.　　Weathers generally to a lighter color, often inclined to brownish, with an even surface slightly roughened and pitted by the unequal erosion of its constituents.   See also Nos. 1005, 1006, 1016, and 1055, of Appendix C.

Amphibole-Schist (probably entirely Huronian).—I am convinced, by frequent references in my field note-books, that a schistose variety of Amphibolyte, or a form of Dioryte-Schist in which the Amphibole predominates, occurs in great abundance and in many localities; the facets of Amphibole, or its altered flakes with associated Chlorite, having such a parallel arrangement that a rock is produced which would be called an Amphibole- rather than a Dioryte-Schist. Calcite is sometimes disseminated in tiny amygdules, crystals, or lenses, so as to produce an amygdaloidal or porphyritic structure or a Schalstone.   I have now no specimens of this rock, and will not venture to make any further description ; but it may be easily studied in the vicinity of Negaunee, especially on its west and south sides, where it passes into Amphibolyte and Dioryte.

It is easily distinguished from the Laurentian rock, derived from Gneiss, by the dull lustre, dark green color, and softened condition peculiar to the Huronian Amphibole ; and until the exact nature of the latter has been determined by analysis, the name "Amphibole-Schist" seems preferable to "Hornblende-Schist" for this variety.

Dioryte-Greenstone.—This is a grayish-green rock (belonging both to the Huronian and Laurentian), of rather uncommon occurrence, and seems to be a variety of altered or Chloritic Dioryte. From that rock it differs in its fine-grained—almost aphanitic—texture, in the consequent indistinctness of its constituents, in the predominance of the green color, and in the universal presence of Calcite. In one locality (Ely's point, Marquette), it possesses a remarkable concretionary structure, the concretions varying from an inch to several feet in diameter.   It is made up of about 4 to 6 parts of Feldspar, often more or less altered, and of about 6 to 4 parts either of scales of Chlorite (No. 332), or of altered blades of Amphibole (No. 333), or of both these minerals, together with a little Mica (Nos. 331 and 334).

This rock is remarkable, especially when it approaches an aphanitic texture, for an extremely fissured structure, by which a fresh fracture is hard to be obtained. These fissures are generally lined with films of Chlorite and grayish-white or brownish Calcite (No. 331); the latter often occurs in seams (No. 333), or geodes (No. 332), sometimes associated with Epidote in considerable quantity (No. 333). A characteristic Amygdaloid occurs in a small ridge in the swamp north-west of the Foster mine, the somewhat flattened amygdules reaching from ½ to 2¾ inches in length and being occupied by Calcite, Quartz, Magnetic Iron (?), Epidote, and Feldspar (?); this rock is free from amygdules in some parts, and passes into a coarse Dioryte and apparently an Amphibole-Schist. Weathers unevenly, usually to a darker green, mottled with brownish spots or stripes. See also No. 1025 of Appendix C.

Micaceous Greenstone-Schist.—This is a Huronian rock of infrequent occurrence, which resembles the preceding in texture, color, and general composition, but differs in a more or less decided schistose structure. This is produced by the Chlorite and altered Amphibole being partially (Nos. 31 and 335), or entirely replaced (Nos. 336 and 337), by a reddish-brown (Nos. 335 and 336), or a black (No. 337) Mica, in parallel scales, rarely $\frac{1}{32}$ inch in diameter, which sometimes retain the form of the original fibrous blades of Amphibole (No. 337). The Feldspar also seems to occur, in thin parallel flakes, between the scales of Mica and Chlorite, and this structure is sometimes revealed on the weathered surface (No. 336). The Magnetite, which is a universal, but generally invisible, accessory constituent of all these rocks derived from the decomposition of Dioryte, is sometimes sufficient in quantity to make some specimens affect the magnetic needle.

This rock is evidently closely allied to Kersanton and Kersantite, grouped by Cotta under his class of Mica-Trap rocks (Glimmertrapp). However, the determination of the Feldspar in this rock has not yet been made, and the rock seems to differ from Kersanton, etc., in its schistose structure, homogeneous texture, etc. I have therefore preferred to propose the provisional name—" Micaceous Greenstone-Schist"—rather than employ either the name " Mica-Trap," which would suggest a false idea in regard to its origin, or the local names, Kersanton, etc., which would also require a careful comparison of actual specimens for identification. Weathers

4

unevenly, by the removal of the Mica, to a minutely flaky surface of a reddish- or blackish-brown color.

It is possible that the Mica in some cases becomes so prominent as to entitle the rock to the name " Mica-Schist" (*e.g.* Formation XI., at Republic Mountain).   See also Nos. 1018, 1019, 1020, 1021, 1022, and 1023, and also Nos. 1005, 1006, 1016, and 1055, of Appendix C, and Vol. I., page 100.

Schalstone.—This Huronian rock has been found in four or five localities, but only one specimen occurs in the collection (No. 338), probably corresponding to No. 1025 of Appendix C.   It is a variety produced in the preceding rock by an increased proportion of Calcite, up to 2 or 3 parts.   This mineral is distributed, either in thin lenticular flakes or in amygdules, both probably originating in an amygdaloidal structure.   To this rock probably belongs a part of the Amygdaloid described under Dioryte-Greenstone.   One variety, by no means uncommon, is rich in Chlorite, the grains of Calcite being quite small.   There is also a variety of Greenstone-Ash (Nos. 194 and 205), which contains much Calcite in small grains and might be called a Schalstone.   Weathers unevenly to a greenish-gray surface, sometimes covered with tiny pits of a reddish-brown color.   See also Nos. 1012 and 1025 of Appendix C.

Aphanyte-Schist.—This is a grayish-green aphanitic Huronian rock, of rather rare occurrence (Nos. 70 and 339), whose nature can be determined only by a microscopic examination, or by its association with the preceding rocks.   It is evidently a transition variety of Greenstone-Schist, differing in its aphanitic texture and its universal content of Chlorite.   By the predominance of this mineral, and the consequent production of a thinly laminated structure, the rock passes into the second variety of Chloritic Schists, described under that class (Nos. 182 and 183).   Weathers evenly to a lighter green.

Chlorite-Potstone.—This is a soft, greenish, and mostly aphanitic Huronian rock, also of rather rare occurrence, which resembles the preceding, but is chiefly composed of Chlorite, and is traversed by this mineral in an irregular network (No. 341).

Transition varieties occur, in which the Chlorite is disseminated as usual in scales and irregularly, or by its parallel arrangement produces a schist (No. 73), or decreases in quantity to 2 parts (No. 340); but even these are characterized by their softness and the large quantity of water they lose by ignition. Calcite is also present, sometimes in considerable quantity (No. 73). Weathers unevenly to a darker green.

X. Trappean Dioryte.

This name is proposed provisionally for a peculiar and interesting rock which seems to be identical in composition with the Diorytes, but rather resembles a Doleryte in general appearance and mode of weathering. There is reason to believe (see Vol. I., pages 155 and 156) that it is an intrusive rock, and, as I have not yet been able to identify it with any certainty, the above name will suffice for our present purpose.

The color of this rock is, when unaltered, black (Nos. 342, 343, and 347), but in other cases, greenish-gray (Nos. 344 and 346), grayish-green (No. 350), and blackish-brown (Nos. 345, 348, and 349). Its structure is always massive like that of the unaltered Diorytes, but more crystalline, being porphyritic in regard to both its constituent minerals. Its texture varies from a coarse rock, in which the crystals are usually $\frac{1}{16}$ inch, sometimes $\frac{1}{8}$ inch across (Nos. 342 and 347), to a fine-grained rock in which they appear as glittering points to the naked eye (Nos. 343, 345, and 350).

The Amphibole resembles Augite in appearance, and amounts to 5, sometimes 6, parts of the rock (No. 347); is of a black (Nos. 342 and 347), brownish-black (Nos. 344 and 348), or grayish-green color (No. 350), brownish when altered (No. 345); and weathers out unchanged in color and projecting above the Feldspar. The Feldspar amounts to nearly 5 parts, and its color is grayish-white (Nos. 342, 344, 346, and 347), sometimes inclining to greenish or yellowish, and sometimes greenish-gray (No. 345).

Magnetite is universally present and may be generally distinguished easily upon the weathered surface; so that the magnet separates from 3 to 5 per cent. of the powder, and the rock is feebly magnetic (Nos. 342, 343, and 346).

Chlorite was distinguished in only one specimen (No. 349), in thin films; also Epidote (No. 348), and two minerals resembling Serpentine and Micaceous-Iron, in small quantity (No. 345). In one specimen (No. 342) the rock gives a feeble effervescence in acid.

In weathering, the fine-grained varieties assume a light color (yellowish- or reddish-brown), are traversed by Chlorite, etc., and pass into a soft Wacké (No. 352 and 353); the coarser varieties assume a much lighter color (usually brownish-gray), mottled with the blackish-green and roughened by the projection of the less altered crystals of Amphibole, and the rock is traversed by minute fissures (No. 342), more abundantly than in the Diorytes, becomes very friable (No. 344), and finally disintegrates into a coarse, angular, dark-greenish sand largely made up of weather-worn, separated crystals of the two minerals.

Porphyry.—Only one specimen has been observed (No. 351), consisting of about 3 parts of tiny crystals of brown Feldspar, in about 7 parts of a bluish-green pyritiferous paste. In the latter, crystals of altered blackish-green Amphibole can be distinguished on a polished section.

Wacké.—In the decomposition, by weathering, of the two preceding rocks, the Feldspar becomes softened and resembles Kaolin, assuming a grayish-green (No. 345) or yellowish color (Nos. 352 and 353). The Amphibole is softened, becomes a reddish-brown, and is sometimes associated with Ochre or Micaceous-Iron. The result is a soft earthy Wacké, in which the reddish-brown color predominates (Nos. 352 and 353).

YOUNGER FELDSPATHIC ROCKS.

XI. Dioryte–Aphanyte.

Certain dykes, of a distinctly intrusive character, occur in this region in four inconspicuous localities, represented by Nos. 354 to 357—No. 355 being Laurentian. Their material is always very hard, compact, heavy, and, unless fissured by weathering, tough, but its texture is too nearly crypto-crystalline to allow its exact identification without a more thorough microscopic investigation than I have yet made.

In structure it is either compact (Nos. 355 and 357), or coarsely laminated (No. 354), or possesses the coarse cross-cleavage characteristic of a trap-dyke (No. 356, and also in other varieties of No. 357 not in this collection). In texture the coarsest variety (No. 354) is finer than almost any Dioryte, while others resemble jasper (Nos. 355 and 356) or the finest porcelain (No. 357), with a few coarse specks—but never vitreous. The color varies from grayish-black to grayish-green, with a gray streak, with sometimes a little shining lustre, and almost always minute glittering facets. The fracture varies from conchoidal to even, but, by weathering, usually becomes very irregular and uneven through the formation of innumerable minute fissures. The weathered surface assumes a brownish color, lighter than the fresh fracture, and is generally smooth, giving no clue to the constituent minerals.

The constitution of this rock is, in the main, evidently feldspathic, as revealed by its fusion before the blowpipe, general physical properties, and the determination of the glittering facets under the loupe as tiny crystals of greenish or blackish feldspar.

A hard black mineral also can sometimes be distinguished in facets, feldspathic in appearance, some of which are even $\frac{1}{16}$ inch in length (Nos. 354 and 356, and No. 79 of Appendix B). Much Pyrite is also disseminated, in particles and seams associated with films of grayish-white Calcite (No. 354).

In a very thin microscopic section, tiny crystals of a triclinic feldspar (the facets already referred to) are readily distinguished, and, smaller and more rarely, hexagonal sections of a greenish hornblendic mineral, whose dichroism identifies it as Amphibole—dispersed through a cloudy ground-mass which I have not yet seen satisfactorily resolved.

The most interesting locality to examine this dyke-material is at the extremity of Light-House Point, near Marquette, where a highly metamorphosed rock occurs, in beds dipping about 80° to the north, which in different parts would be called a Chloritic Schist, Talcose Schist, and Amphibole-Schist. This passes in some places into indurated varieties of these rocks, a massive coarse Dioryte,

Dioryte-Schist, Greenstone-Schist, and a dark Dioryte-Greenstone, sometimes concretionary in structure. Towards the east end of the Point, and mostly along with the strike, these schists are traversed, with rare and slight evidences of flexure or any movement by disruption, by numerous small and branching dykes, from less than an inch to 3 or 4 feet across, broken into angular elbows and occasionally enclosing small dislodged fragments of the schist. Their ordinary arrangement may be understood from the description and figures of Credner, in his Article (loc. cit., pages 548 and 549, with Table XII., figs. 3 and 4), but it is also interesting that in the narrower dykes, three or four successive intersections of each other can be made out, as if belonging to successive periods. The wider and coarser dykes consist of the coarse Dioryte, and can mostly be seen to branch out from the larger masses of that rock, which appear to me in general not to be intrusive but merely due to the metamorphism of the original schist. In some of the dykes, as they thin out towards their terminations, the material becomes finer-grained, shows a tendency to cross-cleavage, and passes into the crypto-crystalline texture represented by No. 357. This locality I think well deserves a more thorough study, both for its geological and lithological phenomena.

At another locality, on the Mineral-Branch Railroad, at the west end of the first bridge east of Iron Cliffs (on the line between Sections 18 and 19—T. 47—R. 27), occurs a fine section of a large outcrop of Dioryte-Greenstone overlaid by Chloritic Schist. At the junction of these two rocks a black, heavy, aphanitic rock, with sub-conchoidal fracture, may be observed, which, though not intrusive, appears to be identical in constitution with this class.

C. FRAGMENTAL ROCKS.

Two varieties of rock of, I believe, rare occurrence, have been included in this division. The first mentioned occurs also in pebbles in the Quartz-Conglomerates, and it is probably a variety which has escaped the induration by which the Quartzytes and Quartz-Schists have been produced.

XII. Sandstone-Schist.

The more common variety of this rock (Nos. 358 and 359) is a loosely-aggregated, arenaceous, grayish-white Sandstone, inclining to a banded structure, chiefly composed of minute granules of grayish-white Quartz, with a little Magnetite arranged in the black layers, and small particles of Ochre, Mica, and Chlorite, irregularly dispersed.

The other variety (No. 360) is one of the Kaolinic Sandstone-Schists of the Silurian beds, and is peculiar for a predominance of flakes of Chloritic Schist.

DESCRIPTIVE LITHOLOGY.

The numbers, from 101 to 360 inclusive, are attached to the descriptions, and are those referred to in Vol. I., Part I. The numbers from 688 upward are those attached to the specimens in the collection of T. B. Brooks. The numbers from 1 to 100 are contained in Appendix B.

No. 101 (Specimen 984).—*Ferruginous Crystalline Limestone.*

Huronian.—Section 28—Township 51—Range 31.

Grayish-white, speckled with blackish-gray and brownish-red spots.

A tough, coarsely granular Limestone, sparkling with facets of Calcite, about ⅛ inch across, about one-half of which are blackish-gray and brownish-red in color, and the remainder grayish-white. It is also evident, on the somewhat weathered surface of a fissure, that the facets of Calcite are enclosed and separated by thin films of Siderite, of a yellowish-brown color, and this mineral probably amounts to about ¼ of the bulk of the rock.

Fracture uneven. Streak reddish-white. Effervesces strongly in hydrochloric acid, dissolving readily with very little residue, and the solution contains only a very small quantity of Magnesia.

The weathered surface is of a brownish-red color, deeply and roughly pitted by the erosion of the calcareous grains. The concretionary character of most of the latter is beautifully shown by the projection, around and within the little pit formerly occupied by each grain, of minute laminæ of Siderite, of a yellowish-brown color; six or seven of such concentric circles may be sometimes counted within each cavity, surrounding a tiny solid nucleus of the same material.

No. 102 (Sp. 1231).—*White Saccharoidal Dolomite-Marble.*

Huronian.—S. E. ¼ Sect. 35—T. 42—R. 30.

White, with a slight yellowish tinge, and yellowish streak; sparkling.

A rather fine grained, saccharoidal, compact Dolomite, with a few short parallel but not continuous streaks of a light yellowish-brown color, which suggest its plane of stratification.

Fracture even and smooth. Streak white. Effervesces very slowly in cold hydrochloric acid, like a pure Dolomite, and dissolves with a small, white, siliceous residue.

Weathering even, but a little roughened by the projection of the crystalline grains, about $\frac{1}{16}$ inch in depth, and of a dirty yellowish-brown color. The edges of the laminæ of the rock are rendered apparent as minute crevices on a weathered transverse section.

No. 103 (Sp. 1233).—*Grayish Saccharoidal Dolomite-Marble.*

Huronian.—North ½ Sect. 35—T. 42—R. 30.

Grayish-white, with light-green spots.

A marble similar to No. 102, but grayish-white in color, and without the streaks or any other indication of lamination in the hand specimen.

Broad, irregular-bladed crystals, ⅛–½ inch long, of a very light-green mineral (apparently Tremolite) are dispersed through the specimen.

Fracture uneven. Streak white. Effervesces like No. 102 in acid, and leaves a larger residue.

Weathering similar to that of No. 102, the tabular crystals projecting considerably above the surface.

No. 104 (Sp. 877).—*Fine-grained Greenish-white Dolomite.*

Silurian.—Presqu'isle, near S. end of Island.

Grayish-white, with tinge of green, mottled with light reddish-brown and olive-green specks.

A hard, tough, compact, fine-grained saccharoidal Dolomite, through which many tiny particles and bunches of soft olive-green Serpentine are irregularly dispersed. A few minute fissures occur, sometimes expanding into geodes lined with rhombs of Dolomite.

Fracture rather uneven. Streak greenish-white.

Weathers roughly to a grayish-black color.

No. 105 (Sp. 1242).—*Fine-grained Gray Dolomite-Marble.*

Huronian.—Fence and Deer River.

A light grayish-drab, with a decided rosy tinge, and a few small rose-brown spots.

A very hard and tough, fine-grained, crystalline, compact, siliceous Dolomite, with a little brown Dolomite interspersed in irregular minute seams and tiny bunches.

Fracture even and smooth. Streak grayish-white. Effervesces very feebly, but dissolves almost entirely in hydrochloric acid.

Weathering very thin, of a dirty cream color, streaked irregularly by the blackish-brown parallel edges of minute cherty seams and bunches, which slightly project over all the surface and betoken the lamination of the material.

No. 106 (Sp. 795).—*Coarse Red Dolomite.*

Huronian.—V.—Chocolate Marble Quarry, South of mouth of Carp, L. S.

Light flesh-red, with brown and blackish-brown streaks and spots; glistening.

A tough, coarsely crystalline, compact Dolomite, made up of Dolomite in facets $\frac{1}{16}$ to $\frac{1}{8}$ inch across. Many minute seams and small irregular spots or stains of a brownish or blackish-brown color, and others, not quite so numerous, of green Talc.

Fracture uneven. Effervesces very feebly in cold, strongly in hot acid.

Weathering about ¼ inch in depth, of a brownish-red color (darker than fresh surface), with a surface roughened by the deeper erosion of the talcose layers and bunches.

No. 107 (Sp. 796).—*Banded Dolomite-Marble.*

Huronian.—V.—Chocolate Marble Quarry, South of mouth of Carp, L. S.

Brownish-red, with many grayish-white, reddish-gray, and light flesh-red bands ; glittering.

A tough, finely granular compact Marble, generally much harder than No. 106, made up of alternating layers, usually ⅛ to ½ inch in thickness, of two materials ; the one of a grayish-white or reddish-white color, and the other darker and harder, of a brownish-red color, inclining to rose. The lighter colored layers are made up of coarsely crystallized Dolomite, with facets rarely as large as $\frac{1}{16}$ of an inch. The darker layers consist of a fine-grained, compact mixture of Quartz and Dolomite, and are harder than the others. Many seams cross the lamination irregularly, sometimes with tiny faults filled with brown Dolomite and milky or glassy Quartz, and in the latter small cherty bunches occur.

Fracture rather even, especially on the siliceous layers. Effervesces in acid like No. 106.

Weathered surface smooth and of a dirty light-brown color.

No. 108 (Sp. 797).—*Rosy Siliceous Dolomite.*

Huronian.—Bed V.—Chocolate Marble Quarry, South of mouth of Carp, L. S.

A reddish-brown, inclining to rose, with a very few dirty gray streaks (similar in color to the darker bands in No. 107); glittering.

A very tough, hard, fine-grained, compact Dolomite, with a lamination faintly indicated by parallel bands of a darker shade, inclining to gray. It consists of layers, usually from ½ to 1 inch in thickness, of two materials : the one consists of Dolomite of a reddish-brown color inclining to rose, and so fine-grained as to be almost crypto-crystalline, and the other of aggregations of thin wavy laminæ, about $\frac{1}{16}$ inch in thickness, of Quartz or Hornstone of a very light reddish-brown or a smoky-gray color. The whole rock is also traversed (and so receives a peculiar cleavage) by innumerable minute seams, at an angle of about 60° with the lamination, filled with minute films of silver-gray and light-green scales of Talc. Other more irregular seams sometimes occur, up to ⅛ inch in thickness, and filled with brown coarsely crystalline Dolomite.

Fracture uneven. Effervesces like No. 107, leaving much residue after solution, consisting of white and reddish-white particles.

Weathers very decidedly, the calcareous layers assuming a cream color, with a light reddish-brown shade ; while the siliceous layers project uniformly above the surface, sometimes as much as ¼ inch, unchanged in color, and presenting a beautifully distinct section of the wavy laminæ of which they are composed.

No. 109 (Sp. 798).—*Mottled Dolomite-Marble.*

Huronian.—Bed V.—Chocolate Marble Quarry, South of mouth of Carp, L. S.

Light reddish-brown, inclining to rose, mottled with gray ; minutely glittering.

A very tough, hard, fine-grained, and compact siliceous Dolomite, made up of little angular masses, ⅛ to ¼ inch across, of a reddish-white and of a reddish-brown color, and with minute seams of silvery-gray and light green scales of Talc disseminated throughout.

Fracture uneven. Streak reddish-white. Effervesces more briskly in cold acid than No. 106, and leaves much white residue after solution.

Weathered surface of a dirty cream color, and rendered uneven by the projection of certain harder laminæ (revealing the schistose structure of the rock), and of roughly rhombohedral crystals of Dolomite of a reddish-brown color, inclining to rose, and about ¼ inch across.

No. 110 (Sp. 799).—*Talco-Siliceous Dolomite.*

Huronian.—Bed V.—Chocolate Marble Quarry, South of mouth of Carp, L. S.

Resembles No. 108 in color, structure, and weathering ; but the siliceous layers are not over ⅛ inch in thickness, and without the wavy lamination. The Talc is also more irregularly disposed and in thicker seams.

Fracture uneven. Effervesces rather more briskly in acid than No. 106, leaving much residue after solution, like that of No. 108.

No. 111 (Sp. 800).—*Rosy Talcose Dolomite.*

Huronian.—Bed V.—Chocolate Marble Quarry, South of mouth of Carp, L. S.

Resembles No. 109 in color, and No. 108 in the arrangement of the talcose films ; but coarser and almost devoid of the siliceous laminæ, which are represented only by a few tiny bunches, hardly ½ an inch long. Hence the lamination cannot be distinguished in the hand specimen. A few brownish-red spots on some of the talcose seams.

Effervesces slightly with acid. The residue, insoluble in acid, contains many red particles.

Fracture uneven. Streak reddish-white and greenish-white.

In another specimen, 808, the plane of lamination certainly coincides with that of the talcose seams, being revealed over the dirty light-brown weathered surface by the projection of the thin edges of innumerable, minute, siliceous laminæ. Rather brisker effervescence in acid than with No. 106.

No. 112 (Sp. 809).—*Mottled Dolomite.*

Huronian.—Bed V.—Chocolate Marble Quarry, South of mouth of Carp, L. S.

Greenish-gray, with shade of citrine-yellow, mottled throughout with flesh-red, and with irregular stripes of gray, brownish-gray, reddish-white, and reddish-brown.

A compact, tough, hard, coarsely granular Dolomite, made up of coarse layers, 1 to 3 inches thick, chiefly of a material similar to that of No. 111, but much coarser, partly of a finer material so traversed by talcose and argillaceous films as to assume an obliquely laminated structure, and partly of a rather coarse aggregation of granules of Quartz and Dolomite, and of minute scales of gray Talc.

Fracture uneven. Streak usually reddish-white. Effervesces rather more briskly in acid than No. 106, leaving a very large residue, chiefly white Quartz, with some red granules.

Weathers very roughly, the quartzose layers and laminæ projecting irregularly and considerably above those more calcareous.

No. 113 (Sp. 811).—*Rosy Talcose Dolomite.*

Huronian.—Bed V.—Chocolate Marble Quarry, South of mouth of Carp, L. S.

Resembles No. 108 in color and material, and No. 110 in the abundance and arrangement of the Talc, and in the mode and color of weathering. Differs from both in the indescribably irregular distribution of the brown Dolomite and the somewhat rarer Chert, in broken seams and tiny bunches crossing each other at all angles and almost concealing the plane of lamination.

Fracture uneven. Streak reddish-white. Effervesces more briskly in acid than No. 106.

No. 114 (Sp. 688).—*Black Quartz-Conglomerate.*

Huronian.—N. side Sect. 19—T. 47—R. 27.

Brownish-black, with grayish-white specks ; glistening.

A very tough, hard and compact, coarse Quartzyte, consisting of an aggregate of small, somewhat angular, fragments of smoky Quartz, about $\frac{1}{16}$ inch across, with similar fragments of colorless and milky Quartz, and small flattened particles of reddish-white Quartz, and bluish-brown, brick-red and reddish-brown Jasper, rarely $\frac{1}{2}$ inch in diameter, arranged in mostly parallel planes and so suggesting the plane of bedding.

Color chiefly due to the smoky Quartz, with slight mottling of the other varieties.

Fracture rather uneven. Streak grayish-white.

Weathering to a dark-brown in shade, but with smooth surface.

No. 115 (Sp. 715).—*Gray Quartz-Conglomerate.*

Huronian.—Bed XIV.—Spurr Mountain, Sect. 24—T. 48—R. 31.

Grayish-white, mottled with olive-green and greenish spots.

A tough, hard, compact Quartz Conglomerate, chiefly made up

of about 7 parts of somewhat angular masses of milky Quartz, up to ⅓ inch in diameter, with about 3 parts of white, fine-grained, laminated Quartz, soft, arenaceous Quartz, and green Chloritic Schist, in flat angular fragments, sometimes 1 inch across, with a little smoky Quartz and Chalcedony.

Fracture uneven. Scratches with difficulty. Streak grayish-white. Seams colored brownish by Ochre, apparently from decomposition of the Chlorite.

Weathered surface of the same color as the fresh fracture. Fragments of milky Quartz project decidedly, from the greater softness of the arenaceous Quartz and Chloritic Schist.

No. 116 (Sp. 716).—*Mottled Quartz-Conglomerate.*

Huronian.—Bed XIV.—Spurr Mountain, Sect. 24—T. 48—R. 31.

Grayish-green, mottled with greenish-white spots and small grayish-black glistening specks.

A tough, hard, compact, coarse Quartz-Conglomerate, of which about half the bulk is composed of rounded pebbles of white (sometimes slightly greenish), soft, arenaceous Quartz, up to 1 inch in diameter. The matrix is made up of about equal parts of milky Quartz, inclining to Chalcedony, and smoky Quartz, in small angular fragments. The pebbles sometimes contain minute particles of Pyrite.

Fracture uneven. Streak grayish and greenish-white.

Weathered surface of about the same color as the fresh surface, but a little roughened by the greater softness of the pebbles.

No. 117 (Sp. 717).—*Chloritic Quartz-Conglomerate.*

Huronian.—Bed XIV.—Spurr Mountain, Sect. 24—T. 48—R. 31.

Blackish-green, mottled with grayish-white and light-brown.

A rather tough, compact Conglomerate, of varying hardness and grain. About half its bulk is composed of rounded pebbles, sometimes 1½ inch across, of white and reddish-white arenaceous Quartz. The matrix consists of small fragments of milky and smoky Quartz, mingled irregularly with a soft chloritic mineral, in blackish-green scales, having a light-green streak.

Fracture uneven.   Streak greenish and reddish-white, light-green, and light brownish-yellow.   Minute particles of Pyrite are disseminated through the pebbles and their matrix, but are mostly decomposed, imparting a brownish-red mottling to the pebbles, to the seams of the rock, and to its weathered surface.   Some of the seams are lined with the chloritic mineral in thin fibrous sheets. The same was observed in No. 118.   It also seems to occur sometimes in lenticular masses, nearly ½ inch in thickness.

Weathers roughly and irregularly, the siliceous portion of the matrix generally projecting above the remainder of the rock.

No. 118 (Sp. 718).—*Greenish Quartz-Conglomerate.*

Huronian.—Bed XIV.—Spurr Mountain, Sect. 24—T. 48—R. 31.

Blackish-green, mottled with light yellowish-brown spots and small grayish and greenish-black shining specks.

A tough, hard, compact Quartz-Conglomerate of varying grain. About one-quarter of the bulk of the rock is made up of rounded pebbles of reddish-white, arenaceous Quartz, from ¼ to 1 inch in diameter.   Matrix greenish-black, similar in composition to that of No. 114, but chiefly of much finer texture ; is mottled by small angular fragments, principally of smoky Quartz, and occasionally of green Jasper, crystallized Pyrite, and blackish-green scales of the soft chloritic mineral which occurs in No. 117.

Fracture uneven, sometimes sub-conchoidal.   Streak greenish-white ; a few reddish-brown seams.

Weathered surface reddish-brown and pretty smooth.

In Sp. 719 the pebbles are very few and small, and contain a little more Pyrite; a very tough, and rather fine-grained rock.

Sp. 720 is more deeply decomposed by weathering (nearly ½ inch) and perhaps contains more of the chloritic mineral in its matrix.

In Sp. 721, one of the pebbles reveals, far more decidedly than any in the previous specimens, that it is derived from a laminated material.   It is made up of alternating layers of a white, rose-red, and dark-greenish, arenaceous Quartz, often colored and mottled reddish-brown—apparently by the decomposition of Pyrite.

Sp. 727 contains much more Pyrite, in particles sometimes ¾ inch across.

Weathers roughly, the grains of milky and smoky Quartz projecting above the reddish arenaceous grains and masses, the chloritic mineral being eroded the most deeply of all.

No. 119.—*Kaolinic Hematite-Breccia.*

Huronian.

Gray and dull, minutely speckled with grayish-white, and with large grayish-black spots ; a few minute glittering points.

A compact, heavy, hard, coarse Breccia, made up of about equal parts of flattened angular grayish-black fragments, whose dimensions range from tiny flakes up to one inch in length, and ¼ inch thick, which have mostly a parallel arrangement, and thus impart a schistose structure—in a gray fine-grained paste, speckled throughout with grayish-white particles, some of which are over ¼ inch across and rectangular. The pebbles consist of a Jaspery Hematite, generally of a minutely laminated structure, composed of a dull aphanitic material containing many glittering points, which are revealed under the lens to be octahedra of Martite; its hardness is so great that it gives a streak with a file, which is partly metallic, by abrasion, and partly brownish-red. The paste consists of about seven parts of similar octahedra of Martite, and perhaps scales of Micaceous-Iron, and of three parts of grayish-white Kaolin. Streak brick-red.

Fracture hackly. The specimen is not magnetic. Weathers unevenly and roughly to about the same color as the fresh fracture, covered with a film of brownish-red Ochre.

No. 120 (Sp. 875).—*Red Jasper-Conglomerate.*

Silurian.—Presqu'isle, Marquette, L. S.

Brownish-red and shining, mottled with greenish-gray.

A very hard, compact, tough Conglomerate, ¾ of whose bulk is made up of irregular nodules, 1 to 3 inches across, of brownish-red

Jasper, of impalpable texture, rarely crystalline, sub-conchoidal fracture, and hardly touched by the file, with much white Quartz disseminated throughout in tiny seams, bunches, and yellowish-brown drusy geodes, sometimes $\frac{1}{2}$ inch long. A few films of a reddish and yellowish-brown softer material, with light reddish-brown streak, also traverse the pebbles. The matrix consists of a soft, tough, greenish-gray, fine-grained aggregate, with uneven fracture, and greenish-white streak, of minute granules of white and greenish-white Jasper, smoky Quartz, grayish-white scales of silvery-gray Mica, tiny flat fragments of a brownish-black material, etc., with white and smoky Quartz dispersed throughout in bunches, usually $\frac{1}{4}$ to $\frac{1}{2}$ inch across.

Weathers unevenly, the nodules projecting roughly, unchanged in color.

No. 121 (Sp. 878).—*Brown Jasper-Conglomerate.*

Silurian.—Presqu'isle, Marquette, L. S.

Dark reddish-brown and dull (matrix), mottled with light reddish-brown and sometimes shining (nodules).

Resembles No. 120. The pebbles, however, rarely possess the brownish-red color, but are of a light reddish-brown, sometimes shining, variegated irregularly with specks of smoky Quartz, rarely $\frac{1}{2}$ inch across: under the lens the whole material is seen to be filled with minute particles of smoky Quartz; the color of the pebbles often becomes lighter towards their edges, and white or reddish-white in contact with the matrix. The latter constitutes $\frac{2}{3}$ of the bulk of the rock, and consists of a tough material, harder than the matrix of No. 120, very fine-grained, and sometimes of almost impalpable texture, having an uneven fracture, and light reddish-brown streak. It is also mottled with a very few round spots, $\frac{1}{16}$ to $\frac{3}{16}$ inch across, of a greenish-gray material, exactly like that of the matrix of No. 120, and is apparently only a decomposed variety of the same; shows about the same constituents under the lens, with a little more Mica, a few fragments of brownish Jasper, and a bright blue particle; is also traversed by a few irregular fissures stained blackish-brown, and is sometimes speckled with tiny particles of a soft, white, slightly greenish pow-

5

der. The bunches and geodes of white Quartz are absent from the rock.

No weathered surface on the specimen.

No. 122 (Sp. 1085).—*Micaceous Conglomerate-Schist.*

Huronian.—Bed XIV.—S. W. of the old Washington Mine.

Grayish-black, with irregular but parallel stripes of grayish-white and brownish-gray; glistening.

A compact, hard, fine-grained Mica-Schist, of a remarkably fibrous structure, which consists of about 7 parts of grayish-white, arenaceous Quartz, in minute granules and angular masses, $\frac{1}{16}$ to $\frac{3}{4}$ inch long, and 3 parts of a steel-gray mixture of black and white Mica, in silvery scales just distinguished by the lens, and whose elongated shape and parallel arrangement impart the fibrous structure. Smoky Quartz also occurs in bunches $\frac{1}{8}$ to $\frac{1}{4}$ inch across, and the rock probably contains a little Feldspar.

Fracture uneven. Streak grayish-white, purplish-gray on the micaceous films, suggesting that the black scales may consist partly or wholly of Micaceous-Iron. The cleavage surfaces are mostly stained brownish-gray.

Weathers unevenly, to a dirty iron-black, mottled by grayish-white and reddish-brown.

No. 123 (Sp. 693).—*Quartzose Feldspar-Breccia.*

Boulder from Jackson, Mich.

Greenish-black, with specks of yellowish-green and smoky-gray, and mottled with large salmon-colored spots.

A hard, compact, rather brittle, coarse Breccia, of porphyritic appearance. About 5 parts consist of angular fragments of crystals of a triclinic Feldspar, with good cleavage, usually from $\frac{1}{8}$ to $\frac{1}{2}$ inch across, and often minutely striated. This light salmon color contrasts finely with the darker matrix, and the frequent reddish-brown spots, on their planes of cleavage, are evidence of a process of alteration. Irregular angular fragments of smoky-gray Quartz, $\frac{1}{8}$ to $\frac{1}{4}$ inch across, and of yellowish-green crystalline Epidote, $\frac{1}{16}$ to $\frac{1}{8}$ inch across, are disseminated throughout, each amounting to about 1 part. The matrix amounts to about 3 parts, and appears under the lens to consist chiefly of smoky-gray Quartz, with much greenish-black Epidote (possibly Actinolite?) disseminated throughout in minute needles, often arranged in radiating groups.

Fracture very uneven ; streak grayish and reddish-white ; effervesces slightly in acid.

Weathers unevenly, with a loss of lustre, and a deepening of the reddish-brown color in the Feldspar crystals.

(No material like that of this boulder has yet been found in place.)

No. 124 (Sp. 1487).—*Schistose Jasper-Breccia.*

Huronian.—Sunday Lake outlet series—W. side Sect. 18—T. 47—R. 45.

Greenish-white, mottled and speckled with greenish-gray.

A coarse, hard, compact Breccia, of a material resembling that of the granular layers of No. 167, but much coarser. It consists of angular, and often flat fragments, of greenish-gray Jasper, of all sizes up to $\frac{3}{4}$ inch in length, in a matrix of minute granules of grayish-white Quartz and greenish-gray Jasper. The parallel arrangement of the flat fragments produces a schistose structure.

Fracture sub-conchoidal. Too hard for the file.

Weathers smoothly, to reddish and yellowish-brown, to a depth of $\frac{1}{8}$ to $\frac{1}{2}$ inch.

No. 125 (Sp. 1490).—*Drusy Jasper-Breccia.*

Huronian.—Lowest bed, Sunday Lake outlet series—Sect. 13—T. 47—R. 46.

Reddish-brown spots, mottled with sparkling brownish-gray and grayish-white.

A hard, tough, cellular Breccia, made up of angular fragments, $\frac{1}{8}$ to 2 inches long, of the two varieties of Jasper of No. 173, partially cemented by glassy Quartz, massive and in tiny crystals, so that the rock is filled with small drusy geodes.

Fracture uneven. Streak on some fragments brownish-red and brownish-yellow.

Weathers unevenly, with a slight polish, and to a dirty cream color.

No. 126 (Sp. 990).—*Grayish-White Quartzyte.*

Huronian.—Slate River, Sect. 28—T. 51—R. 31.

Grayish-white, with a light shade of yellow ; shining.

A very hard, tough, compact Quartzyte, of moderate fineness of texture, chiefly made up of grains of glassy Quartz, easily distinguishable on a fresh fracture, through which are disseminated fewer and more minute granules of milky Quartz, and also tiny and rounded particles of a soft yellowish-white substance.

Fracture uneven and rough. A few seams. Streak grayish-white.

Weathered surface a shade darker than the fresh fracture, and taking a good polish under glacial action, which better reveals its texture ; certain bands of slightly grayer color than the bulk of the rock apparently indicate its plane of bedding.

No. 127 (Sp. 991).—*Conglomeritic Feldspathic Quartzyte.*

Huronian.—Sect. 28—T. 51—R. 31.

Grayish-black, with specks of grayish and reddish-white, etc. ; glistening.

A very hard, tough, cellular, coarse, conglomeritic Quartzyte, made up of angular grains, usually $\frac{1}{16}$ inch across. It consists of about 6 parts of black, smoky, and grayish-white Quartz, of 2 parts of reddish-white Feldspar, and 2 parts of grayish, blackish, and greenish-white Feldspar. The Feldspar grains have a good cleavage and lustre, and are sometimes $\frac{1}{8}$ to $\frac{3}{8}$ inch long. A few black fragments resembling Hornblende were observed. The interstices and the Feldspar-grains are very generally stained with films of reddish-brown and brick-red Ochre.

Fracture uneven.

Weathers unevenly and roughly, with a little loss of lustre, to a blackish-brown, to the depth of $\frac{3}{8}$ inch, with a reddish-brown section, terminated inwardly by a blackish-brown band.

No. 128 (Sp. 803).—*Reddish-Brown Quartzyte.*

Huronian.—Bed V.—Chocolate Marble Quarry, South of mouth of Carp, L. S.

Gray, inclining to reddish or light chocolate-brown, with grayish-white specks ; shining.

Material chiefly a mixture of smoky and white and glassy Quartz, many of the grains of which (few larger than $\frac{1}{8}$ inch) may be distinguished. Much Ferric Oxide is disseminated in innumerable minute seams throughout the rock, imparts to it its purple tint, and also covers its larger fissures. On the surface of the latter many tiny geodes of small Quartz crystals occur, but these are generally filled with Ferric Oxide.

Fracture uneven, but pretty smooth. Streak reddish-white.

The weathered differs from the fresh surface chiefly in the absence of all lustre ; is rendered somewhat irregular by the splitting of the rock in flakes, on account of its many minute seams ; and where polished by glacial action, the various grains of which it is composed are very well displayed.

No. 129 (Sp. 1251).—*Light-Brown Quartzyte.*

Huronian.—From near S. $\frac{1}{4}$ post, Sect. 34—T. 43—R. 30.

A light shade of snuff-colored brown, mottled with grayish-white ; shining.

A very hard, tough, rather coarse, but homogeneous, compact Quartzyte, made up of particles readily distinguishable by the eye ; chiefly a mixture of light-brown and white or glassy Quartz, with a few seams containing small crystals of Garnet and Actinolite, and minute scales of silvery-white Mica.

Fracture uneven. Streak grayish-white.

Weathered surface grayish-white, smooth, and often polished by glacial action.

No. 130 (Sp. 1471).—*Flesh-Colored Quartzyte.*

S. $\frac{1}{4}$ post, Sect. 10–47–45.

Flesh-colored, faintly banded with grayish-white ; slightly shining.

A very hard, tough, uniform, fine-grained rock, with granules easily distinguishable, and of laminated structure. The bands are usually about $\frac{1}{4}$ inch in thickness, and consist of alternations of granules of light reddish-brown and glassy Quartz.

Fracture sub-conchoidal and smooth. Streak reddish-white.

Weathered surface a little lighter in color, and somewhat roughened by the irregular projection of some of the laminæ.

Specimen 1472 is more coarsely schistose, composed of the same
material (chiefly of the flesh-colored sort), in layers about an inch
thick, alternating with layers ⅛–¼ inch thick, of a coarse and
crystalline aggregation of granules of milky and glassy Quartz, and
of a soft blackish-green mineral, with many small geodes lined with
crystals of these two minerals.

No. 131 (Sp. 1243).—*Smoky-Gray Quartzyte.*

Huronian.—Michigammi River.—Sect. 25—T. 43—R. 30.

Smoky-gray, minutely speckled with grayish-white, almost without lustre.

A hard, very compact, and tough, rather fine-grained, uniform
calcareous Quartzyte, which appears under the lens to consist of
about equal bulks of gray and grayish-white Quartz, interspersed
with a few granules of smoky-gray Quartz, and a few tiny facets of
Feldspar.

Fracture even. Streak grayish-white. Effervesces slightly with
acid. A little Pyrite also occurs in tiny yellow particles.

Weathered surface smooth, and of an olive-color.

Specimen 907 (Boulder from N. W. ¼ S. 9—T. 49—R. 33) is a
little finer grained, contains no Pyrite, and weathers to an ashy-
gray.

The color of Specimen 909 (Boulder like 907) is of a slightly
lighter shade; a schistose structure can be just distinguished, and it
weathers somewhat unevenly to dirty shades of greenish, blackish,
and brownish-gray. Effervesces decidedly in acid.

No. 132 (Sp. 1459).—*Greenish-Gray Quartzyte.*

Huronian.—N. W. ¼ of S. W. ¼ of Sect. 10—T. 47—R. 45.

Dark greenish-gray, slightly mottled with light brownish-gray;
dull.

A fine-grained, compact, tough, uniform material, with granules
distinguishable by the lens, and of schistose structure, chiefly made

up of smoky Quartz, with a little white or glassy Quartz, and many minute particles, just visible to the eye, of a yellowish or reddish-brown color.

Fracture sub-conchoidal.   Streak greenish-white.

Weathered surface smooth, and colored two or three very light shades of drab.

No. 133 (Sp. 812).—*Rosy-Gray Quartzyte.*

Huronian.—Bed V.—Chocolate Marble Quarry.

Rose-colored, mottled and banded with ashy or brownish-gray ; slightly shining.

A very hard, compact, fine-grained Quartzyte, of sub-schistose structure, the layers being usually from ½ to 2 or 3 inches in thickness.   The thickest layers are of a flesh-color, inclining to rose, the thinner are darker, and incline to grayish ; and both these shades are often mingled in the same layer.   When the color is uniform, the texture is crypto-crystalline, but in the portions of darker and mingled colors, the minute grains are easily distinguishable with a lens.

Fracture sub-conchoidal and smooth, but covered with the edges of tiny flakes which betoken the fineness of the grain.   Streak reddish-white.   One thin layer consists of chocolate-brown Argillyte (with a light pinkish streak), through which are disseminated many very minute seams of silvery-white scales of Talc.

The weathered surface is smooth, lustreless, and banded, the darker layers weathering to a blackish color, and the lighter to a light-brown.

No. 134 (Sp. 816).—*Slaty-Gray Quartzyte.*

Huronian.—South of mouth of Carp, L. S.

Specimen covered with ripple marks ; grayish-white, with the slightest shade of brown.

A rather brittle, tough, hard, fine-grained, compact, schistose Quartzyte, made up of very fine granules, ranging often in size up to $\frac{1}{16}$ of an inch, and generally very distinct.   Layers generally about ½ inch in thickness, the lines of lamination being usually a crevice, and of a darker and yellowish tint; a few minute seams of Quartz crossing the lamination obliquely.

Fracture almost even. Chocolate-brown spots on some of the surfaces of lamination. Streak grayish-white.

No. 135 (Sp. 1473).—*Brownish-Gray Quartzyte.*

Huronian.—S. W. ¼ Sect. 9—T. 47—R. 45.

A light brownish-gray, slightly mottled with light-gray, and covered with large reddish-brown spots, about an inch in diameter; shining.

A very hard, tough, uniform, fine-grained material, with distinguishable granules, chiefly smoky Quartz, with a very little glassy Quartz; while the spots are composed of a loose aggregation of small granules of glassy Quartz, with their tiny interstices lined or partly filled with a brown powder.

Fracture sub-conchoidal and smooth. Streak grayish-white.

Weathered surface smooth and of a light grayish-drab color, spotted with brown.

No. 136 (Sp. 1476).—*Bluish-Gray Quartzyte.*

Huronian.—N. E. corner Sect. 17—T. 47—R. 46.

A cast-iron gray, with a shade of dark bluish-green; dull.

A tough, hard, uniform, calcareous Quartzyte, of impalpable texture, in which any granules can barely and seldom be distinguished by the lens. Entirely composed of smoky Quartz.

Fracture nearly conchoidal and very smooth. Streak greenish-white. Effervesces slightly with acid.

Weathering smooth, of a dirty cream color, and rarely penetrating $\frac{1}{16}$ of an inch in depth.

No. 137 (Sp. 901).—*Manganiferous Smoky Quartzyte.*

Huronian.—L'Anse Iron Range, N. W. ¼ Sect. 9—T. 47—R. 33.

Smoky-gray, with reddish tint, mottled with seams of brownish-yellow; dull.

A very compact, hard, tough, fine-grained Quartzyte, consisting of minute granules of smoky, and, in smaller quantity, grayish-white Quartz, with many minute particles interspersed of brownish-yellow Ochre. Large irregular seams, uniformly lined with brownish-yellow Ochre and with a few tiny bunches, films, and geodes of lustrous brownish-black Pyrolusite; minute glittering crystals of the latter are also disseminated through the Ochre.

Fracture sub-conchoidal, too hard for the file.

Weathered surface uneven and covered with the Ochre.

No. 138 (Sp. 939).—*Feldspathic Quartzyte.*

Laurentian.—N. side of Sect. 16—T. 49—R. 33, south of Plumbago Creek.

Cast-iron gray, closely covered with tiny smoky-gray specks.

A very hard, tough, compact, fine-grained, uniform Quartzyte, made up of smoky-gray and grayish-white Quartz, mostly in indistinguishable particles, but with a few, about $\frac{1}{32}$ inch in diameter, with much Feldspar of the same color disseminated in glistening facets of about the same size, and a few thin flakes, $\frac{1}{8}$ to $\frac{3}{8}$ inch long, of a soft, blackish, laminated mineral, with gray streak, perhaps Argillyte, by whose parallel arrangement a slightly schistose structure is produced. A few irregular fissures. A vein of milky Quartz, about $\frac{1}{4}$ inch thick.

Fracture uneven. Streak grayish-white.

Weathers evenly to a dirty light brownish-gray color.

Another variety may be described as follows :—

(Sp. 977.)—*Feldspathic Quartz-Schist.*

N. side of Sect. 27—T. 51—R. 32.

Brownish-gray ; slightly glistening.

A hard, compact, tough, very fine-grained Quartz-Schist, which appears under the lens to consist of perhaps 7 parts of grayish-white and smoky-gray Quartz, in minute granules rarely $\frac{1}{16}$ inch in diameter, and 3 parts of smoky- or brownish-gray Feldspar, in minute angular grains, rarely in facets with good cleavage and lustre, $\frac{1}{16}$ inch long. Olive-green, shining Chlorite also occurs, in a few minute scales, and in one shining oval flake, $\frac{3}{8}$ inch long.

Fracture uneven. Streak reddish-white. A few fissures stained reddish-brown.

Weathers unevenly to a dirty chocolate-brown, covered with minute cream-colored specks.

No. 139 (Sp. 1478).—*Jaspery Quartzyte.*

Huronian.—$\frac{1}{4}$ post between Sects. 7 and 18—T. 47—R. 45.

Bright brownish-red, and speckled with white and gray spots; dull.

A hard, somewhat brittle, granular, but compact rock, traversed by numerous irregular fissures. Chiefly consists of rounded, sometimes nearly spherical grains, rarely over $\frac{1}{32}$ inch in diameter, of brownish-red Jasper, set in a paste of white and smoky-gray Chalcedony. When the grains are spherical their section presents somewhat of an oölitic appearance. Many other minute particles are revealed by the lens, of a yellowish-white and of a black color, and the separation of the latter from the powdered rock by the magnet identifies them as Magnetic Iron. A hand specimen slightly affects the compass. Some of the surfaces of the fissures and of tiny cavities are drusy with Quartz crystals or covered with white films of Chalcedony.

Fracture even. Hardly touched by a file.

Weathers about $\frac{1}{2}$ inch deep, with a smooth exterior surface, and of dirty reddish and yellowish-brown colors, darker than the fresh surface.

No. 140 (Sp. 1479).—*Magnetic Jaspery Quartzyte.*

Huronian.—$\frac{1}{4}$ post between Sects. 7 and 18—T. 47—R. 45.

Cast-iron gray, mottled with reddish-brown; dull.

Similar in texture to No. 139, but the paste predominates, and is of a slightly darker shade than cast-iron gray, while the Jasper grains are of a dull reddish-brown, larger and more irregular in shape. Contains more Magnetite disseminated and affects the compass more decidedly. The fissures are sometimes occupied by films of exceedingly minute silvery-white scales, of micaceous structure.

Fracture even. Untouched by a file. Powder pinkish-gray and dull. The magnet separates about 12 per cent. of the bulk, in a grayish-black powder.

No. 141 (Sp. 1477).—*Chalcedonic Quartzyte.*

Huronian.—$\frac{1}{4}$ post between Sects. 7 and 18—T. 47—R. 45.

Smoky-gray, with irregular streaks and spots of white and brownish-red ; dull.

A compact, hard mass, of chalcedonic Quartz, through which pass many seams, somewhat parallel, of smoky and glassy Quartz and brownish-red Jasper, with black, irregular grains of Magnetite.

Fracture uneven, or sometimes inclining to sub-conchoidal and smooth. Untouched by a file. Powder brownish-yellow and dull ; the magnet separates about 10 per cent. of the bulk in a blackish-brown powder. A few minute particles of Pyrite.

Weathered surface uneven and of a brownish color, mottled with black.

No. 142 (Sp. 1225).—*Reddish Hematitic Quartzyte.*

Huronian.—-Felch Mountain, Sect. 32—T. 42—R. 28.

Reddish-gray, with a few minute specks of bright brownish-red.

A very hard, compact, tough, fine-grained Quartzyte, chiefly made up of granules of smoky and grayish-white Quartz, with a very few scales of silvery-gray Mica and minute particles of brownish-red Ochre. Hard iron-black micaceous Hematite is disseminated through the rock in large glistening seams and bunches, about ⅛ to ¼ inch thick, associated with thin bunches of finely granular Magnetite.

Fracture even. Too hard to be scratched by a file. Powder of Quartzyte, free from ferruginous veins, is reddish and slightly glittering. Very slightly magnetic. The magnet separates about 4 per cent. of the bulk in black granules.

Weathers smoothly, with duller shade.

No. 143 (Sp. 993).—*Ochrey Cellular Quartzyte.*

Huronian.—Slate River, Sect. 28—T. 51—R. 31.

Reddish-brown, mottled with bright brownish-yellow and smoky-gray.

A hard, tough, cellular Quartzyte, made up of minute granules of smoky-gray and grayish-white Quartz, with its cavities lined with a slightly calcareous aggregation of compact reddish-brown to brownish-black Hematite and brownish-red Hematite-Ochre, in films or irregular layers and bunches, with about an equal quantity of bright brownish-yellow Limonite-Ochre, irregularly intermingled. The Quartzyte appears to constitute about $\frac{2}{3}$ of the bulk of the rock, and is too hard for the file.

Fractured surface exceedingly cellular and uneven. Streak brownish-red and bright brownish-yellow on the bunches of ore. Effervesces feebly with acid.

No weathered surface on the specimen.

No. 144 (Sp. 902).—*Banded Quartz-Schist.*

Huronian.—L'Anse Iron Range.—N. W. ¼ Sect. 9—T. 49—R. 33.

Alternate narrow bands of smoky-gray and yellowish-brown; dull.

A very hard, compact, fine-grained Quartzyte, of almost slaty structure, made up of layers, $\frac{1}{32}$ to ¼ inch in thickness, of two materials. The one consists of minute granules of smoky and grayish-white Quartz, and is too hard for the file. The other, of the same granules, with a greater or less intermixture of yellowish, rarely reddish-brown Ochre, producing a kind of Jasper. The latter are usually the softer, and give a brownish-yellow, rarely a brownish-red streak.

Fracture almost even. A few tiny seams crossing the laminæ transversely or obliquely, with tiny faults, and filled with smoky Quartz; others covered with a black film.

Weathers with an even surface, colored with the Ochre, the harder layers projecting slightly, with the glacial polish.

No. 145 (Sp. 903).—*Banded Quartz-Schist.*

Huronian.—L'Anse Iron Range.

Faint narrow bands of smoky-gray, grayish-white, and light reddish-brown.

A very hard, compact, tough, fine-grained Quartz-Schist, similar to No. 144, but with laminæ of the above-mentioned three colors, composed of very minute granules of smoky Quartz and grayish-white Quartz, intermingled with very minute particles of reddish-brown Ochre. The grayish-white laminæ rarely exceed $\frac{1}{32}$ inch in thickness. Many thin seams crossing the laminæ more or less obliquely, with tiny faults, minutely drusy, or lined with tiny geodes of Quartz often covered with brownish-black stains and films of Pyrolusite.

Fracture uneven, on account of the seams. Too hard for the file.

Weathered surface smooth and strongly marked with the bands.

No. 146 (Sp. 1232).—*Greenish Quartz-Schist.*

Huronian.—S. E. ¼ Sect. 35—T. 42—R. 30.

Greenish-gray, mottled with grayish-white ; shining.

A hard, compact, coarse, schistose Quartzyte, consisting of a mixture of smoky and white or glassy Quartz, without distinguishable grains, with less than $\frac{1}{10}$ of its bulk of a soft, dark-green transparent mineral, in tiny fibrous folia, with grayish-white streak. The laminæ of the latter are generally arranged parallel, so as to impart a schistose structure.

Fracture sub-conchoidal on plane of lamination, and somewhat uneven across it. Streak grayish-white.

Weathered surface slightly darker and rather uneven.

No. 147 (Sp. 1092).—*Chloritic Quartz-Schist.*

Huronian.—Bed XI.—South of Edwards Mine.

Blackish-green, and dull on the fresh fracture, mottled with tiny grayish-white spots, grayish-black and shining on cleavage surfaces.

A compact, tough, hard schist, made up of about 6 parts of grayish, sometimes greenish-white, arenaceous Quartz, in minute granules, and of 4 parts of shining scales of black and brownish-gray Mica and blackish-green Chlorite, usually very minute, but sometimes in scales $\frac{1}{4}$ inch across. A peculiar mottling is imparted to the cross-fracture by the aggregation of the Quartz in angular, often rectangular masses, $\frac{1}{32}$ to $\frac{1}{4}$ inch long, which resemble pseudomorphs after some mineral (perhaps Feldspar?). Many crystals are disseminated through the rock, $\frac{1}{8}$ to $\frac{1}{4}$ inch in diameter, of a brown mineral which resembles brown Garnet.

Fracture somewhat uneven. Streak white to greenish-gray. Cleavage surfaces are often stained to brownish-gray, and a fissure to a blackish-brown.

Weathers unevenly to a reddish-brown, the crystals before-mentioned projecting above the surface. This seems to be a pseudomorphous rock, perhaps after a porphyritic Amphibole-Schist, in which the Amphibole has been entirely altered into Chlorite and Mica and the Feldspar into Quartz.

No. 148 (Sp. 801).—*Calcareous Quartz-Schist.*

Huronian.—Bed V.—Chocolate Marble Quarry, South of mouth of Carp, L. S.

Light flesh-color, with a few yellowish-white and smoky-gray bands.

An exceedingly hard, fine-grained, and compact, calcareous Quartzyte, giving evidence by numerous fissures of a somewhat rhomboidal cleavage. It is made up of minutely laminated layers, about $\frac{1}{8}$ inch in thickness, of yellowish and grayish-white chert, passing into smoky-gray, alternating with layers of reddish-white and flesh-colored siliceous Dolomite.

Fracture even, on account of the cleavage, but it is rather difficult to obtain a fresh surface. Streak white, with slightly reddish tinge. Very feeble effervescence in acid.

Weathers unevenly, and of a dirty reddish-white color.

Another specimen, Sp. 802, has a slight film of Micaceous-Iron on the surface of one fissure. Very feeble effervescence with acid, like 801.

No. 149 (Sp. 891).—*Opaline Quartz-Schist.*

Huronian.—L'Anse Iron Range, near Centre N. W. ¼ Sect. 9—T. 49—R. 33.

Grayish-white and smoky, mottled with glistening brownish-yellow and lustrous brownish-black.

An exceedingly hard, compact, brittle, fine-grained, schistose Quartzyte, composed of granules, hardly distinguishable, of smoky and white Quartz, and with perhaps ¼ of its bulk of bright, brownish-yellow, glistening semi-opal, disseminated throughout in thin layers, somewhat parallel, and in irregular bunches. Many irregular seams lined with films, and sometimes with tiny crystalline bunches, of brownish-black Pyrolusite.

Fracture uneven. Too hard for the file.

Weathers rather evenly, with a smoky color, striped and mottled with yellowish-brown.

No. 150.—*Talcose Quartz-Schist.*

Huronian.—S. of Foster Mine, on the road to Maillet's Camp.

Brownish-gray, mottled with smoky-gray; shining.

A compact, hard, coarse Quartz-Schist, made up of about 7 parts of milky to smoky-gray Quartz, in irregular lenticular bunches, about ½ to 1 inch long, and ⅛ to ¼ inch thick in the centre, and of nearly 3 parts of brownish-gray Talc, with greasy feel and white streak, in thin silvery flakes and films enveloping the bunches of Quartz.

Fracture hackly.

Weathers unevenly to a smoky-gray, mottled with reddish-gray.

No. 151 (Sp. 734).—*Magnetic Quartz-Schist.*

Huronian.—Bed XIII.—Spurr Range, E. side Sect. 23—T. 48—R. 31.

Reddish-brown, inclining to light purple, with a few narrow black bands.

A hard, fine-grained, compact schist, made up of layers of Quartzyte, about an inch thick, alternating with black, glittering, ferruginous layers, about ¼ inch thick. The Quartzyte consists chiefly of minute granules of reddish-brown Quartz, with a little grayish-white Quartz, black scales of Micaceous-Iron (rarely octahedral), and silvery-gray scales of Mica. Irregular veins and bunches traverse it, consisting of an aggregate of granules of yellowish and brownish-white Quartz and black scales of Micaceous-Iron. The ferruginous layers consist of minute granules of reddish-brown Quartz, with a larger proportion of minute, glittering, black scales, some of which are octahedral. When this mineral is finely powdered, about 35 per cent. of the bulk is taken up by a magnet.

Fracture uneven. Streak reddish-brown on the black layers; and the powder, reddish-gray, slightly glittering. The Quartzyte is too hard for the file. Magnetic, and with polarity.

Weathers unevenly to a light yellowish-brown color.

No. 152 (Sp. 740).—*Magnetic Quartz-Schist.*

Huronian.—Bed XIII.—Spurr Range, E. side Sect. 23—T. 48—R. 31.

Speckled reddish-gray, with narrow glittering bands of iron-black.

A fine-grained, hard, compact, and brittle schist, made up of quartzose layers, about $1\frac{1}{2}$ inches thick, with layers of Magnetite, $\frac{1}{8}$ to $\frac{1}{2}$ inch in thickness. The former consist of an aggregate of granules of grayish-white and brownish-red Quartz, particles of a blackish color, and minute silvery scales of grayish Mica. The black layers consist of the usual aggregate of grayish-white and brownish granules of Quartz and minute octahedra of Magnetite.

Fracture uneven. Streak reddish-white on the quartzose, iron-black on the magnetic layers. Many irregular fissures across the quartzose layers, colored light brownish-yellow. Strongly magnetic, and with polarity. Powder of black layers is blackish-gray and glittering. The magnet takes up all the powder, the grayish-white Quartz granules becoming distinct towards the latter part of the operation.

No weathered surface on the specimen. The quartzose layers are soft to crush, and give a lighter reddish-gray, dull powder, from which the magnet separates about 13 per cent. of the bulk in black granules.

No. 153 (Sp. 999).—*Magnetic Quartz-Schist.*

Huronian.—Felch Mountain, Sects. 32 and 33—T. 42—R. 28.

Lustrous cast-iron-gray, inclining to bluish, speckled and slightly striped with brownish-red, rarely with grayish and reddish-white.

A very hard, compact, fine-grained, crystalline rock—an aggregate of minute crystalline particles of Magnetite, without distinct form, which glitter under the lens, and of minute granules of grayish and reddish-white Quartz, which are irregularly disseminated throughout the rock in small particles, lenticular masses, and parallel laminæ, $\frac{1}{16}$ to $\frac{1}{8}$ inch thick, which resemble a coarse Jasper. Small veins and bunches occur, of glistening micaceous Magnetite, sometimes $\frac{1}{2}$ inch long.

Fracture rather even, streak iron-black, dotted with reddish-brown. Very feebly magnetic. Powder reddish-brown and dull; the magnet separates about $1\frac{1}{2}$ per cent. of the bulk.

Weathered surface smooth, but harsh to the touch, the minute granules being irregularly removed.

No. 154 (Sp. 1227).—*Hematitic Quartz-Schist.*

Huronian.—Felch Mountain, Sects. 32 and 33—T. 42—R. 28.

Alternate lustrous bands of bluish-black and of brownish-black, speckled with brownish-gray.

A hard, compact, fine-grained schist, made up of layers, about $\frac{1}{2}$ inch thick, of fine-grained Hematite, consisting of particles visible to the eye, and which under the lens appear somewhat octahedral in form, together with minute granules of brownish-gray Quartz—alternating with thicker layers of Quartzyte, in which granules of white and smoky Quartz greatly predominate. A few glistening scales and bunches of Micaceous-Iron occur.

Fracture uneven. Streak dark reddish-brown. Powder reddish-brown and glittering. Not magnetic. The magnet separates about 1 per cent. of the bulk.

Weathers rather smoothly, the quartzose layers assuming a reddish-white color.

No. 155 (Sp. 1236).—*Hematitic Quartz-Schist.*

Huronian.—Sect. 31—T. 42—R. 29, Upper Menominee Range.

Cast-iron-gray, with bluish shade.

A hard, compact, fine-grained, arenaceous Quartz-Schist, with coarse columnar structure.   Under the lens its minute granules are shown to be grayish-white Quartz and iron-black irregular scales of Micaceous-Iron.   Weathered seams connected with the columnar cleavage, stained reddish-, yellowish-, and blackish-brown, or grayish-white, and sometimes lined with coarser scales of Micaceous-Iron.

Fracture even.   Streak light reddish-brown.   Powder reddish-gray and glittering; the magnet separates about 4 per cent. of the bulk, in black granules.

Weathers, with a slightly ribbed surface, to a blackish-brown color.

No. 156 (Sp. 994).—*Ferruginous Quartz-Schist.*

Huronian.—Slate River, Sect. 28—T. 51—R. 31.

Smoky gray and grayish-white, speckled and mottled with bright brownish-yellow and a few black and reddish-brown spots.

A very hard, tough, fine-grained, schistose Quartzyte, somewhat cellular, but much less so than No. 143.   It is composed of minute granules of smoky and grayish-white Quartz, intermingled with about $\frac{1}{4}$ of its bulk of irregular calcareous veins and bunches of compact reddish and blackish-brown Hematite, of which the core is generally converted into bright brownish-yellow Limonite-Ochre. The small cavities are lined with layers or films of the two ores, and are sometimes drusy with Quartz crystals.   A very few facets of brownish-gray Calcite, sometimes $\frac{1}{4}$ inch across, occur on the surface of the Quartz.

Fracture uneven.   Streak of the bunches of ore reddish-brown, and bright brownish-yellow.   The bedding seams are stained reddish-brown.

No weathered surface on the specimen.

No. 157 (Sp. 883).—*Limonitic Quartz-Schist.*

Huronian.—S. E. ¼ of S. W. ¼ Sect. 9—T. 49—R. 33.

Light-brown, slightly mottled with grayish-white; slightly lustrous.

An exceedingly hard, compact, tough Quartzyte, of somewhat schistose structure (denoted by a few irregular grayish-white bands), and of a very fine-grained texture; consists of minute granules of grayish-white Quartz, more or less intermixed with, and colored by, brownish Ochre.

Fracture uneven to conchoidal. Too hard for the file. Many tiny transverse veins and bunches of white and glassy Quartz.

Weathers unevenly, and with the color unchanged.

No. 158 (Sp. 1484).—*Green Banded Siliceous Schist.*

Huronian.—Sunday Lake Outlet, W. side Sect. 18—T. 47—R. 45.

Greenish-gray, with narrow blackish-gray stripes.

A compact, homogeneous, tough, hard, siliceous schist, of almost impalpable grain, made up of laminæ, from $\frac{1}{32}$ to $\frac{1}{2}$ inch in thickness, of the two colors above mentioned; chiefly composed of Quartz, with a few small scales of Mica, and is probably covered by a small quantity of Chlorite, a few minute fissures, sometimes 2 or 3 inches long, crossing the lamination transversely, occasionally with tiny faults.

Fracture even. Streak greenish-white.

Weathers smoothly, to the depth of about $\frac{1}{8}$ inch, to a reddish-brown color, mottled and banded with brownish-yellow. The transverse fissures and seams of lamination, just below a weathered surface, are often colored brownish or yellowish by the weathering.

Specimen 1499 is a slate of a greenish and brownish-gray color, with lines and stripes of reddish-brown, exactly like the lighter-colored layers of 1484 in material, color, etc., but is calcareous. Effervesces with acid.

Weathers rather unevenly to a reddish-brown color, mottled with yellowish shades; and the crevices also assume these colors.

Specimen 1500 is exactly like the lighter-colored layers of 1484, but with layers ⅜–1 inch thick, colored reddish-brown along the crevice of lamination.   A few fissures covered with a film of Calcite.

Specimen 1493 is a blackish Siliceous Slate.   Alternate narrow stripes of greenish-, blackish-, and brownish-gray, resembling 1484 ; but with layers about ⅛ inch in thickness, and calcareous. Effervesces with acid.

Weathers smoothly to a dirty-brownish color, some of the harder laminæ, of a reddish-brown color, slightly projecting.

No. 159 (Sp. 1508).—Argillaceous Siliceous Slate.

Huronian.—S. side of S. E. ¼ Sect. 10—T. 47—R. 45.

Alternate stripes of light chocolate-brown and brownish-gray.

A compact, fine-grained slate, made up of alternate laminæ $\frac{1}{32}$ to ⅛ inch thick, of brownish-gray Siliceous Slate, and chocolate-brown Argillyte.   Minute scales of Mica or Talc are disseminated throughout.

Streak reddish-white.

Weathers smoothly, with a surface faintly banded with dirty shades of green and brown. A transition rock between Argillyte-Slate and Siliceous Schist.

No. 160 (Sp. 806).—Greenish Siliceous Schist (Novaculyte).

Huronian.—Bed V.—Chocolate Marble Quarry, South of mouth of Carp, L. S.

A very light greenish-gray and reddish-white, much mottled in an irregular manner with reddish-brown ; slightly shining.

A hard, compact, fine-grained schist, made up of the greenish-gray Novaculyte, with an almost equal quantity of the reddish-brown argillaceous material, irregularly intermingled.   The former is as usual chiefly made up of Quartz, with a small quantity of silvery scales of greenish-gray Talc, and with films and scales of greenish-gray Talc so arranged as to impart the finely laminated structure.   Reddish-white and grayish-white Quartz also occurs in segregated veins and spherical bunches of concentric structure, from 1 to 2½ inches in diameter.

Weathers smoothly and of a light brownish-gray, but with the quartzose bunches projecting.

No. 161 (Sp. 807).—*Greenish-Drab Siliceous Slate (Novaculyte).*

Huronian.—Bed V.—Chocolate Marble Quarry, South of mouth of Carp, L. S.

A light shade of greenish-drab, sometimes passing into reddish, mottled and banded with light reddish-brown; slightly shining.

A compact, fissile Siliceous Slate, which is harder than No. 190, and whose stratification, at an angle of 45° with the slaty lamination, is apparently denoted by the bands, about an inch thick, of light reddish-brown color (much lighter than that of No. 190), speckled with minute lenticular olive-green spots. A schistose Novaculyte, apparently made up of Quartz and exceedingly minute scales of greenish-gray Talc.

Weathered surface even and of dirty-brown and reddish-brown shades. Streak greenish-white.

Another specimen, 805, is striped throughout by reddish-brown, parallel, and mostly continuous bands, $\frac{1}{8}$ to $\frac{1}{4}$ inch thick. The plane of these layers forms an angle of about 70° with that of the slaty lamination, and their granular material consists of grains of Quartz, enveloped in argillaceous laminæ, forming little bunches.

In 804 the brown layers are obscure and irregular.

No. 162 (Sp. 1509).—*Banded Talco-Siliceous Slate.*

Huronian.—S. side of S. E. $\frac{1}{4}$ Sect. 10—T. 47—R. 45.

Alternate stripes of brownish-gray and greenish-gray, made up of layers $\frac{1}{32}$ to $\frac{3}{8}$ inch thick, of brownish-gray Quartz, with a little Feldspar, and others of a greenish-gray color, apparently of minute granules of Feldspar, and tiny scales of greenish-gray Talc. The slaty lamination makes an angle of about 25° with the bedding lines.

Streak greenish-white. Before the blowpipe the material of the talcose layers fuses at about 5, while a thin splinter from the siliceous layers is only covered with a film of enamel.

No. 163 (Sp. 1458).—*Ferruginous Siliceous Slate.*

Huronian.—N. side of S. E. ¼ Sect. 7—T. 47—R. 45.

Dark greenish-black and slightly lustrous.

A hard, compact, homogeneous slate, of impalpable texture, in which only a few minute glittering scales can be distinguished by the eye or lens. The specimen is remarkable for a series of several peculiarly sharp cleavage-planes, by three of which the rock is divided up into inclined rhombohedrons, with sharp angles. By one of these cleavages a finely laminated structure is produced, which imparts a fibrous surface to the cleavage plane which crosses the laminæ.

Streak, light brownish-yellow.

No. 164 (Sp. 1503).—*Ferruginous Siliceous Slate.*

Huronian.—Sunday Lake Outlet Series.

Drab, with a slight brownish shade, and a few narrow grayish-white and reddish-brown bands; dull.

A very hard, compact, and fine-grained Siliceous Slate, consisting of very minute granules of brownish-gray Quartz, a little Chlorite (?), and a little Mica in silvery-gray scales, which glitter on a fresh fracture in the sun. Slight differences in the shade of color distinguish the laminæ of the rock, especially near the weathered surface. A few thin layers of grayish-white Chalcedony occur.

Fracture sub-conchoidal. Streak brownish-white, a few seams drusy with Quartz.

Weathered surface smooth, and, like that of many weathered seams, brownish-black; the interior of the rock being reddish-brown, to a depth of ⅛ to ¼ inch.

No. 165 (Sp. 747).—*Hematitic Siliceous Schist.*

Boulder near ¼ post Sects. 34 and 35—T. 48—R. 27, Deer Lake.

Cast-iron gray, with reddish shade, striped with brownish-red lines; dull.

A very hard, compact, homogeneous and fine-grained schist,

with few particles visible to the eye ; but consists of very minute granules of smoky Quartz, intermingled with red Ochre and minute scales, probably of Micaceous-Iron. The Ochre predominates in many of the minute laminæ, marking the stratification and rendering them softer and of a brownish-red color.

Fracture sub-conchoidal. Streak cherry-red.

Weathers unevenly, but smoothly, the harder layers projecting irregularly, and receiving a slight polish.

No. 166 (Sp. 1485).—*Banded Jasper-Schist.*

Huronian.—Sunday Lake Outlet, W. side Sect. 18—T. 47—R. 45.

Narrow bands of reddish-brown, yellowish-brown, brownish-black, and brownish-gray.

An exceedingly hard, compact, brittle schist, made up of layers of fine-grained Jasper, almost of impalpable texture, of the above-mentioned colors, $\frac{1}{16}$ to $\frac{1}{2}$ inch thick. A few seams of a bright brownish-red mineral, sometimes drusy.

Fracture uneven. Streak of some softer laminæ, reddish-brown.

Weathers smoothly, and unchanged in color.

No. 167 (Sp. 1486).—*Banded Jasper-Schist.*

Huronian.—Sunday Lake Outlet, W. side Sect. 18—T. 47—R. 45.

Narrow bands of bright brownish-red, grayish, and gray speckled with red.

A Jasper-Schist resembling No. 166, but having many layers, finely granular, with tiny fragments of smoky, grayish-white, greenish-gray, and reddish-white Quartz, and bright brownish-red Jasper ; others are chiefly composed of the latter Jasper, slightly speckled with greenish-gray Jasper ; and many thin laminæ consist of smoky-gray Chalcedony. Many minute seams occur, crossing the layers obliquely, with tiny faults, and filled with the material of the granular layers.

Fracture sub-conchoidal. Too hard for the file.

Weathered surface smooth, and a little darker in color and duller than the fresh fracture.

No. 168 (Sp. 1491).—*Banded Jasper-Slate.*

Huronian.—Sunday Lake Outlet, Sect. 13—T. 47—R. 46.

Bright brownish-red, with glittering, brownish-black, parallel lines.

Chiefly consists of brownish-red Jasper, not quite so bright as that of No. 173, interlaminated with many thin parallel films of smoky-gray Jasper, often with crevices drusy with brownish-black and yellowish-brown acicular crystals, resembling Göthite, and having a brownish-yellow streak. A few transverse fissures, covered with a drusy film of the same mineral.

Fracture even. Too hard for the file.

Weathers smoothly, with a slight polish and unchanged in color.

Specimen 1492 is a hard, compact, brownish-black layer, $\frac{1}{2}$ inch thick, corresponding to the blackish laminæ in 1491. Consists of smoky-gray Jasper, with minute crystals of the brownish-black mineral disseminated throughout.

Fracture even. Streak brownish-yellow.

No. 169 (Sp. 1510).—*Banded Jasper-Slate.*

Huronian.—N. side of S. E. $\frac{1}{4}$ of Sect. 8—T. 47—R. 45.

Dark greenish-gray and dull, with grayish-white and chocolate-brown narrow bands.

A very hard, compact, tough, and fine-grained slate, made up of films and laminæ of different colors and shades, up to $\frac{1}{8}$ inch in thickness. It consists of very minute granules of grayish-white Quartz, with perhaps a little Chlorite. (?) The color varies in the different laminæ, becoming of a darker green, with a larger intermixture of Chlorite, of a greenish- or grayish-white where the Chlorite is lacking, and of a chocolate-brown where the Chlorite has decomposed.

Fracture even.   Streak greenish-white.

Weathered surface smooth, and covered on a section with alternate cream-colored and chocolate-brown narrow bands.

No. 170 (Sp. 1506).—*Green Jasper-Slate.*

Huronian.—N. side of S. E. ¼ of Sect. 7—T. 47—R. 45.

Dark greenish-gray and dull, with a few narrow glittering bands.

A very hard and brittle, banded Jasper-Slate, made up of loosely compacted layers, about ⅛ inch thick, and consisting partly of green Jasper and partly of very minute granules of smoky and white Quartz with a little Chlorite. (?)   In some layers coarser granules of smoky and white Quartz predominate, whose fresh fracture produces the slight glittering appearance, together with a very few scales of Mica.

Fracture uneven.   Streak greenish-white.

Weathering smooth, and of a brownish-black color, the weathered interior seams assuming yellowish- and reddish-brown shades.

In another variety (1507) the coarser layers are absent.

No. 171 (Sp. 690).—*Magnetic Jasper-Slate.*

Huronian.—Bed X.—Near centre Sect. 19—T. 47—R. 27.

Iron-black, striped with greenish-gray.

A fine-grained, compact, hard, slaty Magnetite, interlaminated with greenish-gray Jasper, translucent on the edges ; layers from $\frac{1}{16}$ to $\frac{1}{4}$ inch thick.   The layers of Magnetite glitter with minute points, which, under the lens, appear almost always to be irregular scales, sometimes rectangular, and rarely octahedral.   These layers are further divided into thin laminæ, by seams whose surfaces are of a dirty yellowish- and reddish-brown color.

Fracture uneven.   Streak iron-black on the layers of Magnetite, those of Jasper being untouched by the file.   Feebly magnetic with slight polarity.   Powder light reddish-brown, and almost dull.

Weathers smoothly, the Jasper layers slightly darkening in color, and those of Magnetite assuming a brownish-black.

No. 172 (Sp. 1480).—*Hematitic Jasper-Schist.*

Huronian.—Sunday Lake Outlet, Sect. 18—T. 47—R. 45.

Dull chocolate-brown, with faint narrow and slightly lustrous bands, and a few minute white specks.

A hard, compact, and very fine-grained schist, made up of layers, alternately dull and slightly lustrous. The former are about $\frac{1}{4}$ inch thick, and consist of exceedingly minute granules of Hematite and of smoky and grayish-white Quartz, the latter greatly predominating, and sometimes so much so as to render the layer decidedly quartzose ; they also contain minute scales of silvery-gray Mica. The lustrous material consists of groups of two or three parallel laminæ, about $\frac{1}{32}$ inch thick, slightly separated by films of the material of the other layers ; their material is the same as that of the other layers, but of much finer grain—a green Jasper—and rendered slightly lustrous on the section by exceedingly minute films of silvery-gray Mica. A few tiny seams and bunches of smoky- and grayish-white Quartz, reddish-brown Ochre, and soft white Kaolin.

Fracture rather uneven. Streak bright reddish-brown.

Weathers smoothly, to dirty greenish and blackish shades of brown, speckled with yellowish- and grayish-white and reddish-brown.

No. 173 (Sp. 1488).—*Hematitic Jasper-Schist.*

Huronian.—Sunday Lake Outlet, W. side of Sect. 18—T. 47—R. 45.

Cast-iron gray, with bluish shade, with reddish-brown streaks ; dull.

A very hard, compact, tough, and fine-grained Jasper-Schist, consisting of minute particles of reddish-brown Jasper and of bluish-black Hematite, interspersed with micaceous scales of the same. Much Jasper is also gathered together in irregular layers or bunches, $\frac{1}{4}$ inch to 1 inch thick, and thus an imperfect schistose structure is produced. A few minute veins of white and glassy Quartz, and seams covered with films of yellowish-brown Ochre or reddish-brown Quartz.

Fracture uneven. Streak reddish-brown.

Weathers unevenly to reddish and blackish-brown shades, the Jaspery layers projecting and somewhat polished.

No. 174 (Sp. 1088).—*Brown Anthophyllitic Quartz-Schist.*

Huronian.—Bed X.—S. E. of old Washington Mine.

Brownish-gray, slightly streaked with grayish-white ; glittering.

A hard, compact, fine-grained schist, which is made up of about 6 parts of grayish-white Quartz, in minute granules, nearly 1 part of Magnetite in minute black particles (apparently associated with smoky Quartz), and 3 parts of brownish-gray Anthophyllite in silvery scales, which have often an elongated bladed form and fibrous structure, and are sometimes gathered in radiating groups.

Fracture irregular and uneven. Streak grayish-white. Many fissures stained reddish-brown. Yields water when heated in a closed tube.

Weathers unevenly, to a reddish-brown.

No. 175 (Sp. 1090).—*Brown Anthophyllite-Schist.*

Huronian.—Bed VIII.—S. E. of old Washington Mine.

Like No. 174, but a little coarser, on account of the somewhat greater length and abundance of the micaceous blades. A few little bunches of grayish-white and smoky Quartz project from the weathered surface.

In Specimen 1091, many tiny bunches are disseminated, sometimes $\frac{1}{4}$ to $\frac{1}{2}$ inch long, of yellowish-, reddish-, and blackish-brown Ochre. A few thin laminæ occur, in which the Magnetite predominates, producing faint parallel blackish streaks.

No. 176 (Sp. 1093).—*Brown Anthophyllite-Schist.*

Huronian.—Bed X.—S. E. of Edwards Mine.

A coarser variety of No. 174, the blades of Anthophyllite being often over $\frac{1}{16}$ inch in length. In parts of the specimen much of this mineral is of a black color, and by this, as well as by the concentration of the Magnetite in certain tiny bunches or layers, the surface of a fracture is mottled with grayish-black and brownish-gray.

Weathers rather unevenly, to a greenish-gray, mottled and streaked with light reddish-brown.

Specimen 1094 is the coarsest variety of No. 174, the blades of Anthophyllite often reaching ⅛ inch in length. Yields more water than No. 174, when heated in a closed tube. The specimen is traversed by a few layers of grayish-white Quartz, ¼ inch thick.

Specimen 1095 is traversed by many of the reddish-brown fissures.

No. 177 (Sp. 1098).—*Brown Anthophyllite-Schist, passing into Magnetite-Schist.*

Huronian.—Bed VIII. (?)—S. E. of Edwards Mine.

This specimen seems to have been taken from the junction of the above two rocks, the former being fine-grained like No. 174, and the latter a strongly magnetic, hard, compact, black schist, of almost impalpable texture, having a few of the micaceous blades disseminated throughout.

Weathered surface smooth and blackish.

No. 178 (Sp. 1116).—*Magnetic Anthophyllite-Slate.*

Huronian.—Bed XIX.—N. E. of Champion Mine.

Blackish-gray, inclining to greenish, covered with thin parallel brownish-gray and blackish streaks ; minutely glittering.

A compact, very tough, and fine-grained slate, made up of about

7 parts of Anthophyllite in fibrous translucent blades, varying in color from brownish-gray to grayish-white, mostly microscopic but partly needles $\frac{1}{32}$ to $\frac{1}{16}$ inch in length, and of 3 parts of black particles of Magnetite, barely to be distinguished by the lens. The predominance of the latter in parallel films covers the section with blackish lines, while certain layers, $\frac{1}{16}$ inch thick, and $\frac{1}{8}$ to $\frac{1}{4}$ inch apart, consist chiefly of an aggregation of the larger needles of Anthophyllite, arranged obliquely to the lamination. Loses much water by ignition in a closed tube. Decidedly magnetic, and with polarity ; the magnet separates about 19 per cent. from the powdered rock.

Fracture uneven. Streak reddish-gray.

Fissures occur, covered with a reddish-brown stain and films of brownish and reddish-brown Quartz.

Weathers evenly but roughly, to a reddish-brown.

The following manganiferous variety may be here inserted.

(Sp. 1155.)—*Black Magnetic Anthophyllite-Slate.*

Greenish-black ; minutely glittering.

A compact, fine-grained slate, which appears, both to the naked eye and to the lens, to be chiefly or entirely made up of minute glistening black scales, chiefly Magnetite, but often of a bladed form, probably Anthophyllite, separated by tiny films of a blackish and greenish-brown color, which seem to consist of Pyrolusite. A schistose, almost slaty, structure is produced by minute parallel films, about $\frac{1}{8}$ to $\frac{1}{4}$ inch apart, which mark a section with dull reddish-brown lines, and with blackish lines somewhat more lustrous than the general surface. Decidedly magnetic, and with polarity ; and the magnet separates about 9 per cent. of the powdered rock.

Fracture rather uneven. Streak shining black, and the least friction of the surface imparts the same lustre. The rock is of medium hardness, but soils paper and the fingers with a greenish-black stain. Loss by ignition, over 5 per cent., much water passing off, and some oxygen being absorbed.

Weathers rather unevenly, to a slightly shining blackish-brown.

No. 179 (Sp. 729).—*Pseudomorphous Chlorite-Schist.*

Huronian.—Bed XIII.—Spurr Range, East Side of Sect. 23--T. 48—R. 31.

Olive-green, inclining to blackish, covered with glittering facets.

A soft, compact, homogeneous, fine-grained Chlorite-Schist, which appears under the lens to consist of minute granules of grayish-white Quartz and scales of olive-green Chlorite, in about equal proportions. Through this matrix are disseminated large numbers, perhaps about 400 to the square inch, of highly lustrous black scales and octahedra, nearly $\frac{1}{32}$ inch across, with greenish-gray powder—apparently pseudomorphs of Chlorite after Magnetite. A few tiny granules of ruby-red color occur, resembling Garnet.

Fracture uneven. Slightly magnetic, with polarity. Streak and powder light olive-green and slightly glittering. The magnet separates about 23 per cent. by weight, in a powder of the same color.

Weathers evenly to a blackish-brown, mottled with olive-green and shades of reddish and yellowish-brown, the black scales and octahedra weathering to bright brownish-yellow dots.

No. 180 (Sp. 730).—*Pseudomorphous Chlorite-Schist.*

Huronian.—Bed XIII.—Spurr Range, E. side of Sect. 23—T. 48—R. 31.

Resembles No. 179, but the scales and octahedra are much smaller—few of them being distinguishable by the eye. Crystals of Amphibole of fibrous structure, of a shining black color, and with irregular acicular terminations, are disseminated throughout the rock, 5 or 6 being visible on a square inch of surface. They vary in breadth from a mere line up to $\frac{1}{16}$ inch, and in length from $\frac{1}{8}$ to $\frac{1}{2}$ inch. The commencement of their alteration is denoted by a film of greenish-gray material, still retaining the original lustre and structure, into which the minute crystals are wholly converted, and the outer coat of the larger : so that the longitudinal section of the latter shows a black band enclosed by two very thin greenish-gray lines. A smoky gray and grayish-white seam, about $\frac{1}{4}$ inch thick, crosses the lamination obliquely, composed chiefly of grayish-white Quartz, sometimes greenish, with a small intermixture in some places of black particles. Golden-yellow Pyrite is disseminated in tiny particles through the rock, the seam, and the crystals of Amphibole. Effervesces slightly in acid. Slightly magnetic. Streak and powder grayish-green and dull ; the magnet separates 2½ per cent. by weight.

Weathers unevenly to shades of yellowish-brown, rendered shining by exceedingly minute brownish-yellow scales.

No. 181 (Sp. 731).—*Pseudomorphous Chlorite-Schist.*

Huronian.—Bed XIII.—Spurr Range, E. side of Sect. 23—T. 48—R. 31.

Resembles No. 180 in color, materials, and general character. No octahedra occur, but many thick, soft, brownish scales, $\frac{1}{32}$ inch across, with a grayish-green streak. Pseudomorphs, probably after Amphibole, are also disseminated throughout, similar in shape, size, and number to the Amphibole crystals of No. 180, but faintly defined and of a grayish-white color. These consist chiefly of aggregated tiny facets of a grayish-white, glistening, laminated mineral, with a small intermixture of dark scales—apparently of Chlorite.

Not magnetic. Streak and powder grayish-green and dull. The magnet separates nothing.

Weathering like that of No. 179.

No. 182 (Sp. 820).—*Dark-Green Chlorite-Schist.*

Huronian.—N. of North-Western Hotel, Marquette.

Dark olive-green, faintly spotted and streaked with reddish brown.

A compact fissile Chlorite-Schist, about as hard as No. 190.

Streak greenish-white, sometimes reddish-white. Fuses at 4.5, to a black glass.

Weathered surface uneven, and, like many of the cleavage surfaces, of a reddish-brown color from the decomposition of the

Chlorite. A very few irregular veins of granular yellowish-white Calcite. Apparently the last stage in the alteration of a Dioryte, through Dioryte-Schist, into Chloritic Schist.

No. 183 (Sp. 828).—*Green Calcareous Chloritic Schist.*

Huronian.—S. of North-Western Hotel, Marquette.

Light greenish-gray, inclining to brownish, with reddish-brown streaks.

A compact, hard, fissile, chloritic, and calcareous schist, with a few layers, about $\frac{1}{4}$ inch thick, of a finely granular Calcite of reddish-brown color. It is apparently composed of Feldspar, Chlorite, many exceedingly minute silvery greenish-gray scales (apparently of Talc), and a little Calcite. Besides the ordinary cleavage fissures, lined with Chlorite or Talc, a few seams of the reddish-brown Calcite occur.

Weathered surface smooth, and of a dirty greenish-gray, mottled with dirty brown ; color lighter than the interior.

Specimen 829 differs from 828 only in the greater abundance of Calcite, in films and seams of a grayish-white and reddish-brown color, and in geodes of minute crystals.

No. 184 (Sp. 1097).—*Garnetiferous Chlorite-Schist.*

Huronian.—Bed VIII.—S. E. of the Edwards Mine.

Blackish-green, and slightly glittering.

A soft, compact, heavy, tough, fine-grained schist, which appears under the lens to consist chiefly of minute scales of Chlorite, with a small intermixture of a grayish-white Mica, in minute scales and acicular blades, visible to the naked eye. Many crystals of brown Garnet, $\frac{1}{8}$ to $\frac{1}{4}$ inch across, are disseminated through the rock, and are partly decomposed.

Fracture uneven. Streak greenish-gray. Many irregular fissures occur, stained reddish-brown.

Weathers rather unevenly, to a dirty greenish-gray, mottled with brown shades, the Garnets projecting above the surface.

No. 185 (Sp. 1130).—*Green Chlorite-Schist.*

Huronian.—Bed XIII.—Lake Superior Mine.

Olive-green, and very minutely glittering, with many blackish-brown glittering specks.

A compact, soft, rather brittle, crypto-crystalline schist, with an irregular fissile structure, apparently made up of about 7 parts or more of olive-green Chlorite, in exceedingly minute glittering scales, and of nearly 3 parts of greenish-white Feldspar, in microscopic particles. A small quantity of altered crystals of Magnetite is distributed throughout, in blackish-brown shining octahedra, less than $\frac{1}{32}$ inch in diameter, whose material is brittle, and soft, and gives a reddish-brown streak.

Fracture hackly. Streak greenish-gray. Surface of the fissures is stained yellowish, mottled with light reddish-brown. Does not affect the magnetic needle, and the magnet separates only a few particles from the pulverized rock.

Weathers unevenly, to a dull and dirty shade of the same color.

No. 186 (Sp. 1148).—*Porphyritic Chlorite-Schist.*

Huronian.—Bed XI.—Lake Superior Mine.

Blackish-green (and shining, on cleavage surfaces), speckled with greenish-black and reddish-gray shining facets.

A compact, tough, coarse schist, made up of about 4 parts of angular, often rhombic, masses or crystals of greenish-black Feldspar, with good cleavage and lustre, in facets $\frac{1}{16}$ to $\frac{1}{8}$ inch across, distributed throughout a crypto-crystalline soft blackish-green matrix, with greenish-gray streak, which amounts to about 6 parts of the rock. This matrix consists of about $\frac{7}{10}$ of soft blackish-green Chlorite, in exceedingly minute glistening scales, and of $\frac{3}{10}$ of grayish-white Quartz in microscopic particles.

Fracture hackly. Surface of fissures stained to a dirty reddish-brown.

Weathers evenly and smoothly, to a grayish-green, speckled with reddish-gray (the Feldspar).

7

No. 187 (Sp. 1543).—*Chloritic Feldspathic Schist.*

Laurentian.—Near W. ¼ post Sect. 19—T. 47—R. 42.

Greenish-gray, minutely speckled with gray; slightly glittering.

Resembles No. 217, but is slightly coarser. The Mica is irregularly dispersed, is mostly black, but in part is silvery-white. Many irregular fissures, covered with films of blackish-green Chlorite, a soft white mineral (perhaps Kaolin?), and a hard brownish-white Feldspar in tiny facets, with good cleavage and lustre. No Quartz is discernible by the lens, but the fresh surface is hard to a knife edge. Streak greenish-white. Fuses before the blowpipe at 5, to a brown glass.

Another variety, 1544, effervesces slightly in acid. Weathers unevenly to a reddish (projecting Feldspar), mottled by blackish-brown (eroded Chlorite), to the depth of $\frac{1}{16}$ to $\frac{1}{8}$ inch, with a section of the same color, terminated by a blackish-brown band.

No. 188 (Sp. 1545).—*Green Calcareous Chloritic Schist.*

Laurentian.—W. branch of Ontonagon River, Sect. 13—T. 46—R. 41.

Dark grayish-green, inclining to olive, faintly striped with gray.

A compact, fine-grained, fissile aggregate of crystalline grains of grayish and reddish-white Feldspar, with fine granular gray Calcite, arranged in thin lenticular seams, about ⅛ inch apart, and separated by abundant films and seams of olive-green Chlorite in minute glistening scales.

Fracture uneven. Streak greenish-white. Effervesces strongly in acid.

No weathered surface on the specimen.

No. 189 (Sp. 692).—*Micaceous Feldspathic Argillyte.*

Boulder, Ann Arbor, Mich.

Gray, covered with fine parallel blackish gray lines; minutely glistening.

A compact, rather soft and brittle, homogeneous, fine-grained schist, which appears under the lens to consist chiefly of minute scales of black and white Mica, rarely distinct to the eye, and minute granules of grayish-white Feldspar (and Quartz ?), and of a blackish-gray mineral, the latter preponderating in parallel films, usually less than $\frac{1}{32}$ inch apart. Bronze-yellow Pyrite is distributed in minute particles, and a bunch occurs, over an inch long, of Pyrite associated with brownish-gray Siderite.

Fracture uneven. Streak grayish-white. Fuses before the blow-pipe at 5.5, to a white blebby enamel.

Weathers evenly to a dirty brownish-gray color, minutely ribbed with the slightly projecting edges of the darker laminæ.

No. 190 (Sp. 794).—*Brown Chloritic Argillyte.*

Huronian.—Bed **V.**—Chocolate Marble Quarry, S. of mouth of Carp, L. S.

Dark reddish or chocolate-brown, with a few bands of lighter shades of brown and of dark olive-green.

A compact, fissile Argillyte, harder than a true Argillyte. On a close examination the original stratification is displayed by a series of minute bands, almost at right angles with the slaty lamination, varying in shade from yellowish-gray to dark reddish-brown, usually uniform in color for about ⅛ inch in thickness ; and in one case in the hand specimen, of an olive-green inclining to brown (probably chloritic in material), and swelling out, in lenticular form, to a thickness over an inch.

Streak slightly reddish-white on the brown layers, and greenish-white on the green layers. · Talc is disseminated throughout the rock in minute bunches and seams of silvery-greenish-gray scales, and to this is apparently due a slightly greasy feel, as well as a minutely granular structure, in the brown material.

Weathered surface rather smooth and even, and of same color.

No. 191 (Sp. 810).—*Brown Feldspathic Argillyte.*

Huronian.—Bed V.—Chocolate Marble Quarry, S. of mouth of Carp, L. S.

Dark reddish-brown, with a few large greenish-white and many tiny light russet-brown spots ; slightly shining.

A compact, rather hard, fine-grained Argillyte, with its slaty lamination at an angle of about 56° to the plane of stratification. It is apparently identical with the brown material of No. 160, and is chiefly made up of Feldspar and Quartz, interspersed with exceedingly minute scales, in layers $\frac{1}{16}-\frac{1}{4}$ inch thick, which appear on a section as a series of bands alternately dull and shining. Many thin seams of the same material, 1 to 2 inches long, cross the layers irregularly, sometimes with tiny faults. Also a few irregular seams and bunches of greenish-gray Feldspar, sometimes 3 inches long, a few thin seams of reddish-gray Calcite and a few tiny bunches of reddish-brown Feldspar.

Fracture uneven. Streak reddish-white.

Weathers smoothly, of same color, and with slight polish.

No. 192 (Sp. 814).—*Banded Chloritic Argillyte.*

Huronian.—Bed V.—Chocolate Marble Quarry, S. of mouth of Carp, L. S.

Dark greenish-brown (sometimes speckled with light yellowish-brown spots), with light chocolate brown parallel bands.

A compact, fissile, slaty Argillyte, differing from No. 190 only in the predominance of the green bands, their usual thickness being ¾ inch, while that of the brown is ⅛ inch. The stratification is, like that of No. 190, nearly at right angles with the slaty lamination, and the Talc is disseminated in the same way but chiefly through the brown bands. Fuses before the blowpipe at about 5.5.

No weathered surface on the specimen.

No. 193 (Sp. 815).—*Banded Chloritic Argillyte.*

Huronian.—Bed V.—Chocolate Marble Quarry, S. of mouth of Carp, L. S.

Parallel stripes of olive-green, yellowish-brown, and chocolate-brown.

A compact, fissile, slaty Argillyte, with stratification at an angle of about 12° with the slaty lamination, and about as hard as No. 190. The olive-green and chocolate-brown bands are identical with those described in Nos. 190 and 192, but the third material is finely granular, of a light reddish or yellowish-brown color, and made up of layers about $\frac{1}{16}$ inch in thickness, composed of loosely aggregated granules of Feldspar and Quartz, separated by minute parallel and continuous films of reddish-brown Argillyte. Fuses before the blowpipe at 5.5, to a greenish-white enamel.

Weathering smooth and unchanged in color, the green bands receiving a polish and the yellowish-brown bands being slightly pitted by the removal of granules.

No. 194 (Sp. 881). —*Micaceous Feldspathic Argillyte.*

Huronian.—Bed V.—L'Anse Iron Range, S. side Sect. 9—T. 49—R. 33.

Greenish-gray ; slightly lustrous.

A soft, compact, tough, calcareous schist, of almost impalpable texture, composed of minute granules of grayish- or greenish-white Feldspar and a smoky-gray mineral (Quartz ?), with many scales of silvery-gray Mica, sometimes distinct to the eye.

Fracture uneven. Streak grayish-white and partially metallic (iron abraded from the knife). Seams of lamination shining and very slightly corrugated, sometimes covered with a film or thin layer of gray Calcite.

No. 195 (Sp. 882).—*Greenish-Gray Shale.*

Huronian.—L'Anse Iron Range, S. E. ¼ of S. W. ¼ Sect. 9—T. 49—R. 33.

Greenish-white, with minute parallel brown lines ; general effect, greenish-gray.

A rather soft, compact, fine-grained, fissile rock, of an imperfectly slaty structure, approaching a shale, made up of exceedingly minute granules of Feldspar and a few scales of Mica, and with reddish-brown Ferric Oxide disseminated throughout in very minute specks, scales, or continuous parallel seams.

Fracture smooth and even. Streak grayish-white, dotted with light brownish specks. Adheres decidedly to the tongue and yields an argillaceous odor when moistened. The Feldspar is probably altered to Kaolin to a considerable extent.   Bedding seams colored dirty reddish-brown.

Weathered surface even, and of a dirty yellowish-brown color.

No. 196 (Sp. 906).—*Siliceous Feldspathic Argillyte.*

Huronian.—L'Anse Iron Range, N. W. ¼ post, Sect. 18—T. 50—R. 33.

Ash-gray, inclining to greenish; minutely glittering in the sunlight.

A compact, homogeneous, crystalline rock of exceedingly fine texture, rather soft and brittle.   Under the lens it appears to be made up of about 9 parts of minute particles of greenish-gray Feldspar, often with a distinctly marked cleavage, whose facets chiefly produce the glittering appearance, with 1 part of irregular grains of dark smoky Quartz (?) and a few silvery grayish-white soft scales (Talc or Mica).

Fracture sub-conchoidal.   Streak grayish-white.

Weathers rather evenly, to a lighter shade of greenish-gray, minutely speckled with grayish-white; or to brownish-white, minutely speckled with black (the Quartz granules).

The weathering is sometimes $\frac{1}{16}$ to $\frac{1}{8}$ inch deep on flat surfaces, with a brownish-gray section; while at the angular corners of a mass it reaches to the depth of half an inch, with a light brown section, terminated inwardly by a grayish-black band.

No. 197 (Sp. 908).—*Greenish-Gray Feldspathic Argillyte.*

Huronian.—L'Anse Iron Range.

Greenish-gray; slightly shining.

A rather hard, homogeneous, fine-grained, and very fissile schist, with curving laminæ, and a very minute fibrous corrugation of its cleavage surfaces; resembles Nos. 335, 339, and 221.

Fracture hackly.   Streak grayish-white.   Fuses before the blowpipe at 4 to a greenish-gray glass.   Under the lens, exceedingly minute scales, like those of Mica, can be distinguished throughout. A very thin seam of Calcite occurs.

Weathers rather unevenly, to light shades of brownish-gray and cream color.

No. 198 (Sp. 917).—*Banded Feldspathic Argillyte.*

(A small weathered pebble.)

Huronian.—L'Anse Bay, E. side, say 1 mile from South end.

Alternate bands of grayish-white, sometimes speckled minutely with black, and of light chocolate-brown, with darker specks and narrow gray bands.

A soft, compact, fine-grained, finely laminated Argillyte, made up of bands about ¾ inch thick. Streak lighter grayish-white and light yellowish-brown. Contains many exceedingly minute silvery-gray scales, perhaps of Talc, to which a very slight greasy feel may be due.

Specimen 918 is a pebble of similar rock to 917. Colors of layers chocolate-brown—grayish-white, with a greenish tinge, with small spherical masses, ⅛ to ¼ inch across, of a softer, light, reddish-brown material—and cast-iron gray, with dark greenish tinge, and traversed by narrow bands of reddish-brown and light greenish-gray. Slaty lamination at angle of about 30° with the bands. Scratched by the nail.

Another specimen, 919, consists of layers ½ to 1 inch thick. Angle of slaty lamination with bands about 36°. Greasy feel a little more decided.

No. 199 (Sp. 920).—*Greenish Feldspathic Argillyte.*

Huronian.—L'Anse Bay, E. side, say 1 mile from South end.

Light greenish-gray, mottled by seams with dark reddish- and yellowish-brown.

A soft slate, of impalpable texture, and finely fissile lamination, which seems to be chiefly composed of grayish-white Feldspar, with much greenish-gray Talc or Chlorite, in silvery scales, not distinguishable by the naked eye. The specimen is traversed, at the same angle with the slaty lamination as in No. 198 (919), by a layer about an inch thick, which appears to differ from the rest of the material only in a slightly granular texture, but on certain cleavage surfaces is weathered sometimes to a tinge of yellowish-brown, and sometimes to a deep reddish-brown. Scratched by the nail and of slight greasy feel.   Streak greenish-white.   A narrow seam, ⅛ inch thick, distinguished by a somewhat granular structure.

Weathers to a lighter shade of greenish-gray, slightly tinged with yellowish or reddish-brown, the surface being minutely furrowed by projecting laminæ.

Another specimen (921) is a shade darker and harder, more compact, and with a slight lustre.   Contains a minute fossil too imperfect for determination.

Specimen 922 consists of the same material, with various lighter and darker shades of greenish-gray, the layers being ¼ to 2 inches thick, and sometimes of a somewhat granular structure, speckled with tiny reddish-brown angular stains.

No. 200 (Sp. 982).—*Gray Feldspathic Argillyte.*

Huronian.—Near centre of Sect. 13—T. 50—R. 32.

Cast-iron gray inclining to greenish ; slightly glittering.

A rather hard, compact, fine-grained schist, in which only minute scales of brownish-gray Mica can be distinguished by the eye ; but under the lens it appears to consist chiefly of a mixture of exceedingly minute granules of smoky Quartz and grayish-white Feldspar.   A few yellow grains of Pyrite also occur.   On a section its schistose structure is seen to be produced by parallel films of a grayish-black material (probably Argillyte), which divide up the rock into laminæ, about $\frac{1}{32}$ inch thick.   The surface of the joints is stained reddish-brown.

Fracture uneven.   Streak grayish-white.

Weathers somewhat evenly, to a dirty blackish-brown, mottled by yellowish-brown, and on the edges of the laminæ to the depth of about $\frac{1}{32}$ inch, with a brownish-white section.

No. 201 (Sp. 992).—*Green Speckled Argyllite.*

Huronian.—N. part of Sect. 21—T. 51—R. 31.

Grayish-green, spotted with brownish-red.

Similar to No. 200, but of a rather brighter shade of green, and with the section speckled over with circular brick-red stains, nearly

⅛ inch across. It is apparently made up of greenish-gray Feldspar, with a little Mica (Talc or Chlorite ?), in minute glistening scales. Its structure approaches a slate.

Streak grayish-white, dotted with brick-red.

Weathers irregularly and roughly, to a dirty greenish-gray, inclining to citrine-yellow, mottled over with faint irregular streaks and spots of reddish-brown.

No. 202 (Sp. 998).—*Brownish-Gray Feldspathic Argillyte.*

Huronian.—Slate River, Sect. 21—T. 51—R. 31.

A rather slaty rock which resembles No. 199, but is of a dark greenish-gray, with brownish tinge, and faintly banded with yellowish-brown. The lamination or "stripe," which forms an angle of about 60° with the plane of cleavage, is chiefly marked by lines of minute rectangular cavities, rarely $\frac{1}{32}$ inch in length, as if derived from the decomposition of some crystallized mineral (Pyrite ?), filled with a soft yellowish-brown Ochre.

Streak reddish-white to light brick-red.

Weathers smoothly, with a slightly reddish tinge, the bedding-lines being somewhat pitted by the weathering of the rectangular cavities.

No. 203 (Sp. 1101).—*Magnetic Feldspathic Slate.*

Huronian.—E. of mouth of Tunnel, Washington Mine.

Blackish-gray, slightly greenish ; minutely glittering.

A compact, tough, very fine-grained and rather slaty rock, which appears under the lens to consist of about 6 parts of particles of greenish-white Feldspar, 3 parts of exceedingly minute black micaceous scales, and 1 part of Magnetite in black octahedra, just visible to the naked eye. A joint occurs, with the surface stained reddish-brown.

Fracture nearly even. Streak grayish-white.

Weathers smoothly and evenly, to a brownish-black.

No. 204 (Sp. 1102).—*Micaceous Feldspathic Slate.*

Huronian.—S. E. of mouth of Tunnel, Washington Mine.

Blackish-gray ; minutely sparkling.

A slate of the same texture as No. 203, consisting of about 4 parts of grayish-white Feldspar, 4 parts of smoky Quartz, and two parts of black, sometimes grayish-white, Mica, in minute glittering scales, often gathered in flakes on a cleavage surface, $\frac{1}{16}$ to $\frac{1}{8}$ inch across.

Fracture sub-conchoidal. Streak grayish-white. Surface of fissures stained brownish-gray.

Weathers rather evenly and smoothly, to the depth of $\frac{1}{16}$ inch, with shallow pits about $\frac{1}{4}$ inch in diameter, to a brownish-gray, covered (as well as the surface of the fissures) with minute blackish specks and parallel lines. This surface shows the Feldspar to exist in angular fragments, about $\frac{1}{32}$ inch across, surrounded by the mixture of Quartz and Mica, while much of the latter is gathered in minute irregularly parallel films or seams, which produce the fine lines barely distinguishable on a fresh fracture, usually $\frac{1}{32}$ to $\frac{1}{4}$ inch apart, but generally running in pairs.

No. 205 (Sp. 1109).—*Amygdaloidal Amphibole-Schist.*

Huronian.—Bed XIII.—Washington Mine, S. end of McConnell's Pit.

Grayish-black, with a few glistening facets, and covered with tiny, round, greenish-gray specks.

A compact, fine-grained schist, the bulk of which is made up of about 4 parts of the usual grayish-, rarely greenish-white Feldspar, in minute particles, of 4 parts of a black mineral in tiny particles, and in facets with slightly marked cleavage, and hardly touched by a file, $\frac{1}{16}$ to $\frac{1}{8}$ inch across, which resembles Amphibole, and of 2 parts of black or grayish-white Mica, in minute silvery scales. Through this matrix are disseminated, to the amount of nearly $\frac{3}{10}$ of the bulk of the rock, many slightly elliptical masses, usually $\frac{1}{16}$ inch across, but sometimes $\frac{1}{8}$ to $\frac{3}{16}$ inch in length, arranged parallel to the stratification, and imparting an amygdaloidal appearance to a section. They consist of a soft material, with greenish-white streak, of a greenish-gray color, passing into reddish-brown, in which only a few very minute scales of Mica can be distinguished.

Fracture uneven.   Streak gray.   Surface of fissures covered with a film of reddish-brown Ochre.

No. 206 (Sp. 1138).—*Greenish Feldspathic Argillyte.*

Huronian.—Bed XIII.—Lake Superior Mine.

Grayish-green, and dull, with many minute black glittering points.

A compact, rather soft, crypto-crystalline schist, which is apparently made up of about 9 parts of greenish-gray Feldspar, in microscopic particles, with about 1 part of Micaceous-Iron, in minute black scales, with a high lustre and reddish-brown powder, which appear under the lens almost all to be triangular scales, evidently derived from the alteration of octahedra of Magnetite.

Fracture rather uneven.   Streak grayish-white.   Surface of fissures stained reddish-brown.   Does not affect the magnetic needle. The magnet separates about 4 per cent. of the pulverized rock.

Weathers evenly and smoothly, to a reddish-brown.

No. 207 (Sp. 1238).—*Micaceous Feldspathic Argillyte.*

Huronian.—Armstrong's Camp, Michigamme River.

Resembles No. 261 (1229) in color and general character, but minutely glittering.

Under the lens it appears to consist chiefly of minute smoky-gray particles (Feldspar ?), often grayish-white, studded with glistening scales of black Mica (like an Ottrelite Schist).

Fracture uneven.   Streak grayish-white.   Yellow Pyrite is disseminated in minute particles.

Weathers unevenly to a dirty brownish-gray.

No. 208 (Sp. 1240).—*Chloritic Argillyte.*

Huronian.—About ½ mile above mouth of Fence River.

Cast-iron-gray, inclining to olive ; shining.

A rather slaty rock, which resembles No. 207, but the glittering scales or films of Mica (or Chlorite) are quite minute. Very little is visible under the lens, and the texture of the rock is consequently much finer and more fissile. The Pyrite also occurs in less quantity; the seams of lamination are dotted with tiny quartzose bunches, and have a uniform lustre. The streak is greenish-white; and a minute transverse vein of brownish-gray quartz occurs.

Weathers smoothly, to a dirty brownish-gray.

No. 209 (Sp. 1249).—*Chloritic Feldspathic Argillyte.*

Huronian.—Michigamme River, about ¼ way from Paint to Grand Portage.

Grayish-green; dull.

Resembles No. 339. A few seams, $\frac{1}{16}$ to $\frac{1}{4}$ inch wide, cross the laminæ, and are occupied by an aggregate of grayish-white Feldspar, with good cleavage and lustre, and smoky-gray Quartz, with geodes of tiny Quartz crystals, surrounded by a little red Ferric Oxide. Fuses before the blowpipe at 4.5, to a black glass.

Weathers to a blackish-brown, mottled by brownish-yellow and reddish-brown rhomboidal spots, usually about ⅛ inch square. These are revealed under the lens to consist of oölitic granules of Quartz of those colors, and are probably quartzose pseudomorphs after Feldspar crystals.

No. 210 (Sp. 1250).—*Micaceous Siliceous Slate.*

Huronian.—Norway Portage, Sect. 15—T. 42—R. 31.

Resembles No. 261 (1229) in color, and No. 207 in the glitter of its surface; but the latter character is much more decided. The material appears under the lens to consist of about 6 parts of minute granules of grayish-white Feldspar, 1 part of smoky Quartz, and about 3 parts of glistening scales of black Mica. The structure is finely laminated, and the Feldspar predominates in many of the layers, which become lighter colored and vary in thickness from a film up to $\frac{1}{16}$ inch; while other layers are quartzose.

Fracture uneven. Streak grayish-white and partially metallic (abraded iron).

Weathers evenly, to a dirty greenish-gray, covered with parallel lines and narrow stripes of grayish and reddish-white.

No. 211 (Sp. 1368).—*Iron-Gray Argillaceous Mica-Slate.*

Laurentian.—S. end of Lake Gogebic, S. E. ¼ Sect. 3—T. 46—R. 42.

Cast-iron-gray, inclining to bluish; shining on cleavage surfaces.

A rather soft fissile rock, of almost impalpable texture. Under the lens appears to consist chiefly of equal bulks of a grayish-white (Feldspar) and grayish-black mineral (Smoky Quartz?) with many minute scales of Mica disseminated throughout. The cleavage surfaces are much corrugated and covered with a shining film of brown Mica.

Streak bluish-white. Fuses before the blowpipe at 4.5, to a greenish-black glass.

Weathers unevenly to a greenish-gray. Strongly resembles a Huronian schist, like No. 197 (908), No. 222, etc., rather than any other Laurentian rock.

No. 212 (Sp. 1369).—*Gray Feldspathic Schist (Siliceous).*

Laurentian.—S. end of Lake Gogebic, S. E. ¼ Sect. 3—T. 46—R. 42.

Gray, slightly reddish, minutely speckled with grayish-white; minutely glittering on cleavage surfaces, almost dull on the section.

A hard, compact, homogeneous, fine-grained schistose rock, made up of the same materials as No. 187, in somewhat larger granules, the scales of Mica being prominent only on the cleavage surfaces.

Fracture uneven. Cuts hard to a knife-edge. Streak grayish-white. Effervesces slightly in acid, fuses before the blowpipe at 5, to a grayish-white glass.

Weathers rather evenly, to a cream color, and to the depth of ⅛ to ¼ inch: on examining the weathered surface with a lens, it is found to be roughened and lightened in color, by projecting granules of Quartz and Feldspar.

No. 213 (Sp. 1379).—*Banded Magnetic Mica-Slate.*

Laurentian.—From iron locality, N. E. corner Sect. 22—T. 46—R. 42.

Gray, inclining to brownish, with minute grayish-white and with also glittering specks ; highly glistening on cleavage surfaces.

Resembles No. 210 in material and structure, but is a little more fissile and contains more and brighter Mica. It is made up, with a loose adherence, of hard laminæ, about $\frac{1}{32}$ inch thick, consisting of Quartz and Magnetite, alternating with laminæ, not quite so hard to the knife-edge, usually ⅛ to ¼ inch thick, consisting of an aggregate of Quartz and Feldspar. The surface of the seams is covered with glistening films, consisting of large scales of brown Mica. Decidedly magnetic, and polarity strongly marked. Fracture hackly. Cuts hard to the knife-edge. Streak grayish-white and partially metallic (abraded iron). Powder ash-gray, inclining to brownish ; the magnet separates 23 per cent. by weight, in grayish-black particles. Fuses before the blowpipe at 4.5, to a black glass.

Weathers rather evenly on the edges of the layers, to a surface covered with narrow parallel bands of light-red and grayish-black, more strongly contrasted and redder than the weathering of No. 210.

No. 214 (Sp. 1380).—*Banded Magnetic Siliceous Schist.*

Laurentian.—From iron locality, N. E. corner Sect. 22—T. 46—R. 42.

Like No. 213 in color and material, but the laminæ are adherent and but faintly distinguishable on a fresh fracture. On the weathered surface, however, the Feldspathic layers are usually ⅛ to ¼ inch thick, and form light-red and brownish-gray bands, while the magnetic quartzose vary in thickness from a film to ¼ inch, and project slightly above the surface as zigzagged brown bands, rarely mottled with grayish-white Quartz, studded with many sparkling octahedra of Magnetite. Strongly magnetic and with decided polarity. Many of the cleavage surfaces are stained brown and blackish-brown by the weathering, to the depth of 1½ inches or more. Powder ash-gray, slightly inclining to blackish ; the magnet separates about 33 per cent. by weight in black particles.

No. 215 (Sp. 1390).—*Greenish Feldspathic Schist (Siliceous).*

Laurentian.—N. part of N. W. ¼ of Sect. 22—T. 46—R. 42.

Greenish-gray, minutely speckled with gray ; minutely glistening.

A hard rock resembling No. 212, but it is a little coarser in texture, with slight traces of schistose structure in the hand specimen ; and appears under the lens to consist chiefly of granules of grayish-white and greenish-gray Feldspar, with good cleavage and lustre, and of a black and blackish-green shining mineral, in micaceous fragments, probably Mica, sometimes with good cleavage and lustre (perhaps fragments of Amphibole) ; much Pyrite is disseminated in yellow granules.

Fracture uneven, approaching sub-conchoidal. Cuts hard to the knife-edge. Streak greenish white.

Weathers evenly and smoothly, to a dirty yellowish-brown, which under the lens is seen to consist of very slightly projecting thin flakes of Quartz, which is thus shown to be one of the chief constituents of the rock.

No. 216 (Sp. 1466).—*Feldspathic Siliceous Schist (Micaceous).*

Laurentian —S. of Sunday Lake, Sects. 16 and 21—T. 47—R. 45.

Greenish-gray, speckled with grayish-white and pale yellow ; glittering.

Resembles No. 215, but it is coarser, some of the grains of grayish-white and greenish-gray Feldspar being $\frac{1}{16}$ to $\frac{1}{8}$ inch long, with good cleavage and lustre. It also contains more Mica, of a brownish-black color, in rather larger scales, and has a decided but irregular schistose structure. Pyrite is abundantly disseminated in pale yellow particles visible to the eye. Fuses before the blowpipe at 4.5, to a blackish-brown glass. Cuts hard to the knife-edge, with a partially metallic streak (abraded iron).

Weathers rather unevenly, to a reddish-brown, with a few tiny lighter-colored and quartzose spots; many of the cleavage surfaces are stained the same color.

No. 217 (Sp. 1467).—*Feldspathic Siliceous Schist (Micaceous).*

Laurentian.—S. of Sunday Lake, Secs. 16 and 21—T. 47—R. 45.

Gray, speckled with grayish-white, and dotted with short, minute, black, glittering, parallel lines.

Resembles No. 216, but the texture is finer, the Feldspar is gray and grayish-white, and above all the elongated scales of gray Mica are peculiarly arranged, being disseminated throughout the material separately and in parallel planes, thus producing a fibrous appearance. A thin seam of grayish-white Quartz occurs.

Weathers smoothly to a dirty brownish-gray; the streak of the weathered surface is partially metallic with abraded iron, and shows the presence of Quartz as a constituent.

No. 218 (Sp. 1474).—*Green Feldspathic Schist (Siliceous).*

Laurentian.—N. side of Sect. 16—T. 47—R. 45.

Greenish-gray and slightly lustrous.

A compact, tough, homogeneous schist, of almost impalpable texture, made up of a greenish-gray Feldspar, grayish-white on thin edges, and of exceedingly minute glittering scales.

A little Quartz is disseminated in tiny bunches and transverse veins; seams covered with a soft, lustrous, sometimes fibrous, black and blackish-green film, traverse the rock and produce apparently a schistose structure.

Fracture uneven. Streak greenish-white. Many irregular seams and tiny cavities, stained reddish-brown.

Weathers unevenly, to a brownish-gray (Feldspar) to the depth of about $\frac{1}{4}$ inch, with greenish-white section; a little Quartz projects here and there in thin flakes.

Specimen 1475 is of a little coarser texture. Much Pyrite is disseminated in pale yellow minute particles, and a seam occurs, $\frac{1}{16}$ inch wide, of grayish- and brownish-white Feldspar, in tiny facets, with good cleavage and lustre.

No. 219 (Sp. 1523).—*Decomposed Chloritic Schist.*

Laurentian.—W. branch of Ontonagon River, Sect. 13—T. 46—R. 41.

Chocolate-brown, mottled with large spots of greenish-gray.

A rather soft, fissile, and rather slaty fine-grained aggregate of scales of greenish-gray Chlorite and Talc. Mostly decomposed into chocolate-brown, with perhaps a little Feldspar. Surface of laminæ somewhat corrugated and shining. A few irregular fissures.

Streak brownish-red or greenish-white.

Weathered surface even, and unchanged in color. Many exceedingly minute silvery greenish-gray scales, apparently of Talc, to which a somewhat greasy feel is due.

Resembles Nos. 190, 192, and 193.

No. 220 (Sp. 1540).—*Green Feldspathic Schist (Siliceous).*

Laurentian.—W. branch of Ontonagon River, Sect. 13—T. 46—R. 41.

Greenish-gray, minutely speckled with gray; slightly glittering.

Resembles Nos. 212 and 215, and seems to be chiefly made up of greenish-gray and greenish-white Feldspar, in minute granules, and probably Quartz, with a little Mica in minute black scales. Irregular fissures occur, covered with films of the Mica and of brownish-white Calcite.

Fracture uneven. Cuts hard to the knife-edge. Streak reddish-white and partially metallic (abraded iron). Fuses before the blow-pipe at 5, to a grayish-white glass.

Weathers evenly and smoothly, to a light reddish-brown, to the depth of $\frac{1}{16}$ inch.

Specimen 1541 is a coarser and altered variety of 1540, of a reddish-brown color, speckled with greenish-gray, the Feldspar being in tiny facets visible to the eye, often minutely striated, and with good cleavage, and much stained with brownish-red films. Effervesces slightly in acid.   Streak reddish-white.

No. 221 (Sp. 968).—*Bluish-Gray Argillyte-Slate.*

Huronian.—1 mile S. of Sturgeon River, Sect. 18—T. 48—R. 34.

Dark bluish-gray ; a slight lustre.

A homogeneous, very fine-grained, and finely-laminated roofing-slate, with a very minute fibrous corrugation of the laminæ.

Streak light bluish-gray.   Fuses before the blowpipe at 6. Under the lens many exceedingly minute, dark, glistening scales are distinguished.

Specimen 969 is similar to 968, but shade of dark-green, rather than blue ; corrugation not so regular ; streak light greenish-gray.

In Specimen 970 the corrugation is a little coarser.

In Specimen 971 the corrugation is less decided and regular.

Specimen 983 (near centre of Sect. 13—T. 50—R. 32) is similar to 968, but not so fissile, and with only a slight fibrous structure.

Streak bluish-white.

Weathers roughly and to an ashy-gray color ; cleavage surfaces lined with films of Calcite.

No. 222 (Sp. 974).—*Bluish-Gray Argillyte-Slate.*

Huronian.—Plumbago Brook, S. W. ¼ Sect. 13—T. 49—R. 34.

Dark bluish-gray ; dull.

Streak bluish-white, not so finely laminated as No. 221, and with the bedding layers suggested by faint parallel lines, slightly darker and more granular.

Weathers smoothly and to a lighter color, revealing the bedding lines, even the more minute, in alternate thin bands of light and dark bluish-gray and bluish-white.   A minute fibrously corrugated structure, but not so regular as in No. 221.

Another specimen (975) is similar to 974, but slightly darker in color, and with a slight lustre. A few parallel small bunchy veins $\frac{1}{16}-\frac{3}{16}$ inch thick, filled with a coarse and irregular aggregate of glassy and milky Quartz and yellowish-brown scales of Mica. A coarse corrugation of the laminæ, which produces another cleavage resembling that of No. 247.

The weathered surface has a minute cross-striation, by the projection of laminæ on the two cleavage planes.

No. 223 (Sp. 976).—*Pyritiferous Argillyte-Slate.*

Huronian.—S. ¼ post Sect. 28—T. 51—R. 31, in Slate River.

Similar to No. 221, but without the corrugated structure, and dotted over with minute specks of yellowish-gray Pyrite.

Streak bluish-gray.

Weathers smoothly, to a lighter shade, speckled over with reddish-brown.

Specimen 979 is similar to 976, but with Pyrite disseminated throughout, in numerous specks and films of a yellowish-gray color.

Streak bluish-white.

No. 224 (Sp. 1104).—*Talcose Feldspathic Argillyte.*

Huronian —Bed XIII.—Washington Mine, Anderson's Pit.

Ash-gray, with a very slight tinge of green, and dull, with reddish-gray stripes; with a few minute glittering points.

A very compact, fine-grained, rather soft and brittle schist, made up of about 8 parts of grayish-, sometimes greenish- or yellowish-white, Feldspar, in minute particles—1 part of grayish-white, reddish-white, or reddish-gray Quartz, and 1 part of minute scales of black Mica and silvery-white scales of Talc. The Quartz is mostly gathered together, with a little greenish-white Feldspar, into layers about ⅛ inch thick and ¼ inch apart, which occur in tiny faults.

Fracture uneven. Streak grayish-white. A few fissures occur, whose surface is colored grayish-black, inclining to greenish, and possesses a greasy feel.

Weathers rather evenly, to a dirty brownish-gray, mottled with greenish-gray.

No. 225 (Sp. 1241).— *Talcose Feldspathic Argillyte.*

?—$\frac{1}{2}$ way from Paint to Grand Portage, Michigamme River.

Greenish-gray, covered with tiny blackish-green dots; dull.

A soft, compact, tough, crypto-crystalline schist, which appears under the lens to consist of exceedingly minute granules of grayish-white Feldspar, covered with greenish-gray scales of Talc; through this are dispersed irregularly oval spots, about $\frac{1}{32}$ inch long, which are produced by tiny parallel films of a blackish-gray material.

Fracture uneven. Streak grayish-white. The feel is slightly greasy, like Talc. Many irregular fissures, stained blackish-brown.

Weathers unevenly to a blackish-brown, mottled with yellowish-brown.

No. 226 (Sp. 1081).—*Magnetic Talc-Schist.*

Huronian.—Bed XIII.—Old Washington Mine.

On cleavage surface, gray and shining, minutely speckled with black and somewhat mottled with brownish-gray; on a fresh fracture, grayish-green and dull, with many glittering black points.

A rather soft, compact, talcose schist, with slightly greasy feel, which appears to be made up of about 5 parts of greenish-gray Talc, in silvery scales (which may be partly altered into a Mica), of about 3 parts of greenish-white Feldspar, and of 2 parts of Magnetite in octahedral crystals, which has been almost entirely converted into black glittering scales of Micaceous-Iron, many of which retain triangular shapes.

Fracture hackly. Streak white. Slightly attracts the magnetic needle. Cleavage surfaces are generally stained with a brownish-gray film and covered with a very minute corrugation.

Weathered surface rather even, and colored to reddish and yellowish shades of brown.

No. 227 (S).—*Porphyritic Talc-Schist.*

Huronian.—Parsons Mine.

Reddish-brown, streaked and speckled with grayish-white ; minutely glittering.

A rather hard, compact, heavy, fine-grained schist, which appears under the lens to consist chiefly of a very fine-grained aggregate of grayish-white Feldspar, minute scales of silvery-white Talc, and reddish-brown Ferric Oxide.

Fracture uneven. Streak grayish-white, dotted with brick-red. Surface of fissures stained reddish-brown.

Weathers rather unevenly, to a uniform chocolate-brown, covered with reddish-white to reddish-gray rectangular specks. These last consist of Kaolin, and reveal the dissemination, to the amount of nearly one tenth of the bulk of the rock, of thin tabular crystals of Feldspar, usually $\frac{1}{16}$ to $\frac{1}{8}$ inch in length, and rarely over $\frac{1}{32}$ inch in thickness, which cannot be distinguished on a fresh fracture.

No. 228 (Sp. 738).—*Tabular Magnetite-Schist.*

Huronian.—Bed XIII.—Spurr Range, Sect. 23—T. 48—R. 31.

Bluish-black, slightly lustrous, and divided into parallel bands of thin glittering streaks.

An exceedingly fine-grained, homogeneous, hard Magnetite, of steely compactness, and of a tabular lamination. The layers are usually regular and parallel, from $\frac{1}{4}$ to $\frac{1}{2}$ inch in thickness, and contain a few octahedra visible to the eye. They are separated from each other by thin.laminæ through which much Mica is disseminated in distinct brownish scales. Many irregular fissures occur, stained with dirty shades of yellowish and reddish-brown.

Fracture rather even.　Streak iron-black.　Powder grayish-black and dull.　Strongly magnetic, and with decided polarity. The magnet separates about 99 per cent. of the bulk.

Weathers roughly, the Mica assuming a golden yellow color and lustre, mingled with a reddish-brown powder.

No. 229 (Sp. 728).—*Fine-Grained Magnetite-Schist.*

Huronian.—Bed XIII.—Spurr Range, E. side Sect. 23—T. 48—R. 31.

Glittering bluish-black, striped with many narrow dull bands.

A brittle and friable, fine-grained, schistose Magnetite, made up of parallel layers, $\frac{1}{4}$ to $\frac{1}{2}$ inch thick, some of which are soft, loose aggregations of glittering crystalline particles, easily visible to the eye, and sometimes having a brownish tinge ; while the others are exceedingly fine-grained, hard, and dull.　They both consist of aggregates of octahedral crystals of Magnetite, varying in size, and more or less perfect in form, and of minute granules of brownish and grayish-white Quartz.

Fracture somewhat uneven.　Streak iron-black.　Strongly magnetic and with decided polarity.　Powder black and glittering ; the magnet separates about 92 per cent. of the bulk.

Weathers rather evenly, and unchanged in color, though slightly streaked with brownish-gray.

No. 230 (Sp. 1502).—*Black Magnetite-Slate.*

Huronian.—Sunday Lake Outlet.

Bluish-black and dull.

An exceedingly hard and brittle Magnetite-Slate, of impalpable texture, showing only a very few glittering points (probably Mica), and made up loosely of laminæ, about $\frac{1}{16}$ to $\frac{1}{8}$ inch thick.

The fissures between the laminæ are stained yellowish-brown. A transverse vein of glassy Quartz, about $\frac{1}{16}$ inch wide.

Fracture of laminæ even.　Strongly magnetic, and with strong

polarity. Hardly touched by the file. Streak and powder brownish-black and dull ; the magnet takes up all the powder.

Weathers smoothly, to a dirty cream color, mottled with light reddish-brown.

No. 231 (Sp. 737).—*Chloritic Magnetite-Schist.*

Huronian.—Bed XIII.—Spurr Range, Sect. 23—T. 48—R. 31.

Lustrous bluish-black, with narrow bands of dark greenish-gray.

A compact, tough, fine-grained schist, made up of laminæ, mostly parallel, but often coalescing, from a film in thickness up to ¼ inch, and of two materials. The one consists of an exceedingly compact steely Magnetite, with lustrous fracture, in which the glittering octahedral and grayish-white granules of Quartz are distinguishable by the lens ; the other of a fissile, soft Chlorite, through which many larger octahedra of Magnetite and minute granules of grayish-white Quartz are disseminated.

Fracture uneven. Streak iron-black, dotted with light greenish-gray. Strongly magnetic, and with decided polarity. Some of the chloritic laminæ are dotted, apparently by decomposition, with minute yellowish-brown specks. Powder dark grayish-green and dull. The magnet separates about 94 per cent. of the bulk.

Weathers smoothly, to dirty shades of reddish and yellowish-brown.

No. 232 (Sp. 733).—*Chloritic Magnetite-Schist.*

Huronian.—Bed XIII.—Spurr Range, Sect. 23—T. 48—R. 31.

Exactly like No. 231, except that many of the layers of Magnetite are coarser and glitter with minute octahedra of Magnetite, and some of the chloritic layers, near the weathered surface, are decomposed irregularly into a soft brown powder. Powder dark grayish-green, slightly glittering. The magnet separates about 80 per cent. of the bulk, in a blackish-green, slightly glittering powder, the remainder being an olive-green, dull mixture of granules of grayish-white Quartz and olive-green Chlorite.

No. 233 (Sp. 1512).—*Green Magnetite-Schist.*

Huronian.—N. side of S. E. ¼ Sect. 8—T. 47—R. 45.

Cast-iron gray, with greenish shade, with faint narrow stripes, slightly darker in color ; glittering in the sun.

A compact, tough, fine-grained Magnetite-Schist, of crypto-crystalline texture, with a laminated structure denoted by many faint dark lines on its section. It consists of exceedingly minute granules of a black color (Magnetite), and of a grayish-white (Feldspar and Quartz ?), with minute silvery-gray scales of Mica (or perhaps Chlorite ?).

Decidedly magnetic, and with decided polarity.

Fracture sub-conchoidal. Streak white. Powder ash-gray, slightly inclining to brownish, grayish, and dull. The magnet separates about 96 per cent. of the bulk, having the same ash-gray color—showing intimate admixture of the constituents.

Weathering yellowish- and reddish-brown, ⅛–⅓ inch in depth, and with an even surface.

No. 234 (Sp. 736).—*Quartzose Magnetite-Schist.*

Huronian.—Bed XIII.—Spurr Range, Sect. 23—T. 48—R. 31.

Bluish-black, with more or less glittering bands, some of which are mottled with grayish-white.

Consists of layers, ⅛ to ½ inch thick, of the two undecomposed materials of No. 236, with others, ¼ to ½ inch thick, which are decidedly quartzose and hard, the grayish-white Quartz granules greatly predominating.

Fracture even. Streak iron-black. One crystal of Pyrite, about ¼ inch square, occurs in a quartzose layer. Powder blackish-gray and dull. Magnetic and with decided polarity. The magnet separates about 97 per cent. by weight.

Weathers of a dirty brownish-yellow color, and rather evenly, the quartzose layers slightly projecting.

No. 235 (Sp. 1230).—*Quartzose Magnetite-Schist.*

Huronian.—Felch Mountain, Sects. 32 and 33—T. 42—R. 28.

Iron-black, slightly lustrous, banded with blackish-gray, mottled with reddish-gray.

A very hard, fine-grained, compact schist, resembling No. 154, made up of layers, about ½ inch thick, of reddish-gray Quartzyte, consisting of grayish-white and brownish-red granules of Quartz and minute glittering scales, perhaps Mica, and of layers of fine-grained Magnetite, generally of almost steely compactness, but sometimes with glittering particles visible to the eye, among which good octahedrons can rarely be distinguished by the lens.

Fracture uneven. Streak reddish-white on the Quartzyte layers, and on the black layers mostly reddish-brown, but in places iron-black. Strongly magnetic, and with decided polarity. A system of transverse parallel cleavage planes, stained reddish-brown. Many minute strings and bunches, sometimes ¾ inch long, of glistening Magnetite, associated with particles of a soft brown Ochre and reddish-white Quartz. Powder reddish-black and somewhat glittering, and is completely taken up by the magnet.

Weathered surface uneven, and of a dirty reddish-brown color.

No. 236 (Sp. 735).—*Ochrey Magnetite-Schist.*

Huronian.—Bed XIII.—Spurr Range, Sect. 23—T. 48—R. 31.

Dull bluish-black, with a few glittering bands, and with others of a reddish-brown color.

A form of No. 229, consisting chiefly of the dull compact layers, but partly of glittering layers which are not so coarse as those of No. 229. Many thin laminæ are partly weathered into a softer reddish-brown Ochre. A few transverse seams occur, colored brownish-yellow. Strongly magnetic, and with decided polarity.

Streak iron-black and reddish-brown. Powder snuff-brown and dull. The magnet separates about 98 per cent. of the weight.

No. 237 (Sp. 689).—*Specular-Iron Schist.*

Huronian.—Bed XIII.—N. side of Sect. 19—T. 47—R. 27.

Iron-black and shining.

A compact, homogeneous schist, of finely fibrous and minutely lamellar structure, with a high lustre, and covered with minute glittering points, which under the lens are shown to be tiny scales of irregular shape. On a fresh fracture it is faintly perceptible (more clearly under the lens) that the ore is made up of thin and irregular lenticular layers, which differ from each other in fineness of grain, height of lustre, hardness, and abundance of the glittering scales; minute granules of grayish-white and reddish-white Quartz are disseminated throughout the ore, occasionally in tiny lenticular or rounded masses visible to the eye.

Fracture uneven. Streak reddish-brown. Powder brownish-black and glittering.

Weathers evenly, but with a fibrous surface, from the thin edges of many irregularly projecting laminæ.

No. 238 (Sp. 1234).—*Quartzose Hematite-Schist.*

Huronian.—Upper Menominee Range, Sect. 31—T. 42—R. 29.

Bluish-black, slightly lustrous, streaked and speckled with reddish-brown.

A rather fine-grained, hard, cellular schist, mostly made up of an aggregate of granules of smoky and grayish-white Quartz, glittering particles of Hematite of bluish-black color, and many of which are revealed by the lens to possess an octahedral form (Martite), and larger scales $\frac{1}{16}$ inch across, apparently of Micaceous-Iron, with much reddish-brown Ochre dispersed throughout in irregular particles and parallel seams, which mark the schistose structure. The smoky and grayish-white Quartz are also often gathered in irregular bunches and lenticular masses, sometimes 1 or 2 inches long.

Fracture uneven. Streak reddish-brown. Powder reddish-brown and glittering, from which the magnet separates a very few black particles.

Weathers very unevenly, to a brownish-black color, the quartzose layers and bunches projecting irregularly.

No. 239 (Sp. 1235).—*Quartzose Hematite-Schist.*

Huronian.—Upper Menominee Range, Sect. 31—T. 42—R. 29.

Sparkling bluish-black, exactly like the color of No. 229.

A compact, homogeneous, and somewhat brittle Hematite-Schist, rather fine-grained, but with distinct particles, and having a sub-schistose structure. Under the lens most of the particles appear to be irregular scales, but many retain an octahedral form (Martite). Granules of grayish Quartz are also revealed; in some places the Quartz is gathered in tiny particles and bunches visible to the eye.

Fracture uneven. Streak reddish-brown. Powder reddish-brown and glittering. The magnet separates about 1 per cent. of the bulk.

Weathers rather unevenly, with a diminution of lustre.

No. 240 (Sp. 1237).—*Quartzose Hematite-Schist.*

Huronian.—Upper Menominee Range, Sect. 31—T. 42—R. 29.

Cast-iron gray, with bluish shade; glittering.

A very hard, compact, tough, homogeneous, fine-grained Hematite, of imperfectly schistose structure, chiefly made up of minute glittering irregular scales of iron-black Micaceous-Iron, together with granules of grayish-white Quartz, only to be distinguished by a lens. A few irregular fissures, stained reddish- and yellowish-brown.

Fracture uneven, but approaching sub-conchoidal on large surfaces. Streak reddish-brown. Slightly magnetic. Powder blackish-brown and glittering. The magnet separates only a few black particles.

Weathered surface smooth and somewhat polished, of a dirty shade of blackish-brown.

No. 241 (Sp. 1429).—*Ochrey Quartzose Hematite-Schist.*

Huronian.—W. line of Sect. 18—T. 47—R. 45.

Blackish-brown, irregularly mottled with brownish-red and reddish-gray; dull.

A soft, compact, somewhat schistose Hematite, mostly of impalpable texture, in which grayish and yellowish-white Quartz and brownish-red Ochre are disseminated, in irregular tiny bunches, and a very few minute scales of silvery-gray Mica.

Effervesces slightly with acid. Thin films of a grayish-white and yellowish-brown color traverse the rock irregularly.

Fracture uneven. Streak bright reddish-brown.

Weathers unevenly, assuming lighter shades of color.

No. 242 (Sp. 872).—*Calcareous Ochrey Siliceous Schist.*

?—Near North end of Presqu'isle.

Grayish-white, striped throughout with yellowish-brown.

A tough, fine-grained, ferruginous, schistose rock, traversed throughout by layers about $\frac{1}{16}$ inch thick and apart, largely composed of hard grayish-white crystalline Calcite, somewhat but irregularly parallel, and with thinner laminæ crossing at all angles. The chief material is a brownish-yellow, siliceous Ochre, through which are disseminated small scales of brownish-black Hematite and tiny crystalline masses of a light green mineral—probably Talc.

Fracture uneven. Streak brownish-white. Effervesces briskly with acid, the grayish-white layers dissolving out.

Weathers smoothly and of same color, the calcareous laminæ sometimes projecting above the brown oxide, where somewhat separated from each other.

No. 243 (Sp. 995).—*Ochrey Calcareous Hematite.*

Huronian.—Slate River, Sect. 28—T. 51—R. 31.

Blackish-gray, mottled with reddish-brown and bright brownish-yellow; glistening.

A compact, coarsely crystalline aggregate of Calcite, in large facets, often ¼ to ½ inch across, with irregular crystalline bunches of calcareous reddish-brown Hematite, smaller bunches of Limonite and of grayish-white fine-grained Quartz being interspersed in less proportion. Effervesces strongly with acid.

Fracture uneven. Streak white, reddish-brown, and bright brownish-yellow.

Weathers unevenly, to dirty shades of yellowish and reddish-brown, the Hematite projecting above the Calcite, and the surface of the latter being minutely furrowed by the weathered-out edges of its harder laminæ.

No. 244 (Sp. 896).—*Kaolinic Ochre-Schist.*

Huronian.—L'Anse Iron Range, Sect. 9—T. 49—R. 33.

Stripes of gray and reddish-brown.

A soft, compact, finely granular rock, made up of layers ¼ inch thick of two materials ; the one being reddish-brown and composed of Hematite-Ochre, and amounting to about 6 parts ; and the other being a mixture, of a gray color, speckled with white, of red Ferric Oxide with a very soft white Kaolin, amounting to about 4 parts. Many irregular fissures, one of which is mottled with black and possesses a high polish of slickensides.

Streak light reddish-brown. No weathered surface on the specimen, which is a decomposed variety of a schist associated with the specular ores.

No. 245 (Sp. 890).—*Brown Limonite-Schist.*

Huronian.—L'Anse Iron Range, near centre N. W. ¼ Sect. 9—T. 49—R. 33.

Blackish-brown, with reddish shade.

A compact, hard, rather brittle rock, of rather slaty structure, made up of minute granules of light reddish-brown Quartz, particles of Limonite, and minute micaceous scales.

Fracture even. Streak light yellowish-brown. A few tiny geodes lined with Limonite, and others filled with brick-red Ochre.

Weathered surface smooth, and covered with reddish-brown Ochre.

No. 246 (Sp. 879).—*Carbonaceous Slate.*

Huronian.—Lower Bed.—L'Anse Iron Range, S. side of Sect. 9—T. 49—R. 33.

Blackish-brown ; dull.
A compact, hard, fine-grained, fissile, Carbonaceous Argillyte, with a few minute seams of a light brown color. Consists of minute grains of gray Quartz, scattered through the black schistose material.
Streak glistening black, and rock receives a high polish by a little friction. Soils paper by rubbing.
Weathers smooth and of same color.

No. 247 (Sp. 904).—*Carbonaceous Shale.*

Huronian.—Lower Bed.—L'Anse Iron Range, S. W. ¼ of Sect. 13—T. 49—R. 34.

Grayish-black.
A rather hard, compact, slightly Carbonaceous Argillyte, with a finely fibrous corrugation of all the laminæ, which imparts a minute and peculiar cleavage in 2 planes at right angles to each other. On the cleavage plane of corrugated surface, the color is blackish-gray and slightly shining ; on the surface of the other cleavage plane (which divides the rock into thin flakes) the color is blackish-gray and slightly shining, speckled with grayish-black spots without lustre. In a diffused light, with no reflection from the shining surfaces, the color of the rock is grayish-black.
Streak greenish-white. Does not soil paper, with carbon, by rubbing.

No. 248 (Sp. 880).—*Quartzose Carbonaceous Shale.*

Huronian.—Lower Bed.—L'Anse Iron Range, S. side of Sect. 9—T. 49—R. 33.

Color like No. 246, but a shade blacker ; dull.
A rock similar to No. 246, but softer, and soiling paper more readily. Contains seams of glassy Quartz, ¼ inch thick ; also small veins and bunches, distributed irregularly, and filled with an aggregate of Quartz, yellowish-brown Ochre, and minute scales of Mica.

No. 249 (Sp. 898).—*Quartzose Carbonaceous Slate.*

Huronian.—Lower Bed.—L'Anse Iron Range, N. W. ¼ of Sect. 9—T. 49—R. 33.

Similar to No. 246, but a little blacker and softer, and containing a seam of glassy Quartz, $\frac{1}{16}$ inch thick.

No. 250 (Sp. 899).—*Graphitic Shale.*

Huronian.—Lower Bed.—L'Anse Iron Range, N. W. ¼ of Sect. 9—T. 49—R. 33.

Resembles No. 246, but with many layers covered with a glistening graphitic film, some layers harder and more compact than others. Contains large bunches of an aggregate of Quartz and yellow and brownish-yellow Ochre. A few minute transverse seams, filled with the same material as the shale, but of more granular structure.

No. 251 (Sp. 900).—*Graphitic Shale.*

Huronian.—Lower Bed.—L'Anse Iron Range, N. W. ¼ of Sect. 9—T. 49—R. 33.

Similar to No. 250, but of a laminated structure, some layers being graphitic.

Weathered surface smooth, the graphitic layers being more polished so as to impart a banded appearance. A seam filled with an aggregate of Quartz and brownish-yellow Ochre, and covered with indistinct impressions of fucoidal remains.

No. 252 (S).—*Coarse Red Granite.*

Laurentian.—Foster Mine.

Light salmon-colored spots, surrounded by grayish-black; shining.

A coarse Granite, made up of about 7 parts of angular masses of Orthoclase, with good cleavage and lustre, 1 to 2 inches across, in an aggregate of about 2 parts of smoky-gray to grayish-white Quartz, in angular grains about ¼ inch across, and grayish-black Mica, inclining to greenish, in soft scales, giving a gray streak, inclining to greenish.   Much of the Quartz is also interlaminated, in thin films and leaves, through the cleavage seams of the Orthoclase.

Fracture very uneven.   Irregular fissures, slightly stained blackish and brownish.

Weathers unevenly, the Feldspar being a little brightened in color, but losing its lustre.

No. 253 (Sp. 1228).—*Ferruginous Granite.*

Huronian.—Dyke.—Felch Mountain, Sects. 32 and 33—T. 42—R. 28.

Reddish-gray, mottled with light brown and black.

A hard, tough, coarse, compact rock, consisting of Feldspar and Quartz, with a little Micaceous-Iron and Mica.   The Feldspar, apparently Orthoclase, constitutes about 6 parts of the bulk, and consists of small masses of grayish-white color, passing into the softer brownish-red material, with a few large irregular glassy crystals, $\frac{1}{2}$ to 1 inch long, of a light-brown color.   The Quartz constitutes nearly 3 parts of the bulk, and is smoky-gray, rarely greenish-white, and occurs in small masses.   The Micaceous-Iron amounts to nearly one part, and occurs in tiny bunches and thin seams, often 1 to 2 inches long, running and crossing each other irregularly.   The Mica is present in very small quantity, in minute silvery-gray scales, and seems to be replaced by the Micaceous-Iron: so that this rock, to judge by the hand specimen, resembles and may be identical with the Eisen-Granit of the Germans.

Fracture uneven.

Weathers unevenly, by the removal of the Micaceous-Iron and decomposition of the Feldspar, and to a reddish-white color.

No. 254 (Sp. 741).—*Fine-Grained White Granite.*

Boulder, near 34th Mile Post, M. & O. Road.

Grayish-white, with minute blackish-brown specks disseminated throughout; glittering.

A hard, compact, tough, fine-grained Granite, made up of 4

parts of grayish-white Feldspar, often with good cleavage, minutely striated and iridescent ; of 5 parts of smoky-gray Quartz, in grains, like those of the Feldspar, rarely ⅛ inch across ; and of one part of soft brownish-black Mica, with gray streak, in minute scales, disseminated throughout, without any parallel arrangement. A coarse bunch occurs, in which the scales of Mica are ⅛ inch across. A little of the Mica inclines to a massive or fibrous structure, resembling an altered Amphibole ; and under the lens many minute grains are seen to be associated with it of a translucent yellowish-green color, and with a glassy fracture (Epidote).

Fracture sub-conchoidal. Streak white.

Weathers smoothly to a slightly reddish-white, some of the small grains of Feldspar becoming soft and reddish.

No. 255 (Sp. 746).—*Fine-Grained Black Gneiss.*

Boulder, near 34th Mile Post, M. & O. Road.—Lake Michigamme, Sect. 3—T. 47—R. 30.

Grayish-black, minutely speckled with gray ; glittering.

A hard, compact, rather brittle, fine-grained Gneiss, made up of minute scales of black Mica and granules of grayish-white Feldspar and smoky Quartz, just distinguishable by the eye. Pyrite occurs in a very few tiny particles.

Fracture even. Streak gray and grayish-white. Effervesces slightly in acid. Fuses before the blowpipe at 4, to a brownish-black blebby enamel. A few seams occur, covered with films of yellowish- and reddish-brown Ochre.

Weathers to an even surface, of a reddish-white color, minutely speckled with gray and reddish-brown scales, and with a few angular fragments projecting, about ¼ inch long, of a coarse reddish-white Feldspar.

No. 256 (Sp. 1248, B).—*Fine-Grained Black Gneiss.*

?—Michigamme River.—E'ly part of Sect. 21—T. 42—R. 31.

Blackish-brown, speckled with gray ; decidedly glittering.

A hard, compact, tough, minutely porphyritic, fine-grained

Gneiss, made up of nearly 4 parts of blackish-brown Mica, in minute glittering scales, of 4 parts of a gray Feldspar, in thin plates $\frac{1}{32}$ to $\frac{3}{16}$ inch long, and of over 2 parts of grayish-white Quartz, in minute granules. A little yellow Pyrite is disseminated in small particles.

Fracture uneven and rough. Streak grayish-white. A thin seam of reddish-brown Feldspar crosses the specimen, and a fissure stained reddish-brown.

Weathers unevenly, to a blackish-brown, speckled with yellowish-brown.

No. 257 (Sp. 1252).—*Fine-Grained Grayish-Black Gneiss.*

?—Long Portage.—Sects. 32 and 33—T. 42—R. 31.

Grayish-white, minutely speckled with black ; glittering.

A hard, tough, compact, and very fine-grained, uniform, laminated Gneiss, which consists of about 1 part of tiny scales of black Mica, about 4 parts of grayish-white Quartz, in minute grains, and 5 parts of smoky-gray or blackish-gray Feldspar, in tiny crystalline grains.

Fracture almost even. Streak white. A transverse seam of blackish-green, glistening scales of Chlorite, with a few yellow grains of Pyrite.

Weathers unevenly, to a brownish-black, the scales of black Mica becoming silvery-gray. Somewhat resembles a Slate-Gneiss (Cotta)—Schiefer-Gneiss (Germ.).

Another variety, 1253, resembles 1252, but the amount of Feldspar is much less, and the color of the rock is lighter. A few tiny, short, lenticular seams of grayish-white Quartz occur ; and the weathered surface is of a dirty reddish-brown.

No. 258 (Sp. 935).—*Coarse Reddish Gneiss.*

Laurentian.—Head of 2 miles Portage in Sect. 18—T. 45—R. 29.

Mottled grayish-white, reddish-brown, smoky-gray, and black.

A compact, hard, tough, coarse, porphyritic Gneiss, with a parallel arrangement of all its constituents, especially of the Mica.

The Feldspar constitutes over 6 parts of the bulk of the rock, and mostly occurs in large angular masses, often 1 inch by ¼ inch, of a grayish and grayish-white color. Along the edges of the facets and throughout many of the smaller masses, it passes into a somewhat softer material, of a brownish-red color, inclining to deep orange, and with a reddish-white streak, which is evidently the result of decomposition. The Quartz, which amounts to over 2 parts, occurs in smaller masses, rarely ½ inch long, of a grayish-white and smoky-gray color. The Mica is very generally disseminated in tiny bunches and somewhat parallel short seams, consisting of minute black scales, rarely silvery-gray, which are soft and give a greenish-gray streak, from partial decomposition.

Fracture uneven. Tiny yellowish-brown coatings occur on the Mica.

Weathers unevenly, to a grayish-black color and to a depth of about ⅛ inch, being brownish-black and shining on the fresh fracture.

In Specimen 936, the Feldspar is a shade whiter, the gneissic structure is less marked, and the weathering smoother, thinner, and of a brownish-black color.

Specimen 937 contains very little Mica, the Quartz is nearly equal in bulk to the Feldspar, and the weathering is like that of 936.

No. 259 (Sp. 947).—*Grayish-White Gneiss.*

Laurentian.—From State Road L'Anse to Champion, T. 49—R. 33.

Grayish-white, with black specks and streaks.

A compact, hard, tough, fine-grained Gneiss, of which the Mica is arranged in parallel seams, but is chiefly disseminated in a few layers, about ½ inch thick. The Feldspar is grayish-white, often minutely striated, occasionally decomposed into a softer light brownish-red material, occurs usually in tiny particles, but renders the micaceous layers porphyritic with masses sometimes ¼ by ½ inch, and constitutes about 6 parts of the bulk of the rock. The Quartz is the same as in No. 258, but occurs in smaller particles, and constitutes nearly 4 parts of the bulk of the rock. The Mica is the decomposed variety of No. 258, is not so generally diffused, and is present in small quantity. Yellowish-green Epidote occurs in small quantity, in minute particles, through a micaceous layer, and in tiny crystals in a transverse vein of smoky-gray Quartz.

Fracture rather even.

Weathers rather evenly to a reddish-gray color.

No. 260 (Sp. 1548).—*Mottled Gneiss.*

Laurentian.—From N. ¼ of T. 46—R. 41.

A small fragment of Gneiss, coarser than 1546, chiefly made up of angular masses of a brownish-red and a grayish-white Feldspar, and smoky-gray Quartz, about ¼ to ½ inch across, in about equal quantities. A little Mica, with silvery-gray scales, is also disseminated in tiny seams.

Fracture uneven. A few fissures.

The specimen is too small to distinguish the feldspars (which may both be varieties of one species). The angular crystalline masses may also entitle it to the name porphyritic. This specimen may be from a vein in No. 296.

No. 261 (Sp. 1226).—*Black Hornblende-Gneiss.*

Laurentian.—Felch Mountain, Sects. 32 and 33—T. 42—R. 28.

Black and glittering, speckled with gray.

A rather fine-grained, uniform Gneiss, resembling Nos. 262 and 265, and is composed of about 5 parts of black Amphibole, in fibrous facets of high lustre, slightly altered and softened, rarely $\frac{1}{16}$ inch across, and with a decided parallel arrangement, and of a gray mixture of about 3 parts of grayish-white Quartz and 2 parts of grayish-white Feldspar, in particles not distinguishable by the eye.

Fracture nearly even. Streak greenish-white. A few fissures stained reddish-brown.

Weathers evenly but roughly, to a grayish and reddish-white color, speckled with blackish-green to a depth of ¼ inch.

The following two varieties illustrate the common alteration of the Amphibole of these Gneisses, partially (Sp. 1229) or entirely (Sp. 1224) into a black Mica.

(Sp. 1229.) *Fine-Grained Black Gneiss.*

Dark cast-iron gray, inclining to a slight tinge of purplish or greenish in different lights; slightly lustrous.

A rather hard, compact, tough, fine-grained Gneiss, of quite fissile structure, which appears under the lens to consist of about 2 parts of minute granules of grayish-white Quartz, 4 parts of gray Feldspar, and 4 parts of minute narrow-bladed scales of black and blackish-brown Mica. Seams of lamination often stained reddish-brown. A few transverse irregular veins, $\frac{1}{8}$ to $\frac{1}{4}$ inch wide, sometimes widening into bunches, 1 inch across, filled with a fine-grained aggregate of gray and grayish-white Feldspar, grayish-white Quartz, and black Amphibole, with greenish-gray streak, sometimes in crystals $\frac{1}{4}$ inch long.

Fracture uneven. Streak grayish-white.

Weathers evenly, the veins slightly projecting, to a lighter greenish-gray, mottled with grayish-white and dirty brownish-gray.

(Sp. 1224.) *Fine-Grained Black Gneiss.*

Blackish-gray; slightly glittering.

A hard, tough, compact, very fine-grained Gneiss, whose imperfectly schistose structure is chiefly shown in the shape of the specimen. It appears under the lens to consist of about 3 parts of minute granules of gray Quartz, 4 parts of minute scales of black Mica, which glitter on the section, and 3 parts of grayish-white to brownish-gray Feldspar, in minute granules—a single crystal of which was observed, $\frac{1}{8}$ inch long.

Fracture uneven. Streak greenish-white. A few fissures stained reddish-brown, yellowish-brown, and white.

Weathers unevenly, to grayish-black minutely speckled with brownish-gray, the surface being studded with reddish-white rectangular spots. The spots consist of irregular rectangular masses, dispersed at intervals of about $\frac{1}{2}$ inch apart, $\frac{1}{8}$ to $\frac{1}{4}$ inch long, of a reddish-white fine-grained aggregate of grayish-white Quartz and reddish-white Feldspar, appearing to be altered crystals of Feldspar and producing a porphyritic appearance.

No. 262 (Sp. 949).—*Black Hornblende-Gneiss.*

Laurentian.—From State Road L'Anse to Champion, S. $\frac{1}{4}$ of T. 49—R. 33.

Greenish-black, with minute specks and narrow bands of grayish-white ; glittering.

A hard, compact, tough, finely crystalline Gneiss, with a few coarse-grained layers, varying irregularly from $\frac{1}{8}$ to $\frac{1}{2}$ inch in thickness.   It consists of slightly altered greenish-black Amphibole, in tiny fibrous crystals, just distinguishable on a fresh fracture, of grayish-white and smoky-gray Quartz, and of milky-white and grayish-white Feldspar (?), in minute particles.   The coarse thin layers consist of an aggregate of the last two, the facets of Feldspar being often $\frac{1}{4}$ inch across.

Fracture even.   Streak greenish-white.   A few irregular broad seams, covered with films of shining Amphibole.   A little Pyrite is disseminated throughout, in particles, generally minute, but sometimes $\frac{1}{16}$ inch across.

Weathers rather evenly, the coarse layers slightly projecting, of a reddish-white color, with smoky-gray specks ; while the finer material is reddish-white, speckled with the dark-green crystals of Amphibole.

No. 263 (Sp. 742).—*Coarse Altered Hornblende-Gneiss.*

Laurentian.—Near 34th Mile Post, M. & O. Road, Lake Michigamme.

Grayish-white, speckled throughout with spots and irregular parallel streaks of greenish-black ; glittering.

Apparently a coarse vein from No. 254, and consists of the same materials.   The Feldspar constitutes about 4 parts and the Quartz 3 parts, in facets and grains $\frac{1}{16}$ to $\frac{1}{8}$ inch across.   Through this matrix are disseminated, to the amount of about 3 parts, bunches $\frac{1}{16}$ to $\frac{1}{8}$ inch thick and often $\frac{1}{2}$ inch long, sometimes irregular and isolated, but generally gathered in long aggregations with a parallel arrangement. These consist of about equal quantities of the brownish-black scales of Mica, and fibrous masses of black Amphibole, both soft and with gray streak, and of the yellowish-green mineral (Epidote ?)—each in masses about $\frac{1}{16}$ to $\frac{1}{8}$ inch across, and therefore distinguishable without the lens. Effervesces but very slightly in acid.

Fracture uneven, almost sub-conchoidal.

Weathered surface uneven, and differs from the fresh fracture in a slight reddish tinge to the Feldspar, and a bronze-yellow tinge to the Mica.

No. 264 (Sp. 744).—*Altered Hornblende-Gneiss.*

Laurentian.—Near 34th Mile Post, M. & O. Road, Lake Michigamme.

A vein, about two inches broad, of the material of No. 254, crossing a coarse Gneiss like No. 263. It differs from those specimens in the general mottling of the Feldspar with spots and streaks of a reddish-white, sometimes brick-red color; in the occurrence of a few thin seams or films of crystalline Epidote; in the occurrence of a few particles of Pyrite in the grains and seams of Epidote; and in the association of a little silvery-white Mica, in minute scales, with the black Mica of some parts of the vein.

No. 265 (Sp. 954).—*Altered Hornblende-Gneiss.*

Laurentian.—From State Road, L'Anse to Champion, T. 49—R. 33 and S. E.

Grayish-white, speckled and streaked with blackish-green, and with a few grayish-white bands; glittering.

A compact, tough, fine-grained, hard Hornblende-Gneiss, chiefly made up of about 6 parts of grayish-white Feldspar, in facets rarely $\frac{1}{16}$ inch across—of about 3 parts of similar grains of Quartz, grayish-white inclining to smoky—and of about 4 parts of a fine-grained aggregate of the three minerals of No. 268, denoted a, b, and c, viz., blackish-green softened fibrous Amphibole, greenish-black scales of Mica, and minute particles of the yellowish-green Epidote. This last dark-green mixture is arranged in decidedly parallel scales, giving the section a streaked or laminated appearance. A few bands, about ⅜ inch thick, chiefly composed of a coarse aggregate of the Quartz and Feldspar, the latter in facets sometimes nearly ⅛ inch across. A little Pyrite is disseminated, in minute yellow particles.

Fracture even. Streak greenish-white.

Weathers smoothly, to a grayish-white color, divided on a section by dark-green lines into narrow stripes and bands.

No. 266 (Sp. 1086).—*Chloritic Hornblende-Gneiss.*

Huronian.—Bed XI.—Old Washington Mine.

Blackish-green, minutely streaked with grayish-white; glittering.

A compact, tough, hard Gneiss, which consists of nearly 6 parts of grayish-white Quartz, in minute granules, of probably about 1 part of greenish or grayish-white Feldspar, in exceedingly minute granules, of over 2 parts of Amphibole, in black and greenish-black blades, $\frac{1}{16}$ to ⅛ inch long, and of 1 part of silvery scales of a grayish-white (Mica?) and blackish-green (Chlorite?). Much of the Quartz is gathered in thin lenticular, greenish-white flakes, $\frac{1}{16}$ to ¼ inch long, which contrast with the crystals of Amphibole; and certain layers, ⅛ to ⅜ inch thick, consist almost entirely of the greenish-white Quartz-granules.

Fracture uneven. Streak greenish and grayish-white. A few particles of yellow Pyrite are disseminated through the layers.

Weathers unevenly to dirty shades of greenish-gray, mottled by reddish-brown.

No. 267 (Sp. 1087).—*Hornblende-Gneiss.*

Huronian.—Bed XI.—Old Washington Mine.

Blackish-green, minutely speckled with black and grayish-white; glittering.

A hard, compact, tough, homogeneous, fine-grained Gneiss, with no evidence of stratification in the hand specimen except its flattened shape. It seems to be made up of the same constituents as No. 266, and about the proportion of 4 parts of Amphibole, in blades rarely exceeding $\frac{1}{16}$ inch in length, of 4 parts of grayish-white Quartz, and of 2 parts of Feldspar. The micaceous scales are not distinguishable. A very few glistening flakes occur, showing cleavage, sometimes nearly $\frac{3}{16}$ inch long, which appear to be partially altered facets of Feldspar. A little Pyrite occurs in rather larger particles than in No. 266.

Fracture nearly even. Streak greenish-white. Surface of fissures is stained reddish-brown.

Weathers to the depth of $\frac{1}{4}$ inch, with a surface which is even but rough, and of a greenish-gray color, the crystals of Amphibole assuming a blackish-green and projecting above the other grayish-white constituents.

No. 268 (Sp. 1361).—*Banded Hornblende-Gneiss (Epidotic).*

Laurentian.—Near centre S. W. $\frac{1}{4}$ Sect. 19—T. 47—R. 42.

Blackish-green, speckled with grayish-white, and mottled with greenish-gray and with reddish-white parallel stripes ; glittering.

A compact, tough, calcareous Hornblende-Gneiss, of rather coarse texture, made up of somewhat wavy layers, some dark and speckled, $\frac{1}{2}$ to 1 inch thick, separated by others which are reddish-white, about $\frac{1}{4}$ inch thick. The latter consist of an aggregate of grains of varying fineness, rarely exceeding $\frac{1}{16}$ of an inch, of glassy grayish-white Quartz and crystalline reddish-white Feldspar ; thin seams, of the same material but finer grained, sometimes run obliquely across and connect two adjacent layers. The dark layers consist, to the extent of about $\frac{1}{2}$ their bulk, of the same aggregate, as a matrix with irregular crystals of the three following minerals disseminated throughout, the first greatly predominating :

a—Blackish-green Amphibole, with a slight lustre, in facets $\frac{1}{8}$ to $\frac{1}{4}$ inch long, but having about the hardness equal to 2, and greenish-gray streak ; the greater dimension of the facets is usually parallel to the lamination.

b—Glistening scales of black Mica, never over $\frac{1}{32}$ inch in diameter, soft and giving a greenish-white streak. The same Mica as that of No. 258.

c—A rather soft, gray mineral (probably Epidote), with tinge of yellowish-green, giving a white streak, which occurs abundantly, sometimes in amorphous particles, or in facets having the fibrous structure, cleavage and general appearance of those of Amphibole. These particles are generally concentrated in certain portions of a layer, imparting to it their color.

Fracture of the rock rather uneven. Effervesces with acid.

Weathers roughly to a dirty-gray color, with tiny spots of blackish-green (facets of Amphibole), the white layers and seams projecting slightly as ridges over the surface.

No. 269 (Sp. 1363).—*Chloritic Hornblende-Gneiss.*

Laurentian.—Near W. ¼ post Sect. 19—T. 47—R. 42.

Blackish-green and highly glistening, speckled and banded with brownish-gray and greenish-white.

A compact, tough Gneiss, of medium texture, with grains and scales about $\frac{1}{32}$ inch across. The Feldspar constitutes about 5 parts of the rock, occurring in gray, grayish-white, and brownish-gray glistening facets, often minutely striated, which are easily distinguishable in certain coarsely crystalline layers, about ½ inch thick, made up of the Feldspar and Quartz. The latter is grayish-white and smoky gray, in distinct grains, and constitutes nearly 3 parts of the rock. The third mineral is apparently an altered Amphibole, constitutes over 2 parts of the rock, occurs in glistening scales, often ⅛ to ¼ inch across, which resemble Amphibole in fibrous structure and cleavage, and have a blackish-green color by reflected light, but are soft, give a greenish-gray streak, and have a light yellowish-green color by transmitted light.

Fracture uneven.

Weathers evenly, to a light flesh-red color, mottled with blackish-green.

In another variety (Sp. 1362), described below, the Amphibole has been completely altered into Chlorite.

(Sp. 1362.)—*Green Chloritic Gneiss.*

Olive-green, with glistening greenish-black specks and greenish-gray streaks.

A compact, tough, fine-grained, rather hard schist, made up of about equal quantities of soft olive-green Chlorite, minutely crystalline, but enclosing many brownish-, sometimes greenish-black glistening scales of altered Mica, often $\frac{1}{4}$ inch across—of tiny grains of glassy Quartz, varying in color from grayish-white to grayish-black, and of greenish-white Feldspar, which can only be distinguished in certain grayish-white and greenish-gray layers, which are coarsely crystalline and contain little Chlorite.

Fracture uneven.   Streak greenish-gray.

Weathers unevenly, to a dirty yellowish-green, inclining to citrine-yellow, bespangled with brownish scales of weathered Chlorite.

No. 270 (Sp. 1370).—*Altered Hornblende-Gneiss.*

Laurentian.—Near W. $\frac{1}{4}$ post Sect. 19—T. 47—R. 42.

Blackish-green and glistening, with grayish-white specks, traversed by broad brownish-gray bands.

A hard, compact, tough, coarse calcareous Gneiss, in which occurs a lighter-colored band, $\frac{1}{2}$ inch thick.   The dark matrix consists of about 5 parts of blackish-green Amphibole, altered like that of No. 269, in fibrous facets $\frac{3}{16}$ inch long—of 2 parts of grayish-white and smoky-gray Quartz, in tiny granules—and of 3 parts of grayish-white, often smoky or reddish, Feldspar, in tiny facets, often minutely striated.   The facets of Amphibole are generally parallel to the bands, and produce the schistose structure.   The lighter-colored band consists of a coarser aggregate of the Feldspar and Quartz, in grains sometimes $\frac{1}{16}$ inch across, with tiny crystals of Amphibole scattered throughout in small quantity.

Fracture rather uneven.   Effervesces decidedly in acid, especially the material of the lighter-colored bands.   This is apparently a coarse seam in Amphibole-Gneiss.

Weathers rather unevenly, to a dirty reddish-brown, speckled with blackish-green and reddish-white.

No. 271 (Sp. 1689).—*Black Hornblende-Schist.*

Huronian.—Bed IX.—Old Washington Mine.

Black, minutely speckled with grayish-white ; glittering.

A compact, hard, tough, coarse rock, with a feebly schistose structure in the hand specimen, which consists of about 7 parts of black Amphibole, with greenish-gray streak, in fibrous shining plates, $\frac{1}{16}$ to $\frac{1}{8}$ inch in diameter,—of 2 parts of greenish-gray Feldspar, and perhaps nearly 1 part of grayish-white Quartz. Blackish-green scales (of Chlorite ?) are abundantly associated with the facets of Amphibole and denote their partial alteration.

Fracture uneven. A few fissures occur, stained grayish-black. A small segregated vein lines the side of the specimen, consisting of crystals of Amphibole and grayish-white Quartz, with cleavable crystalline masses of grayish and reddish-white Feldspar.

Weathers very unevenly and roughly, to a reddish-brown (the projecting Amphibole), speckled with reddish-white.

No. 272 (Sp. 946).—*Chloritic Hornblende-Schist.*

Laurentian.—From State Road L'Anse to Champion, T. 49—R. 33 and S. E.

Blackish-green and shining, minutely mottled with yellowish-green, with a few spots and streaks of reddish-white.

A rather hard, compact, tough, fine-grained, slightly calcareous schist, chiefly made up of a softened blackish-green Amphibole, with light greenish-gray streak, sometimes in tiny fibrous facets which produce a granular texture, but usually in soft glistening and slightly fibrous films (Chlorite ?), which give the rock a scaly lamination in many irregular planes, the filmy scales enveloping the granular masses in all directions. The interstices between the films are occupied by massive yellowish-green Epidote, which also occurs in tiny bunches and thin scales. Grayish-white Feldspar and grayish and reddish-white Quartz are also disseminated in particles through the rock, and gathered in bunches and veins, sometimes $\frac{1}{2}$ inch thick.

Fracture uneven. Streak grayish-white. Effervesces very feebly in acid.

Weathers unevenly, to a brownish-gray, mottled with yellowish-green.

No. 273 (Sp. 948).—*Chloritic Hornblende-Schist.*

Laurentian.—From State Road L'Anse to Champion, T. 49—R. 33 and S. E.

Blackish-green and glittering, sometimes with grayish-white specks.

A tough, compact, rather hard, uniform, finely-crystalline, slightly calcareous schist, chiefly made up of tiny, irregular, fibrous facets of altered Amphibole, harder than those of No. 272, giving a greenish-white streak. A few films also occur, whose approximately parallel arrangement imparts to the rock a faintly distinguishable schistose structure. Grayish-white and smoky-gray Quartz and white Feldspar are disseminated, in particles rarely distinguishable without a lens, but sometimes appearing as whitish specks on the dark-green ground. A vein of a coarse aggregation of these two minerals occurs, about ¼ inch thick, the facets of Feldspar being sometimes ¼ inch across.

Fracture uneven. Effervesces feebly in acid.

Weathers evenly, but with a slightly pitted surface, to a blackish-green, mottled with light-brown.

No. 274 (Sp. 950).—*Chloritic Hornblende-Schist.*

Laurentian.—From State Road L'Anse to Champion, T. 49—R. 33 and S. E.

Dark grayish-green, with glistening spots; shining on planes of lamination.

A coarsely crystalline, tough, soft, homogeneous, slightly calcareous schist, which resembles No. 272 in color and general structure. Appears to the eye and to the lens to be entirely made up of large fibrous facets of softened Amphibole, with greenish-gray streak, which are conspicuous on the cross-fracture, together with more or less Chlorite in minute scales. Their frequent parallel arrangement produces a decidedly schistose structure.

Fracture uneven.

Weathers quite unevenly and roughly to a dirty greenish-brown.

No. 275 (Sp. 1393).—*Greenish Chloritic Gneiss.*

Laurentian.—N. ¼ of N. W. ¼ of Sect. 14—T. 47—R. 43.

Greenish-gray, with reddish-white and glittering blackish-green spots.

A rather coarse, compact, tough, hard, uniform, feldspathic rock, with very little evidence of schistose structure in the hand specimen. It consists of about 3 parts of greenish-white Quartz—1 part of greenish-black to black Chlorite, in tiny glistening soft scales, with greenish-gray streak—3 parts of reddish-white Feldspar, in crystalline facets, often ⅛ inch across—and 3 parts of a greenish-gray, finely granular, crystalline, apparently feldspathic mineral, with slightly greenish-white streak, in undefined masses, about ⅛ inch across.

Fracture uneven. A few irregular minute seams of reddish-brown Ochre.

Weathering uneven, with a surface of dirty gray, but imparts a deep reddish-brown color to the depth of about ¼ inch.

No. 276 (Sp. 867).—*Chloritic Gneiss.*

Laurentian.—Mouth of Dead River, near Marquette.

Greenish-gray, with specks of smoky-gray, black, and reddish-white, and occasionally small rusty reddish-brown spots.

A very compact, tough, rather hard, uniform, Chloritic Gneiss The Feldspar is grayish-white, often greenish-white, reddish-white, or light brownish-red, often minutely striated, with white or reddish-white streak, in tiny massive grains, and constitutes about 4 parts of the rock. The Quartz is smoky-gray, with a lighter or deeper blackish tint, in tiny grains uniformly distributed, and amounts to about 4 parts. The Chlorite constitutes about 2 parts of the rock being uniformly distributed in soft minute particles or scales of blackish-green, in a somewhat parallel arrangement, and is sometimes mixed with a few glistening, silvery-gray, micaceous scales. Many large irregular seams occur, covered with a film of Chlorite.

Fracture rather uneven.

Weathers to a rusty reddish-brown color, evenly, but with many grains of Quartz projecting.

No. 277 (Sp. 870).—*Epidotic Chloritic Gneiss.*

Laurentian.—Mouth of Dead River, near Marquette.

Resembles No. 276, contains however very little Chlorite, arranged in thin parallel scales, and nearly a quarter of the bulk of the rock consists of light yellowish-green, translucent Epidote, with greenish-white streak, in tiny masses uniformly distributed. Also broad seams occur covered with films of Epidote of a deeper green.

Weathered surface rather reddish, with tiny specks of yellowish-white.

NOTE.—The following rock occurs as a narrow vein in Chloritic Gneiss :

(Sp. 874.)—*Epidotic Greenstone.*

Blackish-green, minutely speckled with greenish-gray ; glittering.

A compact, tough, homogeneous rock, of medium hardness and very fine texture, which appears under the lens to consist of about 4 parts of grayish and reddish-white Feldspar, in tiny facets, with good cleavage and lustre—of 3 parts of minute scales of blackish-green and greenish-white Chlorite—and of 3 parts of crystalline grains of yellowish-green translucent Epidote. Pyrite is also disseminated in pale yellow particles. A few tiny bunches of grayish-white and flesh-red Feldspar are disseminated, and much yellow Pyrite, in minute particles, is disclosed on a polished section.

Fracture uneven. Streak greenish-white.

Weathers evenly to a yellowish-green, mottled by flesh-red and minutely speckled with dark-green—the surface being roughened by the removal of the Chlorite. The weathering is about $\frac{1}{8}$ inch deep, its section being greenish-white, shading inwardly to grayish-green.

No. 278 (Sp. 938).—*Chloritic Gneiss.*

Laurentian.—N. E. side of Sect. 16—T. 49—R. 33.

Dark grayish-green and glittering, with tiny grayish-white specks arranged in parallel lines.

A rather soft, compact, tough, fine-grained, uniform, calcareous schist, made up of tiny particles, rarely $\frac{1}{16}$ inch across, of an aggregate of about 2 parts of grayish-white and smoky-gray glassy Quartz, —4 parts of grayish-white Feldspar, in facets often minutely striated—and 4 parts of a dark grayish-green mineral, with light greenish-gray streak, which appears under the lens to consist of exceedingly minute glittering scales. The last mineral, which may be altered Amphibole, is disseminated in thin seams or lenticular flakes, with a parallel arrangement which produces a schistose structure. A little Pyrite is disseminated in minute golden-yellow crystals and irregular particles. A few thin seams or films of grayish- or brownish-white Calcite cross the layers obliquely. Effervesces with acid.

Fracture rather uneven.

Weathers evenly but roughly, to a dirty-brown color, mottled with dark-green, some surfaces being covered with tiny pits and others roughened by the irregular weathering of certain scales.

No. 279 (Sp. 941).—*Red Chloritic Gneiss.*

Laurentian.—N. E. side of Sect. 16—T. 49—R. 33.

Brownish-red, minutely speckled with grayish-white, mottled and streaked with olive-green ; dull.

An exceedingly hard, compact, tough, calcareous Chloritic Gneiss, with a peculiar fibrous structure, composed of about 7 parts of brownish-red Feldspar, minutely crystalline, almost impalpable in texture—1 part of grayish-white Quartz in particles which can be barely distinguished, even by the lens—and about 2 parts of soft olive-green Chlorite, irregularly distributed in certain seams, or concentrated in certain thin layers, perhaps an inch apart, approximately parallel. The Chlorite also has a minutely fibrous structure, so as to impart the same to the rock. Silvery-gray Mica is also associated, in exceedingly minute scales, with the chloritic layers, rendering their surface glistening. Many transverse seams or films of Calcite occur.

Fracture uneven. Streak reddish and greenish white. One weathered seam has a greenish-brown color, inclining to citrine, some of the projecting layers of Feldspar being polished. Effervesces very feebly with acid.

Weathers unevenly, of a light flesh-red color, streaked with greenish-gray.

No. 280 (Sp. 942).—*Red Chloritic Gneiss.*

Laurentian.—N. E. side of Sect. 16—T. 49—R. 33.

Bright brownish-red, inclining to orange, slightly speckled with grayish-white ; glistening.

Resembles No. 279, but is a very coarse aggregate of crystalline Feldspar, with ill-defined glistening facets, $\frac{1}{4}$ to $\frac{1}{2}$ inch across, and of grayish-white Quartz, distributed in minute or tiny bunches, sometimes $\frac{1}{8}$ inch, rarely $\frac{1}{2}$ inch across ; olive-green Chlorite is also disseminated in small quantity, in tiny bunches and films of a fine-grained aggregate of minute glittering scales.

Fracture uneven.   Streak reddish-white.

Weathers smoothly to a dirty reddish-brown, mottled with iron-black.

No. 281 (Sp. 951).—*Porphyritic Chloritic Gneiss.*

Laurentian.—From State Road L'Anse to Champion, T. 49—R. 33.

Reddish-gray, mottled with greenish-black.

A compact, hard, tough, coarse Porphyry, in which a schistose structure is produced by the parallel arrangement of the Feldspar crystals.   The latter constitute about 3 parts of the rock, are usually $\frac{1}{2}$ to 1 inch long, by $\frac{1}{4}$ inch wide, and consist of grayish-white, passing into softer reddish-white, Feldspar.   The Quartz amounts to less than 3 parts of the rock and occurs in small inconspicuous masses.   The Mica amounts to over 3 parts of the rock, is of the same decomposed variety as in No. 258, and occurs in tiny bunches and seams of rather larger scales, often $\frac{1}{16}$ inch in diameter.   Much yellowish-green Epidote, in tiny crystals and crystalline masses just visible to the eye, is disseminated throughout, in association with the Mica.

Fracture somewhat uneven.

Weathered surface of a grayish-white color, even and very rough —being deeply pitted by the removal of the bunches of Mica and a slight projection of the larger Feldspar crystals.

10

Another variety (Sp. 953) is of a light brownish-red color, with the Mica flakes arranged in greenish-black parallel streaks; weathered surface reddish-white and even.

No. 282 (Sp. 952).—*Greenish Chloritic Gneiss.*

Laurentian.—From State Road L'Anse to Champion, T. 49—R. 33.

Grayish-green, with minute reddish-white, slightly glittering specks.

A hard, compact, tough, fine-grained, uniform, calcareous Gneiss, composed of grains, never over $\frac{1}{32}$ inch in diameter, of the following :—

a. About 5 parts of the rock, of reddish-white, often grayish-white, and smoky-gray Feldspar, minutely striated.

b. About 3 parts of the rock, of grayish-white Quartz, and

c. Minute soft olive-green scales of Chlorite, hardly distinguishable by the lens, whose frequently parallel arrangement produces the faintly-marked schistose structure. Small bunches occur of a coarse crystalline aggregate of the Feldspar and Quartz, in facets, $\frac{1}{16}$ to $\frac{1}{8}$ inch across, with a few minute particles of yellow Pyrite.

Fracture rather uneven. Streak greenish-white. Effervesces decidedly in acid. A few seams, covered with a film of the Chlorite, which appears under the lens to consist largely of minute glistening scales.

Weathers nearly $\frac{1}{2}$ inch deep, with an even surface, of grayish-white color, with a slight reddish tinge, the particles of Chlorite being more distinct on this lighter ground than on the fresh fracture.

No. 283 (Sp. 955).—*Coarse Chloritic Gneiss.*

Laurentian.—From State Road L'Anse to Champion, T. 49—R. 33.

Grayish-white, mottled with light brownish-red ; glistening.

A coarse, hard Gneiss, composed of the same materials as No. 258, viz.:

a. About 6 parts of grayish-white crystalline Feldspar, partially decomposed into light brownish-red, in facets $\frac{1}{4}$ to $\frac{1}{2}$ inch across.

b. About 4 parts of grayish-white and smoky-gray glassy Quartz, in masses ⅛ to ¼ inch across, but partially in tiny, flat, thin, lenticular, parallel masses. A blackish-green soft altered Mica or Chlorite, in minute glistening scales, with greenish-gray streak, is distributed throughout in small quantity, in parallel thin lenticular masses, ¼ to 1 inch long.

Fracture uneven. A few fissures, stained reddish-brown.

Weathers rather evenly, to a white or reddish-white, mottled with smoky gray.

No. 284 (Sp. 956).—*Fine-grained Chloritic Gneiss.*

Laurentian.—From State Road L'Anse to Champion, T. 49—R. 33.

Grayish-green ; glittering.

A hard, tough, homogeneous, and very fine-grained, calcareous rock, made up of the same materials as No. 282, with the addition of minute scales of softened brown Mica. The scales of Chlorite help to produce the minutely glittering appearance, and the Feldspar occurs in thin flat crystals, which appear in section as exceedingly minute glistening lines, $\frac{1}{32}$ to $\frac{1}{8}$ inch long. A few yellow particles of Pyrite can be distinguished by the lens. The hand specimen does not reveal a schistose structure. A few thin seams occur, which are somewhat parallel and occupied by films of grayish-white Calcite.

Fracture sub-conchoidal. Streak grayish-white. Effervesces decidedly in acid. Fuses at 5 to a black glass.

By weathering, the color becomes a dirty greenish-gray, the edges are rounded, and the surface is covered with shallow cavities, slightly roughened by projecting particles of Feldspar and the edges of the Calcite-seams. Apparently a fine-grained variety of No. 282, in which no schistose structure can be distinguished in the hand specimen.

No. 285 (Sp. 1128).—*White Chloritic Gneiss.*

Laurentian.—Champion Mine.

Grayish-white, speckled with bluish and reddish-white ; shining.

A compact, hard, brittle, coarse rock, which is made up of about equal parts of a grayish to bluish-white Feldspar, with good lustre and cleavage, and white streak, in facets $\frac{1}{16}$ to $\frac{1}{2}$ inch across, and of grayish to reddish-white and smoky Quartz, in tiny granules, which surround the grains of Feldspar, with a small quantity (much less than one-tenth) of a soft altered grayish-green Mica (Chlorite ?), with greenish-gray streak, in tiny films, rarely over $\frac{1}{16}$ inch in length, made up of minute scales. The latter are irregular and sparsely distributed, and their slight predominance in one layer in the specimen faintly suggests a gneissoid structure.

Fracture uneven.

Weathers rather evenly and smoothly, to the depth of $\frac{1}{8}$ inch, to a dull grayish-white, speckled with dirty blackish-green.

No. 286 (S. 1367).—*Fine-grained Chloritic Gneiss.*

Laurentian.—S. W. part T. 47—R. 42, W. of Lake Gogebic.

Greenish-gray, minutely speckled with reddish-white.

A tough, compact, fine-grained Gneiss, consisting of Feldspar, Quartz, and Chlorite. No traces of stratification can be distinguished in the hand specimen. The Feldspar constitutes about 4 parts of the rock, and consists of minute granules of reddish-white or brownish-red color. The Quartz occurs in about equal quantity, in similar particles of a smoky-gray and grayish-white color. The Chlorite occurs in minute, soft, olive-green scales. Small bunches occur of coarse aggregations of these materials, the Chlorite traversing them in thin layers.

Fracture almost even. Streak greenish-white. A few fissures stained reddish-brown.

Weathers smoothly, to a dirty reddish-brown.

No. 287 (Sp. 1375).—*Banded Chloritic Gneiss.*

Laurentian.—N. E. $\frac{1}{4}$ of S. W. $\frac{1}{4}$ of Sect. 33—T. 47—R. 42.

Greenish-black, with minute specks and narrow bands of brownish-gray ; glittering.

A compact, tough, hard, fine-grained, Chloritic Gneiss, made up of regular layers, which vary in thickness from a film up to $\frac{1}{3}$ inch, and in color in proportion to the amount of Chlorite in each layer. The Feldspar and Quartz resemble those of No. 269 (Sp. 1363), in grains rarely $\frac{1}{8}$ inch in diameter. The Chlorite consists of soft greenish-black scales, like those of No. 269, but never as large even as $\frac{1}{32}$ inch across. Several of the layers contain Pyrite in golden-yellow particles.

Fracture sub-conchoidal, but rough. Streak greenish and grayish-white.

Weathered surface even, and of a greenish-black color, with brownish tinge.

No. 288 (Sp. 1377).—*Chloritic Gneiss.*

Laurentian.—W. of Lake Gogebic, S. part of T. 47—R. 42.

Grayish-white, with blackish-green and white specks; slightly shining.

A compact, tough, hard, fine-grained Chloritic Gneiss, with its constituents uniformly distributed. The Feldspar constitutes about 6 parts of the rock, and differs slightly from the ordinary form, presenting a dead white appearance, slightly inclined to milky-white, often minutely striated, and occurs in tiny crystalline grains or perfect crystals, rarely exceeding $\frac{1}{32}$ inch in diameter, but in one case $\frac{1}{2}$ inch long. The Quartz occurs in tiny grains of smoky-gray, constituting 3 parts of the rock. The Chlorite occurs in minute scales, with almost as high lustre as those of No. 287. One layer occurs, chiefly feldspathic, and traversed by innumerably minute transverse films of a yellowish-green Epidote.

Fracture uneven.

Weathering even, but rough, and a reddish-white color, with white specks.

No. 289 (Sp. 1378).—*White Chloritic Gneiss.*

Laurentian.—In brook N. E. corner of Sect. 22—T. 46—R. 42.

Grayish-white, inclining to smoky, and with minute dark-green specks; glittering.

A compact, hard, tough, rather fine-grained, uniform, white Chloritic Gneiss, composed of Quartz and Feldspar. The Feldspar is grayish-white, with a smoky tinge, gives a white streak, and occurs coarsely crystallized ; so that the section is covered with glittering facets, often minutely striated, about $\frac{1}{16}$ inch across. The Quartz occurs in about equal quantity, grayish-white in color, and in tiny masses uniformly distributed among the Feldspar. The micaceous scales are of two kinds : the one greenish-black, soft, glistening, fissile, and with greenish-gray streak—the other blackish-green, still softer, dull, particles of Chlorite, with greenish-white streak ; the latter are the more abundant.

Fracture even.

Weathering smooth, and of a dirty olive-green, minutely speckled with black, and stains the rock with a light reddish-brown to the depth of ⅛ to ¼ inch.

No. 290 (Sp. 1381).—*Banded Chloritic Gneiss.*

Laurentian.—Near N. W. ¼ of Sect. 29—T. 47—R. 42.

Olive-green, faintly banded with light flesh-red ; slightly shining.

A hard, compact, tough, fine-grained, Chloritic Gneiss, made up of regular layers, faintly visible on a section, from a film up to ⅛ inch in thickness. The Feldspar constitutes about 6 parts of the rock, and consists of flesh-red and reddish-white minute crystalline grains, very rarely exceeding $\frac{1}{32}$ inch in diameter ; its predominance in certain layers imparts to them their reddish tint. The Chlorite is disseminated in thin films, mostly parallel, soft, olive-green, and slightly shining, because made up of very minute greenish-black, glistening scales, which can just be distinguished by the lens. Its predominance in films and layers produces the olive-green bands. Smoky-gray Quartz occurs in a very few minute grains, and a little yellowish-green crystalline Epidote in grains sometimes ¼ inch long. A little Pyrite is disseminated in minute golden-yellow particles.

Fracture uneven.

Weathers rather evenly, and without change of color.

Specimen 1383 is a layer from 1381, in which the proportion of the constituents is about 5 parts of Feldspar, 3 parts of Quartz, and 2 parts of Epidote, with only a very few scattered scales of Chlorite.

No. 291 (Sp. 1391).—*Decomposed Chloritic Gneiss.*

Laurentian.—N. ½ of N. W. ¼ of Sect. 14—T. 47—R. 43.

Reddish-white and shining, with faint short lines of blackish-green and brownish-yellow.

A very hard, tough, compact, fine-grained, Chloritic Gneiss, made up chiefly of about equal quantities of reddish and grayish-white Feldspar, in tiny crystalline grains, often minutely striated, and of grayish-white and smoky-gray Quartz, with a very small amount of Chlorite, uniformly distributed in tiny parallel glistening blackish-green scales. Many of these have been decomposed, and their places are occupied by a brownish-yellow Ochre. Irregular seams occur, covered with soft bright brownish-yellow and reddish-brown Ochre.

Fracture almost even.

Weathers smoothly, to a dirty greenish-brown.

No. 292 (Sp. 1392).—*Decomposed Chloritic Gneiss.*

Laurentian.—N. ½ of N. W. ¼ of Sect. 14—T. 47—R. 43.

Light flesh-red, mottled with reddish-brown and brownish-yellow.

A very hard, compact, tough, ochrey rock, made up of Feldspar and Quartz, like those of No. 291, the former predominating.

Fracture uneven. Streak white. It is traversed by many irregular fissures, by some of which a schistose structure is produced, and which are covered with soft films and folia of reddish-brown and brownish-yellow Ochre.

This is a variety of No. 291, in which the original Chlorite is entirely decomposed—the last stage in the decomposition of the Chlorite in a Chloritic Gneiss.

No. 293 (Sp. 1398).—*Banded Chloritic Gneiss.*

Laurentian.—N. W. corner of Sect. 29—T. 47—R. 42.

Apparently identical with No. 287, except in a lighter shade of green, and in the absence of Pyrite. (Hand specimen too small for any further distinctions.)

Specimen 1399 is lighter in color, the altered Mica constituting less than ⅛ of the rock, and arranged in irregular but parallel thin seams, by which the section is covered with thin dark-green streaks, ⅛ to ¼ inch apart.

No. 294 (Sp. 1400).—*Red Chloritic Gneiss.*

Laurentian.—Near centre of N. W. ¼ of Sect. 29—T. 47—R. 42.

Brownish-red, streaked and speckled with smoky-gray, with broad flat surfaces speckled with blackish-green.

A compact, hard, tough, coarse Gneiss, with many seams, ⅓ to ½ inch apart, which produce a decidedly schistose structure. The Feldspar amounts to about 6 parts and is brownish-red, with reddish-white streak, and coarsely crystalline—the depth of its color being probably due to weathering. The Quartz amounts to about 3 parts, and is smoky-gray, and disseminated in bunches and seams, often ¼ inch thick. The seams are covered with thin films and tiny bunches of grayish-white Calcite and soft blackish-green Chlorite, with greenish-white streak, usually intermingled in the bunches. A few tiny geodes of Quartz crystals occur.

Fracture uneven.

Weathers smoothly and without change of color.

No. 295 (Sp. 1402).—*Chloritic Gneiss.*

Laurentian.—Near centre of N. W. ¼ of Sect. 29— T. 47—R. 42.

Grayish- and blackish-green, speckled and mottled with reddish and grayish-white.

A hard, compact, tough, Chloritic Gneiss, of medium texture. It consists of about 6 parts of crystalline Feldspar, in tiny facets, rarely $\frac{1}{16}$ inch across, of a reddish and grayish-white and greenish-gray color, of 3 parts of grayish-white and smoky-gray Quartz, and 1 part of soft blackish-green or bright grayish-green scales of Chlorite, with greenish-gray streak. The latter has a parallel arrangement which produces the schistose structure ; and it is also somewhat irregularly disposed, so that small bunches and streaks in the rock are colored reddish-white by the predominance of the Feldspar.

Fracture uneven.

Weathers to the depth of about ⅛ inch, with an uneven surface of a dirty cream color or reddish-white, with tiny crystalline grains of Feldspar projecting.

No. 296 (Sp. 1546).—*White Chloritic Gneiss.*

Laurentian.—From trail running N. Easterly from Ontonagon River in T. 46—R. 41.

Grayish-white, speckled with reddish-white and black.

A compact, tough, fine-grained, Chloritic Gneiss. The Feldspar constitutes about 6 parts of the bulk of the rock, and consists of tiny masses, rarely ¼ inch across, of grayish-white color, passing into reddish-white, and sometimes minutely striated. The Quartz is smoky-gray, and amounts to nearly 4 parts of the rock. The Chlorite is disseminated in minute soft olive-green scales, with some-what parallel arrangement, and does not amount to 1 part of the rock. A few crystals of yellowish-green Epidote occur.

Fracture even.

Weathers rather evenly, to a gray color, dotted with white crystals of Feldspar.

Another variety, 1547, is a reddish-white Chloritic Gneiss, of still finer grain, and the weathered surface is of a reddish-white, speckled with white ; contains no Epidote.

No. 297 (Sp. 940).—*Talcy Chloritic Gneiss.*

Laurentian.—N. side of Sect. 16—T. 49—R. 33.

Resembles No. 290 (Sp. 1381), is not banded, but has a more deci-dedly and uniformly laminated structure from the arrangement of the Feldspar, in parallel lenticular flakes, usually $\frac{1}{16}$ inch thick and $\frac{1}{8}$ to $\frac{1}{2}$ inch long. Contains no Pyrite, but many minute reddish-brown particles, as if from its decomposition. A little grayish-white Quartz is disseminated throughout in tiny granules, not easily distinguished by the eye. A little Talc seems to be associated with the Chlorite in minute greenish-gray or gray glistening scales.

No. 298 (Sp. 944).— *Talcy Chloritic Gneiss.*

Laurentian.—N. side of Sect. 16—T. 49—R. 33.

Light brownish-red, with specks and streaks of greenish-gray, grayish-white, and smoky gray; slightly shining.

A compact, hard, brittle, uniform, decidedly schistose Chloritic Gneiss, made up of about 4 parts of light brownish-red Feldspar, in tiny masses, rarely crystals, $\frac{1}{32}$ to $\frac{1}{16}$ inch across, of about 3 parts of grayish-white and smoky-gray Quartz, usually in still smaller grains, and of grayish-green Chlorite, with greenish-gray streak, and of greenish-gray Talc, with grayish-white streak, in greasy parallel films, which consist of minute glittering scales. The Feldspar grains are generally separated from each other by the Quartz and a somewhat porphyritic appearance is produced on a small scale.

Fracture uneven.

Weathers evenly, unchanged in color.

No. 299 (Sp. 945).— *Talcy Chloritic Gneiss.*

Laurentian.—N. side of Sect. 16—T. 49—R. 33.

Resembles No. 298 in general character, but is coarser. The Talc is present in much smaller quantity; the Feldspar predominates, occurring in crystalline masses, sometimes $\frac{1}{2}$ inch across, and the Quartz occurs in parallel, irregular, lenticular flakes. A seam occurs, stained reddish-brown.

Streak of the greenish films, sometimes greenish-gray, but generally greenish-white.

No. 300 (Sp. 1389).—*Brownish-gray Mica-Slate.*

Laurentian.—N. part of N. W. ¼ of S. 22—T. 46—R. 42.

Like No. 214, but the parallel films of brownish-gray Mica so predominate as to convert the rock into a Mica-Slate.

Effervesces decidedly in acid. Fuses before the blowpipe at 4.5, to a black glass.

Weathers rather evenly to a brownish-gray—the cleavage surfaces within being stained brown, often to the depth of an inch or more.

A transition rock from Feldspathic Argillyte into Mica-Slate.

No. 301 (See No. 61, Appendix B).—*Staurolitiferous Mica-Schist.*

Huronian.—Formation XIX.—Island in Michigamme Lake.

Brownish-black, minutely streaked with brownish-gray ; glistening.

A rather hard, compact, fine-grained Mica-Schist, of a finely fibrous and somewhat nodular structure. It is made up of about 6 parts of grayish-white Quartz, in minute granules, and 4 parts of brown, blackish-brown, and black Mica, in minute narrow bladed scales, rarely over $\frac{1}{16}$ inch in length, the two materials being uniformly intermingled. Crystals of Staurolite, ⅛ to ¼ inch long, and sometimes over $\frac{1}{16}$ inch broad, are dispersed through the rock, both in separate blades and in twins, associated with irregular masses, sometimes ¼ inch across, of a brownish-yellow mineral ; the bending of the micaceous laminæ around these minerals, sometimes in broad continuous films, and in separate scales, $\frac{1}{16}$ inch across, produces the nodular structure.

Fracture hackly. Streak white.

Weathers to a reddish-brown.

No. 302 (Sp. 743).—*Altered Porphyritic Dioryte.*

Huronian.—Sect. 3—T. 47—R. 30. South of Lake Michigamme.

Greenish-black and glittering, speckled with greenish-gray and reddish-white.

A hard, compact, tough, coarse Dioryte. The hornblendic mineral amounts to nearly 6 parts, and occurs in irregular masses, scales, and long thin blades, usually $\frac{1}{16}$ to $\frac{1}{8}$ inch wide, and $\frac{1}{4}$ to $\frac{5}{8}$ inch long, of a high lustre, greenish-black color, sometimes iridescent, and with grayish-white and greenish-gray streak. These scales and blades have a feebly marked transverse striation, instead of the usual longitudinally-fibrous structure of Amphibole ; and a minute dull line often runs down the middle of the long blade, like the midrib of a lanceolate leaf. Minute films of a light-green and of a grayish-white color sometimes cover these facets, and perhaps consist of Epidote and Calcite. The Feldspar amounts to about 4 parts, is generally greenish-gray, often reddish-, greenish-, and yellowish-white, gives a grayish-white streak, has generally a very feebly marked cleavage and dull lustre, and occurs in grains $\frac{1}{16}$ to $\frac{1}{8}$ inch across. A very few grains of smoky-gray Quartz and bronze-yellow Pyrite also occur, $\frac{1}{16}$ to $\frac{1}{8}$ inch across.

Fracture uneven. Effervesces but very slightly in acid. Not magnetic. Powder greenish-white. The magnet separates 5 per cent. in black particles.

Weathers unevenly to a reddish-brown, the crystals of Amphibole projecting and unchanged in color.

No. 303 (Sp. 1103).—*Black Dioryte.*

Huronian.—Bed VII. or IX.—Washington Mine.

Greenish-black and glistening.

A hard, compact, very tough, and rather coarse Dioryte, which consists of about, or over, 5 parts of greenish-black Amphibole, in fibrous facets, $\frac{1}{16}$ to $\frac{1}{8}$ inch long, of somewhat micaceous structure, greenish-gray streak, and glistening lustre—of nearly 4 parts of grayish-white Feldspar, in crystalline masses with very feebly marked cleavage—and about 1 part of smoky Quartz (?), yellow Pyrite, scales of blackish-green Chlorite, and particles of black Magnetite : which can all be distinguished by the lens, especially on the weathered surface.

Fracture uneven. Streak greenish-white. Fissures stained reddish-brown.

Weathers evenly but roughly, to a reddish-white (Feldspar), speckled with blackish-green (Amphibole). The flattened shape of the specimen and a few fissures suggest that it may be a Dioryte-Schist.

No. 304 (Sp. 1244).—*Green Dioryte.*

Huronian.—Grand Portage, Sect. 25—T. 43—R. 30.

Greenish-gray, minutely speckled with greenish-white; glittering.

A compact, tough, hard, rather fine-grained rock, consisting of about 6 parts of grayish-green fibrous facets of Amphibole, $\frac{1}{16}$ to $\frac{1}{8}$ inch long—3 parts of greenish-white Feldspar, in crystalline particles without cleavage—and nearly 1 part of minute yellow particles of Pyrite.

Fracture uneven, but approaching sub-conchoidal. Streak greenish-white.

Weathers rather evenly, to blackish-brown, mottled by yellowish-brown ; the constituents appear to weather equally.

No. 305 (Sp. 1246).—*Green Altered Dioryte.*

Huronian.—1¼ miles above Paint Portage.

Dark green, speckled with brown ; glittering.

A hard, compact, tough, minutely porphyritic Dioryte, of medium grain, made up of about equal bulks of blackish-green Amphibole, in slightly fibrous blades, usually from $\frac{1}{16}$ to $\frac{1}{8}$ inch, sometimes $\frac{1}{4}$ inch in length—of a brown Feldspar in thin plates of the same size, with good cleavage—and of a crystalline light green paste, which seems to be made up of minute scales, perhaps of Chlorite. Much Pyrite is also disseminated in bright yellow crystals or particles, $\frac{1}{16}$ inch across.

Fracture uneven. Streak greenish-gray. A fissure occurs, covered with a film of brownish-white Calcite.

Weathers rather unevenly, to a yellowish-brown, mottled with reddish-brown.

No. 306 (Sp. 1409).—*Black Porphyritic Dioryte (Micaceous).*

Boulder in Sect. 18—T. 47—R. 45.

Black, with reddish-white specks ; glittering.

A very compact, hard, tough, coarse, calcareous Dioryte, composed of about equal parts of slightly altered black Amphibole, in fibrous facets about ⅛ inch long, with greenish-gray streak, and of reddish or grayish-white Feldspar, in massive grains, rarely over $\frac{1}{16}$ inch across. Mica also is disseminated in brown scales, and yellow Pyrite in unusual quantity, in minute particles or strings, often crossing the facets of Amphibole.

Fracture rather uneven. Effervesces decidedly in acid.

Weathers unevenly to a light yellowish-gray, speckled with black and reddish-white. Resembles an Amphibole-Gneiss rather than any other Dioryte, on account of the slight alteration and bright lustre of its Amphibole, but I cannot distinguish any Quartz.

No. 307 (Sp. 1427).—*Black Dioryte.*

Huronian.—W. line of Sect. 18—T. 47—R. 45.

Black, minutely speckled with gray ; decidedly glittering.

An unaltered, minutely porphyritic Dioryte, resembling No. 306, but of a fine texture, the crystals rarely exceeding $\frac{1}{16}$ inch in length. The Feldspar is usually grayish-white. Pyrite is disseminated in minute particles, and there is no Mica nor Calcite.

Fracture sub-conchoidal. Streak grayish-white. A thin seam of brownish-red Feldspar occurs. Very feebly magnetic. Powder ash-gray, inclining to greenish ; the magnet separates 7½ per cent. by weight in grayish-black particles.

Weathers unevenly, but smoothly, to a brownish-red enamel.

No. 308 (Sp. 1432).—*Altered Porphyritic Dioryte (Magnetic).*

Copper Trap.—Just N. of S. E. corner of Sect. 7—T. 47—R. 44.

Blackish-green, with greenish-gray specks ; decidedly glittering.
A very hard, compact, heavy, tough rock, of medium texture,

made up of about 6 parts of greenish-gray and grayish-white translucent Feldspar, with good cleavage and high lustre, in sharply
crystallized blades, usually ⅛ inch, some ⅜ inch, in length,—of
3 parts of a blackish-green, apparently amorphous mineral (altered
Amphibole)—and nearly 1 part of irregular grains of black Magnetite. Much Pyrite is disseminated through the rock, being often
enclosed in the crystals in minute bright yellow particles.

Fracture uneven. Streak greenish-white. Many irregular fissures, stained yellowish-brown. Decidedly magnetic, and polarity
strongly marked. Powder greenish-gray. The magnet separates
8½ per cent. by weight, in blackish-gray particles.

Weathers evenly to a light chocolate-brown, to the depth of ¼
to 1 inch ; on the surface occurs a tiny geode of Quartz crystals, so
that the whole rock may be quartzose.

No. 309 (Sp. 1454).—*Fine-grained Gray Dioryte.*

Laurentian.—S. side of Sect. 16—T. 47—R. 45.

Gray, inclining to greenish, minutely speckled with gray ; glittering.

Resembles No. 256, but is a little finer-grained, and consists of
about equal parts of brownish and greenish-black Amphibole, and
grayish-, sometimes yellowish-white Feldspar, both with good cleavage and lustre. A little smoky Quartz may also be present. It
contains no Mica and little Pyrite. Very feebly magnetic. Powder
ash-gray, slightly inclining to greenish ; the magnet separates 2.8
per cent. by weight, in grayish-black particles. Many fissures
occur, stained blackish-brown.

Weathers evenly but roughly, to a dirty reddish-brown, to the
depth of $\frac{1}{32}$ to ⅛ inch, with a section of the same color, terminating
in a dark brown band.

No. 310 (Sp. 1498).—*Fine-grained Blackish-green Dioryte.*

Huronian.—Sunday Lake Outlet.

Blackish-green, with very minute gray specks ; glittering.
A very fine-grained, compact, hard, tough, homogeneous, mi-

nutely porphyritic, altered Dioryte, in which the crystals are rarely $\frac{1}{32}$ inch long.　Under the lens it appears to consist of about 6 parts of fibrous facets and needles of blackish-green altered Amphibole, and 4 parts of minute plates of grayish-white Feldspar, with many bright yellow particles of Pyrite disseminated throughout.

Fracture sub-conchoidal.　Streak greenish-gray.

Weathers unevenly, to a reddish-brown; the color may be due to disseminated Chlorite.

This specimen differs to the eye from all the other Diorytes in its extremely fine grain, its peculiar uniform green color, and the indistinct blending of its constituent minerals.

No. 311 (Sp. 1501).—*Fine-grained Black Dioryte.*

Huronian.--Sunday Lake Outlet.

A minutely porphyritic, unaltered Dioryte, resembling No. 310; but its texture is not so fine, the crystals being often $\frac{1}{16}$ inch long. The Amphibole also is of a black color.　Many irregular fissures occur, stained yellowish, and reddish-brown.

Fracture uneven.　Streak white, slightly grayish.　Effervesces slightly in acid.　Very feebly magnetic.　Powder ash-gray, perhaps slightly greenish; the magnet separates 5 per cent. by weight, in grayish-black particles.

Weathers evenly, to shades of yellowish- and reddish-brown.

No. 312 (Sp. 1504).—*Greenish Altered Dioryte.*

Laurentian.—Near E. $\frac{1}{4}$ of Sect. 24—T. 47—R. 46.

Blackish-green and glittering, speckled with greenish-white.

A hard, compact, tough rock, of medium texture, made up of equal quantities of a blackish-green mineral (altered Amphibole?), in shining narrow facets, usually about $\frac{1}{8}$ inch long, and sometimes fibrous, and of greenish-gray Feldspar, partly massive and partly in tiny tabular crystals, with good cleavage.

Fracture uneven.　Streak grayish-white.

Weathers evenly, to dirty shades of reddish-brown.

In another variety, 1505, bronze-yellow Pyrite is disseminated in tiny particles.

Weathers to the depth of $\frac{1}{16}$ inch, with an even surface of a reddish color, speckled with blackish-green, and roughened by the irregular weathering and slight projection of the harder crystals of the two minerals.

No. 313 (Sps. 1549, 1550, 1551).—*Fine-grained Black Dioryte.*

Laurentian.—Say N. E. ¼ of Sect. 22—T. 46—R. 41.

Black, speckled with grayish-white ; glittering.

A compact, hard, tough, fine-grained rock, minutely porphyritic, and resembling No. 332, etc. ; but is made up of about 6 parts of grayish-white Feldspar, in thin plates, with good cleavage and high lustre, and sometimes minutely striated, and of 4 parts of ill-defined short blades and facets of a black and blackish-green Amphibole, passing into blackish-green scales of Chlorite, which sometimes retain the bladed form.

Fracture uneven.   Streak grayish-white.

Weathers evenly to a yellowish-brown, reddish-brown, and brick-red, to the depth sometimes of $\frac{1}{16}$ inch.

No. 314 (Sp. 1720).—*Quartzose Porphyritic Dioryte.*

Huronian.—Marquette Quarry near Cleveland Dock.

Blackish-green, speckled with brownish-red ; glittering.

A compact, tough, heavy, coarse Dioryte, made up of about equal parts of green Amphibole, with good lustre, and greenish-white streak, in fibrous facets, usually $\frac{1}{16}$ to $\frac{1}{8}$ inch, sometimes $\frac{1}{4}$ inch, in length, and of a bright brownish-red to salmon-colored Feldspar, in facets rarely over $\frac{1}{16}$ inch across, generally with good cleavage and lustre, and grayish-white streak, but often showing alteration by dullness of lustre and color, and lack of good cleavage. The arrangement of these constituents varies at one end of the specimen, one or other of the constituent minerals predominating ; and the extreme corner consists of a mixture of the same coarseness, of equal parts of the Feldspar and of grayish-white to smoky Quartz, entirely free from Amphibole.

Fracture uneven. A few irregular fissures, covered with films of dull blackish-green Amphibole, or reddish to yellowish-brown Ochre.

Weathers rather evenly, to a dirty blackish-green, speckled with dull brownish-red.

Specimen 1721 is a larger specimen of the quartzose aggregate which occurs on a corner of 1720. The Quartz is occasionally gathered in bunches, $\frac{3}{16}$ inch across, and a few isolated crystals of greenish-black Amphibole are interspersed. A seam of greenish-gray material, $\frac{1}{8}$ inch thick, lines one face of the specimen, and is described under No. 315.

No. 315 (Sp. 1723).—*Quartzose Porphyritic Dioryte.*

Huronian.—Marquette Quarry near Cleveland Dock.

A coarser variety of No. 314, the blades of Amphibole often varying in length from $\frac{1}{4}$ to $\frac{1}{2}$ inch, and the facets of Feldspar from $\frac{1}{8}$ to $\frac{1}{4}$ inch, with rare evidence of cleavage and dull lustre and color, the two minerals being irregularly mingled in different parts of the specimen. It is traversed by a seam, apparently of segregation, from $\frac{1}{4}$ to $\frac{1}{2}$ inch thick, of a grayish-green material, almost impalpable in texture and resembling green Jasper. It gives a grayish-white streak, slightly metallic from the file, and may be a fine-grained aggregate of Quartz and greenish-gray Feldspar.

No. 316 (Sp. 1724).—*Epidotic Porphyritic Dioryte.*

Huronian.—Marquette Quarry near Cleveland Dock.

A variety of No. 314, with the coarseness of No. 315, consisting of about 7 parts of brownish-red Feldspar, with good cleavage and lustre, often in bunches $\frac{1}{8}$ to $\frac{1}{4}$ inch across, and 3 parts of greenish-black Amphibole, in fibrous shining facets, $\frac{1}{8}$ to $\frac{3}{8}$ inch long, the two minerals being somewhat irregularly mingled. A little yellowish-green translucent Epidote is interspersed in crystalline masses, with good lustre, sometimes $\frac{1}{8}$ to $\frac{1}{4}$ inch across, always attached to, or surrounding, the blades of Amphibole. The coarseness of the rock, high lustre of the minerals, and fine contrast of the colors, render this the most beautiful and characteristic of the Diorytes.

Specimen 1725 is a seam, $\frac{1}{4}$ to $\frac{1}{2}$ inch thick, from the Dioryte represented by Specimens 1720 to 1724. It consists entirely of brownish-red Feldspar, with good cleavage and lustre, and apparently unaltered, in facets $\frac{1}{8}$ to $\frac{3}{8}$ inch across. Many tiny geodes occur, lined with small crystals of the Feldspar, the surface of the geodes and of the cleavages being mostly covered or mottled with brownish or brownish-black stains.

No. 317 (Sp. 1733).—*Porphyritic Dioryte.*

Huronian.—Pic Nic Rocks, Marquette.

Resembles No. 316, in general appearance and characteristics; but the Amphibole occurs in about equal quantity to the Feldspar. The latter is very much lighter in color ; very little Epidote can be distinguished; and a very little Quartz is associated with the Feldspar grains.

The weathered appearance is striking : the crystals of Amphibole remaining undimmed in color and lustre, but more deeply worn than the Feldspar—while the latter projects in angular masses of a reddish-white color, without lustre, the surface being thus rendered rather uneven and very rough.

No. 318 (Sp. 1734).—*Quartzose Porphyritic Dioryte.*

Huronian.—Pic Nic Rocks, Marquette.

About half of this specimen consists of a very coarse Dioryte, like Nos. 316 and 317, containing a very little Epidote, Quartz, and bronze-yellow Pyrite, and in which the blades of Amphibole are often from $\frac{1}{8}$ to over $\frac{1}{2}$ inch long, and from $\frac{1}{8}$ to $\frac{1}{4}$ inch wide. This passes quite suddenly into very hard, fine-grained, compact, grayish-green rock, somewhat resembling the flinty seam in No. 315, but consists not only of Quartz and grayish-white and greenish-white Feldspar, but of microscopic blades of Amphibole. Much

Pyrite is disseminated through this fine-grained rock, in tiny parti-cles and in thin films, sometimes $\frac{1}{4}$ inch across, and it is also crossed irregularly by thin seams of blackish-green Amphibole, and by others of greenish-gray color, from whose material the Amphi-bole seems to be absent. The specimen is traversed by a few fis-sures, covered with films of Ochre of a brownish-red and yellow color.

Weathers somewhat unevenly but smoothly, on the fine-grained rock, to a light shade of greenish-gray, striped by the seams with reddish-white, and mottled by the fissures with reddish-brown and yellowish-gray.

No. 319 (J).—*Coarse Green Amphibolyte.*

Huronian.—N. part of N. W. ¼ of S. W. ¼ of Sect. 11—T. 47—R. 27 (N. of Mar-quette Mine).

Blackish-green, speckled with grayish-green ; shining.

A tough, compact, heavy Amphibolyte, made up of about 7 parts of blackish-green Amphibole, in rather soft, fibrous, thinly lami-nated facets, $\frac{1}{8}$ to $\frac{1}{4}$ inch across, which give a greenish-white streak, and of 3 parts of a minutely granulated Feldspar, of a greenish-gray, grayish-white, and yellowish-green color, in thin scales or in tiny granules.

Fracture uneven. Thin seams traverse this rock, containing a light-purple feldspathic mineral, in radiating groups, associated with green Quartz and a little Chlorite in minute scales.

No. 320 (Sp. 745).—*Coarse Green Amphibolyte.*

Boulder from S. 3—T. 47—R. 30, South of Lake Michigamme.

Blackish-green ; shining.

A compact, tough, coarse Amphibolyte of medium hardness, made up of about equal bulks of Amphibole and a very fine-grained matrix of the same color. The former occurs in fibrous facets, about $\frac{1}{2}$ to $\frac{3}{4}$ inch square, inclined irregularly in all direc-tions, and gives a greenish-gray streak. The matrix appears under the lens to consist of scales of silvery-white Mica, needles of Amphibole, and granules of grayish-white Feldspar, with a little yellowish-white Quartz.

Fracture very uneven. Many seams and films traverse the rock and the crystals of Amphibole, weathered to rusty shades of reddish-brown.

Weathers rather evenly and smoothly to a blackish-green, minutely speckled with reddish-white (Feldspar), the Amphibole crystals appearing as spots of a lighter shade of blackish-green than on a fresh fracture. In some parts of the weathered surface, minute yellowish-green spherules (of Epidote) appear under the lens.

No. 321 (Sp. 876).—*Black Serpentine.*

Dyke like Presqu'isle.—E. side of Presqu'isle.

Iron-black ; slightly glittering.

A rather hard, compact, brittle, fine-grained rock, almost homogeneous to the eye, but which under the lens appears to consist of about 7 parts of tiny black angular masses, in a yellowish-green paste, probably Serpentine. The former is partly crypto-crystalline, but mostly granular, presenting many minute facets visible to the naked eye and traces of cleavage (altered Amphibole). A small quantity of scales of blackish-green Chlorite appears to be present, and a few particles of yellow Pyrite. Many irregular fissures, stained reddish-brown, or covered with films of a black enamel and of brownish-white Calcite.

Fracture very uneven. Streak gray.

Weathers very unevenly and roughly to a blackish-brown.

No. 322 (Sp. 1245).—*Green Magnesian Dioryte (Serpentine).*

Dyke like Michigamme River, Sect. 28 or 29—T. 42—R. 31.

Greenish-gray, mottled with black ; dull.

A rather soft, compact, brittle, crypto-crystalline rock, whose appearance slightly resembles that of an Ophiolyte, consisting of about 7 parts of angular black masses, of irregular shapes, usually ¼ to ½ inch long, in about 3 parts of a greenish-gray paste. The latter presents many minute facets under the lens, sometimes slightly striated, and appears to consist of a Feldspar. The black masses seem to consist of about equal bulks of particles of the same greenish-gray Feldspar, and of black scales, sometimes fibrous, perhaps of altered Amphibole. Many irregular fissures in all directions, stained or mottled with reddish-brown.

Fracture uneven. Streak greenish-gray on the black masses and grayish-white on the paste.

Weathers unevenly to shades of reddish-brown. This rock contains much Lime and Magnesia, but no Chromium, and appears to show one of the last stages in the alteration of a Dioryte into Serpentine.

No. 323 (Sp. 1247).—*Black Magnesian Dioryte (Serpentine).*

Huronian (?)—Sect. 22—T. 42—R. 31.

Iron-black and dull, speckled with greenish-gray, and glittering.

A brittle, coarse rock, resembling No. 322, made up of about 7 parts of black irregular angular masses, $\frac{1}{8}$ to $\frac{1}{4}$ inch across, in 3 parts of a greenish-gray paste. The former is generally dull, crypto-crystalline and homogeneous; but under the lens it sometimes shows an imperfect columnar structure (Amphibole). The greenish-gray paste consists of crystalline grains of a Feldspar, with good cleavage and lustre, passing into grains of the same color without cleavage, and possessing a greasy lustre, which may be Serpentine. A little brown Mica is also interspersed, sometimes in scales $\frac{1}{8}$ inch long; Pyrite occurs in a few yellow particles; Calcite, associated with red Ferric Oxide in grayish-white and reddish-brown films ; and a translucent greenish-gray mineral, with grayish-white streak, apparently Serpentine, in a thin enamel-like seam.

Fracture uneven. Streak gray and grayish-white.

Weathers very unevenly, to reddish-brown, mottled with blackish-brown.

No. 324 (Sp. 1530).—*Chloritic Dioryte.*

Laurentian (?).—W. branch of Ontonagon River, Sect. 13—T. 46—R. 31.

Blackish-green, minutely speckled with brown ; slightly glittering.

A hard, compact, heavy, tough, fine-grained rock, which appears under the lens to consist of about 6 parts of blackish-green Amphibole, in minute glittering blades, and of 4 parts of brown Feldspar, with ill-defined form and cleavage, and feeble lustre.   Many irregular fissures stained reddish-brown, and one also lined with tiny scales of brown Mica and perhaps a little Chlorite.

Fracture uneven.   Streak greenish-white, dotted with light brownish-red.

Weathers rather evenly, to dull shades of reddish and yellowish-brown.

Another variety (1531) is a little coarser.

Specimen 1532 contains also a light green paste, filled with minute scales resembling Chlorite.   A seam of yellowish- and reddish-white Quartz, ⅛ inch thick, crosses the specimen.   Effervesces slightly in acid.

Specimen 1533 is traversed by more reddish-brown films.

Specimen 1534 contains much more Mica, both disseminated throughout and in a thin seam.   Another thin seam consists of grayish-white and reddish-brown Feldspar.

Effervesces slightly in acid.

Weathers evenly to a blackish-green, and to the depth of over ⅛ inch, with a reddish-brown section.

Specimens 1535, 1536, and 1537, are like 1534, with much Mica disseminated in minute scales, and with the other minerals rather ill defined.

Weathers to reddish-brown.

Specimen 1538 rather resembles No. 332, but most of the scales appear to be a brown Mica.   Films of Calcite traverse the rock, so that it effervesces strongly in acid.

Streak grayish-white and brownish-red.

Specimen 1539 is like 1538, but it is a little coarser, and seems to contain more Chlorite.

No. 325 (Sp. 1428).—*Chloritic Dioryte-Wacké.*

Laurentian.—W. line of Sect. 18—T. 47—R. 45.

Reddish-brown, almost dull.

A decomposed variety of No. 307, the Feldspar being reddish-brown, the Amphibole blackish-green, and hardly distinguishable without a lens, and the interstices between them being occupied by brick-red particles. Many irregular fissures covered with films of brick-red and reddish-brown Ochre, a brownish-gray substance, and blackish-green Chlorite.

Streak brick-red.

Weathers unevenly to a yellowish-brown, mottled by reddish-brown.

No. 326 (Sp. 818).—*Chloritic Dioryte-Schist.*

Huronian.—N. of North-Western Hotel, Marquette.

Greenish-gray, minutely speckled with reddish-brown; minutely glittering.

A tough, hard, compact, fine-grained calcareous schist, which appears under the lens to consist of about 4 parts of a reddish-brown mineral in fibrous facets (altered Amphibole), of 3 parts of minute scales of grayish-white Mica and blackish-green Chlorite, and of 3 parts of a grayish-white crystalline Feldspar, in minute particles.

Fracture even. Streak reddish-white. Effervesces decidedly in acid. The fissures of lamination are stained chocolate-brown and often covered with films of grayish-white Calcite and olive-green Chlorite.

In another specimen, 823, a very little of the Feldspar is reddish-white.

No. 327 (Sp. 1099).—*Blackish-Green Dioryte-Schist.*

Huronian.—Edwards Mine.

Blackish-green and glittering.

A hard, compact, heavy, homogeneous rock, chiefly of rather fine texture, and with a slight tendency to a flaky structure. It appears to consist mostly of greenish-black Amphibole, sometimes in fibrous facets $\frac{1}{16}$ to $\frac{1}{8}$ inch across, often iridescent, and rather micaceous in cleavage, but chiefly in minute scales or flakes, probably associated with a large quantity of Chlorite. A very little grayish- or greenish-white Feldspar, in minute particles, can also be distinguished by the lens.

Fracture uneven. Streak greenish-white. A few irregular fissures, with reddish-brown stains or covered with films of brownish-white Calcite.

Weathers rather unevenly, by the splitting off of the flakes, to a dirty brownish-gray, inclining to green.

No. 328 (Sp. 1384).—*Greenish Dioryte-Schist.*

Laurentian.—S. W. corner Sect. 12—T. 47—R. 47.

Greenish-black, speckled with grayish-white; glittering.

A very hard, tough, compact, homogeneous, calcareous, porphyritic rock, of medium grain, composed of about 7 parts of greenish-black Amphibole, in narrow fibrous facets, rarely distinct crystals, $\frac{1}{16}$ to $\frac{1}{4}$ inch long, and of 3 parts of brownish and grayish-white Feldspar, in massive particles just visible to the eye. A little Pyrite is disseminated in minute yellow particles. A few fissures and seams stained reddish-brown.

Fracture rather uneven. Streak greenish-white. Effervesces slightly in acid.

Weathers evenly and smoothly, to a brownish-black.

No. 329 (Sp. 1385).—*Greenish Dioryte-Schist.*

Laurentian.—S. W. corner Sect. 12—T. 47—R. 47.

Resembles No. 328, but lighter colored.

The proportion of the Amphibole to the Feldspar is about 5 to 3. The Amphibole is often of a blackish-green color. Minute scales of blackish-green Mica are disseminated in small quantity. There is a slightly schistose structure, and the weathered surface is greenish-gray and slightly ridged and minutely pitted by the removal of the Amphibole and Mica and projection of tiny laminæ of Feldspar.

No. 330 (Sp. 1401).—*Greenish Dioryte-Schist.*

Laurentian (?)—Near centre of N. W. ¼ of Sect. 29—T. 47—R. 42.

Greenish-black, speckled with greenish-gray; glittering.

A compact, hard, tough Dioryte, of medium texture and apparently of coarsely schistose structure. Its constituents, which are visible to the eye, are a greenish-black Amphibole, in tiny facets, and irregular grains of greenish-gray, sometimes reddish-white, altered Feldspar, generally massive, but often showing a cleavage or an imperfect crystalline shape. The facets of Amphibole are much broken up by the irregular insertion of particles of the Feldspar. Much bronze-yellow Pyrite is disseminated in tiny grains. Parallel seams occur, lined with a fibrous film of Chlorite, with greenish-gray streak, and produce the apparent schistose structure.

Fracture uneven. Streak greenish-white.

Weathers to the depth of ⅛ inch, with an even surface of reddish-white color, roughened and speckled by projecting crystals of weathered greenish-gray Amphibole.

No. 331 (Sp. 821).—*Calcareous Dioryte-Greenstone.*

Huronian.—N. of North-Western Hotel, Marquette.

Olive-green, mottled with chocolate-brown.

A compact, hard, brittle, fine-grained, calcareous rock, which appears under the lens to be chiefly composed of minute scales of olive-green Chlorite, in many spots altered into chocolate-brown, with a few acicular blades (altered Amphibole?) of the same colors, and many minute silvery-gray glistening scales, disseminated throughout. A few grayish and greenish-white particles (Feldspar?) can also be distinguished. The alteration of the Chlorite is sometimes so produced as to mark the section with narrow chocolate-brown concentric bands.

Fracture uneven. Streak grayish-white, often more or less reddish. Effervesces decidedly in acid. Many irregular fissures in all directions, rendering it difficult to obtain a fresh fracture, and occupied by films of grayish-white and reddish-brown Calcite, and blackish-green Chlorite, partly altered into chocolate-brown.

Weathers unevenly to blackish-green, mottled with chocolate-brown.

No. 332 (Sp. 1527).—*Fine-grained Dioryte-Greenstone.*

Laurentian.—W. branch of Ontonagon River, Sect. 13—T. 46—R. 41.

Grayish-green, glittering.

A soft, compact, tough, homogeneous, fine-grained rock, made up of about 6 parts of minute scales of soft, light-green to blackish-green Chlorite, and 4 parts of plates of grayish-white, sometimes brown, Feldspar, with good cleavage—both minerals having a high lustre.

Fracture uneven. Streak greenish-white. Effervesces slightly in acid.

Weathers evenly to reddish-brown.

In another variety, Specimen 1528, a little Calcite occurs in tiny geodes, while, in 1529, a larger part of the Feldspar is colored brown.

No. 333 (Sp. 819).—*Epidotic Dioryte-Greenstone.*

Huronian.—Lower Bed, N. of North-Western Hotel, Marquette.

Chocolate-brown, streaked and mottled with yellowish-green ; dull.

A compact, hard, tough, rather fine-grained calcareous rock, made up of about 6 parts of reddish-brown, grayish- and reddish-white Feldspar, in minute crystalline facets, of 1 part of reddish-brown scales or needles without lustre (altered Amphibole ?) and uniformly disseminated, and of 3 parts of a yellowish-green translucent mineral, resembling Epidote, in tiny masses, and especially in many seams, mostly parallel, usually about $\frac{1}{16}$ inch thick. These seams possess a marked transverse cleavage, which produces a fibrous structure on their section. Many irregular seams also occur, from a film up to $\frac{1}{16}$ inch in thickness, of grayish-white Calcite, in crystalline plates $\frac{1}{4}$ inch across, of grayish-white glassy Quartz, associated with the latter, and of soft chocolate-brown fibrous films, with brownish-red streak, resembling altered Amphibole.

Fracture rather uneven. Streak reddish-white. Effervesces decidedly in acid.

Weathers rather evenly, but roughly, to a blackish-green, mottled with chocolate-brown and yellowish-brown stripes.

No. 334 (S).—*Dioryte-Greenstone.*

Huronian.—Lower Bed (West of Marquette Mine).

Grayish-green, faintly spotted by blackish-green ; minutely glittering.

A tough, hard, compact, heavy and very fine-grained calcareous rock, which consists of about equal bulks of somewhat rounded blackish-green masses in a greenish-gray paste. The former often indicate traces of cleavage in feebly shining surfaces, and are apparently altered blades of Amphibole.

The light-colored paste appears, under the lens, to consist chiefly of greenish-gray Feldspar (greenish-white on thin edges), with many minute silvery-white scales or narrow blades, as of a Mica.

The surface of the fissures is covered with films of brownish-gray Calcite, and reddish-brown Ochre.

Fracture rather uneven. Streak greenish-white. Effervesces strongly in hydrochloric acid.

Weathered surface very rough and uneven, being pitted in a peculiar manner, by the erosion of the blackish-green masses, into irregular rounded cavities, $\frac{1}{8}$ to $\frac{1}{2}$ inch across and $\frac{1}{4}$ inch deep—the general color being greenish-gray, mottled by dirty reddish-brown spots at the bottom of the cavities.

No. 335 (Sp. 826).—*Micaceous Greenstone-Schist.*

Huronian.—Lower Bed—South of North-Western Hotel, Marquette.

Grayish-green, with minute dull chocolate-brown and glittering reddish-brown specks, mottled with chocolate-brown on cleavage surfaces.

A rather brittle, calcareous schist (almost a slate), chiefly made up of a greenish-gray feldspathic material of impalpable texture, resembling that of No. 339, but dotted with many tiny chocolate-brown spots and streaks, usually $\frac{1}{32}$ inch across, and containing much Mica and Chlorite disseminated throughout in reddish-brown glistening irregular scales, rarely over $\frac{1}{32}$ inch across. The seams of lamination are covered with soft films of Chlorite, of a blackish-green, much mottled with bright chocolate-brown.

Fracture uneven. Streak greenish and reddish-white. Effervesces strongly in acid. Differs from No. 339 in the apparently increased proportion of Chlorite.

Weathers evenly, to shades of reddish-brown.

No. 336 (Sp. 827).—*Micaceous Greenstone-Schist.*

Huronian.—South of North-Western Hotel, Marquette.

Greenish-gray, sometimes with slight reddish tinge; glittering very slightly.

A rock of fine-grained texture which reveals its constituents under the lens. It resembles No. 335, but is coarser, and the schistose structure is more irregular and less distinctly marked. It appears to consist of about equal quantities of minute granules of reddish-white Feldspar, and minute scales of reddish-brown Mica, dispersed throughout. The seams of lamination are covered with a film of soft greenish-black Chlorite, made up of exceedingly minute scales, which produce a shining surface.

Fracture very uneven. Streak grayish-white, sometimes reddish or greenish-gray. Effervesces decidedly in acid. Fuses at 4.5 to a black and grayish-white enamel.

Weathered surface uneven, and in spots very rough and cellular, by the weathering out of the Mica; has a blackish-brown color, mottled in the rough spots by reddish-brown. This roughness is produced by the projection of the parallel scales of Feldspar and Mica, and reveals more clearly the schistose texture of the rock.

No. 337 (Sp. 1096).—*Micaceous Greenstone-Schist.*

Huronian.—Lower Bed—Edwards Mine.

Grayish-black and glittering.

A very fine-grained, homogeneous schist, which consists of about

6 parts of grayish-white Feldspar (and smoky Quartz?) and of 4 parts of black Mica, mostly in minute scales, but much of which is in blades, often fibrous and suggesting altered Amphibole. A little blackish-green Chlorite is also disseminated throughout.

Fracture uneven. Streak grayish-white, often inclining to greenish. Somewhat magnetic. Fissures stained to a dirty reddish-brown.

Weathers unevenly, to a brownish-gray, grayish-brown, and covered with minute black granules of Magnetite.

No. 338 (Sp. 1100).—*Schalstone.*

Huronian.—Lower Bed—Washington Mine.

Blackish-gray, slightly greenish, minutely streaked with grayish-white.

A hard, compact, very tough and fine-grained schist (almost a slate), which consists of about 4 parts of greenish-white, sometimes grayish-white, Feldspar, in minute granules—4 parts of a Mica, in minute brown or blackish-brown scales—and 2 parts of grayish-white crystalline Calcite. The latter is mostly gathered in many thin, lenticular, parallel flakes, $\frac{1}{16}$ to $\frac{1}{4}$ inch in length, whose grayish-white color contrasts with the prevailing dark color of a section. One feldspathic bunch occurs in the specimen, $\frac{1}{4}$ inch long.

Fracture uneven. Streak grayish-white.

Weathers very unevenly, to a dirty greenish-gray, the surface being covered with circular pits, $\frac{1}{8}$ to $\frac{3}{8}$ inch across, whose bottoms are usually colored reddish-brown.

No. 339 (Sp. 824).—*Green Aphanyte-Schist.*

Huronian.—Lower Bed—S. of North-Western Hotel, Marquette.

Grayish-green ; dull.

A compact, tough, homogeneous rock, of impalpable grain, and rather schistose structure, which appears under the lens to consist of a greenish-gray translucent Feldspar, sometimes slightly speckled by reddish-gray Mica and blackish-green Chlorite. Of the latter many exceedingly minute glistening scales are disseminated throughout.

Fracture rather uneven. Streak greenish-white. A few tiny veins, sometimes swelling into lenticular masses $\frac{1}{4}$ inch across, of a material in which the glistening scales predominate. A few fissures lightly stained to a yellowish- and reddish-brown, slightly mottled with a light greenish-gray. Fuses at 4, to a black glass.

Weathers evenly and rather smoothly, to a greenish-gray, with yellowish-white specks, revealing a few scales of the Mica to the lens.

Specimen 825 resembles 824. Fuses at 4, to a greenish-black glass.

Weathers, with an even surface soft to the touch, to a dirty greenish-gray, tinged with reddish-brown; which glistens slightly and appears under the lens to be covered with minute projecting scales of Mica.

No. 340 (Sp. 817).—*Greenish-gray Chlorite-Potstone.*

Huronian.—Lower Bed—N. of North-Western Hotel, Marquette.

Light greenish-gray, mottled, by fissures, with light reddish-brown.

A soft, compact, finely granular, schistose rock, apparently made up of about 8 parts of grayish-white Feldspar, and 2 parts of minute scales of a grayish-white Mica (possibly Talc), and greenish-gray Chlorite. Contains much less Chlorite than No. 341. A few minute veins of white Quartz occur, and many fissures running irregularly, but so as to impart the schistose structure, and lined with a film of reddish-brown material with greasy feel (probably decomposed Chlorite). Effervesces slightly in acid. Streak greenish-white. Fuses at 5.5, to a greenish-brown glass.

Weathered surface uneven, and of a darker, dirty-green color.

No. 341 (Sp. 1494).—*Green Chlorite-Potstone.*

Huronian.—Lower Bed—Sunday Lake Outlet.

Grayish-green, mottled with grayish-brown.
A very soft, compact, friable, highly altered chloritic rock, of

impalpable texture, consisting of about 3 parts of brown, vaguely defined, irregular masses, about ⅛ inch across, in a grayish-green paste. In one part of the latter a slight cleavage and lustre were observed, resembling those of a Feldspar. Many brownish films traverse the rock in all directions.

Fracture very uneven. Streak brownish-red and grayish-green. Effervesces slightly in acid. Yields a very large amount of water, on ignition in a matrass. This rock seems to show the last stage in the alteration of a Dioryte into a species of Chlorite-Potstone.

Another variety (Specimens 1495, 1496, and 1497) is traversed by a network of soft, fibrous, apple-green films of Chlorite.

No. 342 (Sp. 884).—*Black Trappean Dioryte.*

Huronian.—Lower Bed—L'Anse Iron Range.

Black, speckled with greenish-white and reddish-brown; glittering.

A hard, tough, compact, coarse, heavy rock, made up of about 5 parts of black Hornblende in irregular crystalline lamellar masses, usually $\frac{1}{16}$ inch long and often showing facets of high lustre—and of 5 parts of greenish-yellow and sometimes grayish-white Feldspar, in irregular tabular crystals, $\frac{1}{16}$ inch long. Many of the interstices of the Feldspar, and many irregular fissures, are stained reddish- and yellowish-brown.

Fracture uneven. Streak grayish-white. The crystals both of Hornblende and Feldspar are sometimes ⅛ inch long and the latter are sometimes covered with a minute striation. Feebly magnetic. Powder ash-gray, inclining to brownish. The magnet separates 5 per cent. by weight, in grayish-black particles.

Weathers rather unevenly to a dirty brownish-gray, and finally disintegrates into an angular sand.

In another specimen (885) the fissures are more minute and the cleavage surfaces are stained reddish-brown; so that it is difficult to obtain a fresh unaltered surface only an inch square. Effervesces but very feebly in acid.

Weathers evenly to a blackish-green, speckled with grayish- and reddish-white.

No. 343 (Sp. 886).—*Black Trappean Dioryte.*

Huronian.—Lower Bed—L'Anse Iron Range.

Resembles No. 342, but its texture varies in fineness down to a grain in which the crystals become glittering points which can hardly be distinguished by the eye. Few of the interstices have the yellowish-brown stain. The specimen does not perceptibly affect the compass, but the magnet separates about 4 per cent. from the pulverized rock.

The weathered surface of the coarse parts of the rock is roughened by the projection of the greenish-black crystals of Hornblende and a few black octahedra of Magnetite.

No. 344 (Sp. 888).—*Trappean Dioryte.*

Huronian.—Lower Bed.—L'Anse Iron Range.

Greenish-gray, speckled with black ; glittering.

Resembles No. 342, but consists of about equal parts of imperfect crystals of Hornblende and Feldspar. The former occurs in short brownish-black, imperfect crystals, often showing a lamellar structure, and sometimes a slight iridescence on a cleavage surface. The Feldspar is greenish-white, very rarely grayish-white, glassy and translucent to semi-transparent ; its fusibility is about 3.5, and it is almost insoluble in boiling hydrochloric acid. Very feebly magnetic. Powder yellowish-gray. The magnet separates 2 per cent. by weight of grayish-black particles. The interior portion of this specimen, 2 or 3 inches below the weathered surface, is converted into a very friable mass, in which the crystals cohere very loosely—those of Feldspar assuming a brownish-gray to greenish-gray tint.

No. 345 (Sp. 889).—*Altered Trappean Dioryte.*

Huronian.—Lower Bed.—L'Anse Iron Range.

Chocolate-brown, with glittering greenish-gray specks, banded with grayish-green.

A soft, compact, fine-grained, weathered rock, which appears under the lens to consist of about 7 parts of tiny dull plates or particles, sometimes laminated, of a brick-red and reddish-brown color, (altered Hornblende), with about 3 parts of tiny glittering facets of greenish-gray Feldspar, often grayish-green and soft. A few parallel bands and a short transverse seam occur, of a greenish-gray color, and about ⅛ inch thick, in which the soft grayish-green material predominates, having a greasy feel and resembling Serpentine, with a few scattered brown masses of Hornblende. The seam is traversed by a thinner seam of fibrous structure and reddish-brown, brick-red, and blackish-green color—apparently altered Hornblende. A very few minute glittering black scales occur, apparently of Micaceous-Iron.

Weathered surface rather even and smooth, about $\frac{1}{32}$ inch deep, and of a brownish-yellow color, mottled with greenish-black—the section being grayish-green.

No. 346 (Sp. 905).—*Speckled Trappean Dioryte.*

Huronian.—Lower Bed.—L'Anse Iron Range near W. line Sect. 18—T. 49—R. 33.

Resembles No. 344, but is a little coarser, many of the crystals being ⅛ inch long, and about half the Feldspar is of a grayish-white color.

Feebly magnetic. Powder ash-gray, inclining to greenish. The magnet separates 3 per cent. by weight, in grayish-black particles.

Weathered surface even, but roughened by projection of the crystals of Hornblende and harder plates of Feldspar, and of a dirty cream color, speckled with blackish-green.

No. 347 (Sp. 912).—*Black Trappean Dioryte.*

Huronian.—Lower Bed.—L'Anse Iron Range.

Iron-black, speckled with gray; glittering.
A hard, compact, tough, rather coarse, highly crystalline rock,

made up of about 7 parts of iron-black lamellar Hornblende, in irregular masses and plates, and 3 parts of a grayish and yellowish-white Feldspar, with decided cleavage, in crystals and plates which cover a section with facets and minute lines $\frac{1}{8}$ inch long. A minute seam crosses the specimen, filled with a reddish-brown Ochre, and a few minute irregular fissures, stained reddish-brown.

Fracture uneven. Streak grayish-white, sometimes dotted with reddish-brown.

Weathers to the depth of about $\frac{1}{32}$ inch, with a rather even surface of a brownish-gray color, roughened by projecting grains of the Hornblende.

No. 348 (Sp. 913).—*Brown Trappean Dioryte.*

Huronian.—Lower Bed.—L'Anse Iron Range.

Blackish-brown, speckled with gray ; glittering.

Like No. 347, but of a little finer texture, and with a blackish-brown substituted for the iron-black Hornblende. Many fissures occur, mostly parallel, and generally occupied by a film of a yellowish-green color, apparently Epidote.

No. 349 (Sp. 915).—*Brown Trappean Dioryte.*

Huronian.—Lower Bed.—L'Anse Iron Range, S. of L'Anse, Sect. 9—T. 49—R. 33.

Like No. 348, but has the coarseness of No. 347, and is traversed in all directions by blackish-green films of Chlorite, giving greenish-gray streak.

No. 350 (Sp. 996).—*Fine-grained Green Trappean Dioryte.*

Huronian.—Lower Bed.—W. of Slate River, Sect. 28—T. 51—R. 31.

Dark grayish-green, speckled with brown and grayish-white ; glittering.

A compact, tough, hard rock, which resembles Nos. 342, 343,

and 346, but is finer-grained and poorly crystallized. It appears to consist of about equal bulks of grayish-white Feldspar, in thin tabular flakes, and a brown Feldspar in tiny facets, both about $\frac{1}{16}$ inch across, and irregular grains of grayish-green crystalline Hornblende.

Fracture uneven. Streak greenish-white.

Weathers unevenly to a reddish-brown, mottled by gray, and the constituents appear to weather equally.

Another specimen (997), is a fine-grained and tougher variety. The surface of the joints is stained reddish-brown.

No. 351 (Sp. 911).—*Green Porphyry.*

[Huronian.—Lower Bed.—L'Anse Iron Range, N. W. ¼ of Sect. 9—T. 49—R. 33.

Dark bluish-green; dull, with brown glittering specks.

A rather hard, brittle, compact, heavy, crystalline rock, made up of about 3 parts of a brown and orange-brown or copper-colored Feldspar, with good cleavage, in about 7 parts of a dark bluish-green, dull, aphanitic paste.

Fracture uneven. Streak greenish and reddish-white. Many minute fissures in all directions, stained with films of yellowish and reddish-brown.

Weathers unevenly to a reddish-brown.

On a polished section, under the lens, the paste is resolved into 3 minerals: well defined, dull, blackish-green, crystals of altered Hornblende, amounting to about 3 parts of the rock—a green homogeneous paste, probably chloritic, amounting to about 3 parts— and nearly 1 part of Pyrite, in yellowish-white, angular particles.

No. 352 (Sp. 887).—*Brown Wacké.*

Huronian.—Lower Bed.—L'Anse Iron Range.

Reddish-brown, mottled with light-yellow; mostly dull, but with a few glittering points.

A very soft and friable, fine-grained, decomposed rock, produced by the weathering of the preceding rock, in which the Feldspar predominates over the Hornblende, both occurring in tiny altered grains, distinguishable by the eye. In the yellow parts of the specimen, the Feldspar is light-yellow to yellowish-white, and the Hornblende blackish-green ; and in the reddish-brown, the color is due to the reddish-brown altered crystals of the latter mineral. The cleavage and general characteristics of both minerals are indistinct.

No. 353 (Sp. 914).—*Speckled Wacké.*

Huronian.—L'Anse Iron Range, N. side of above Dioryte Dyke.

Yellowish-white, minutely speckled with reddish-brown.

A rather soft and brittle, compact, fine-grained rock, made up of about 6 parts of reddish-brown, soft, irregular grains, apparently of a reddish Ochre, derived from alteration of Hornblende, in a soft yellowish-white paste, which imparts a greasy feel to the rock and apparently consists of a Feldspar, altered to Kaolin. It is apparently a decomposed form of a finer grained variety of Nos. 347 and 348. A few minute glittering black scales, apparently of Micaceous-Iron.

Fracture uneven. Streak brownish-red, dotted with yellowish-white.

No. 354 (Sp. 1110).—*Black Dioryte-Aphanyte.*

Huronian.—Dyke.—Washington Mine.

Grayish-black ; minutely glittering.

A compact, tough, hard, fine-grained rock, which appears to consist of about equal bulks of grayish-white Feldspar, in minute particles, and of a black mineral, with high lustre, (resembling the black mineral of No. 205,) in minute flakes, scales, or blades, sometimes $\frac{1}{16}$ inch long. Much bronze-yellow Pyrite is disseminated throughout, in particles and films, sometimes over $\frac{1}{4}$ inch across, especially in seams associated with films of grayish-white Calcite.

Fracture conchoidal. Streak gray. Fissures occur, stained greenish-black and greenish-gray.

No. 355 (Sp. 1382).—*Black Dioryte-Aphanyte.*

Laurentian.—Dyke.—N. W. ¼ of Sect. 29—T. 47—R. 42.

Grayish-black, slightly glittering.

An exceedingly hard, compact, heavy, tough, homogeneous, almost crypto-crystalline rock, which appears under the lens to consist of about 3 parts of minute facets of grayish-white Feldspar, with good cleavage and lustre, in 7 parts of a dull black paste, hardly touched by the file.

Fracture even. Streak gray.

Weathers evenly, to a dirty yellowish-brown, to the depth of $\frac{1}{32}$ inch, with a surface rendered harsh to the touch by minute projecting points.

No. 356 (S).—*Black Dioryte-Aphanyte.*

Dyke near Forestville.

Like No. 355. Facets of a black Feldspar, with high lustre, can also be distinguished, which are sometimes $\frac{1}{32}$ to $\frac{1}{16}$ inch long. Surface of fissures stained a light brownish-red, or brownish to yellowish-gray ; possesses the strongly marked cross-cleavages (in 3 planes at right angles to each other) peculiar to a dyke.

No. 357 (S).—*Green Dioryte-Aphanyte.*

Dyke, half an inch wide, crossing obliquely a Huronian Dioryte-Schist.
Light-House Point, Marquette.

Grayish-green and dull.

A very hard, compact, heavy, crypto-crystalline rock, of the texture of porcelain or many Felsytes, resembling a green Jasper. Nothing can be distinguished in it, even by the lens, but a few tiny particles of Pyrite.

Fracture rendered exceedingly uneven, by the whole rock being traversed irregularly by small fissures, stained reddish-brown ; and it is for the same reason difficult to obtain a fresh fracture half an inch square. The hardness is less than that of a Felsyte. No trace visible in this specimen of the cross-cleavage of No. 356. Streak greenish-white.

Weathers rather unevenly, to a light brownish-gray, the vein sometimes sharply projecting above, and sometimes sharply sunken below, the surface of the schist.

No. 358 (Sp. 732).—*Arenaceous Sandstone-Schist.*

Huronian.—Bed XIII.—Spurr Range, Sect. 23—T. 48—R. 31.

Gray, mottled with grayish-white, with many tiny specks of dark greenish-gray.

An arenaceous schistose Sandstone, almost exactly like No. 359, without the bands, made up of minute granules of glassy Quartz, sometimes intermixed with a greenish-gray substance (probably Chlorite), and tiny particles and seams of a dirty yellowish and reddish-brown color. The surfaces of the layers are covered with films of a gray color, mottled with dirty shades of yellowish and reddish-brown, containing many minute scales of brownish-gray Mica.

Fracture rather even. Streak grayish-white. Slightly magnetic, and with polarity, from a thin adhering layer of Magnetite.

Weathers smoothly to dark brownish shades.

No. 359 (Sp. 739).—*Magnetic Arenaceous Sandstone-Schist.*

Huronian.—Bed XIII.—Spurr Range, Sect. 23—T. 48—R. 31.

Grayish-white, with bluish-gray, reddish-brown, and blackish-gray bands.

A rather brittle and friable, loosely aggregated, fine-grained, arenaceous, laminated Sandstone, almost of a slaty structure. This rock is made up of laminæ, usually varying in thickness from $\frac{1}{32}$ to $\frac{1}{4}$ inch, most of which are gray, grayish-white, and bluish-gray, and consist of arenaceous Quartz ; and some of which, at intervals of an inch or more, are light reddish-brown and black, glittering, rarely more than $\frac{1}{8}$ inch in thickness, and consist of mixtures of Magnetic Iron and ferruginous Quartz. On examination by a lens, the gray and grayish-white laminæ are seen to consist of minute grains of milky Quartz ; the bluish-gray laminæ, of grains of smoky Quartz ; the reddish-brown, of ferruginous and milky Quartz ; and the black, which are always associated with the last, of a mixture of octahedral crystals of Magnetite, with ferruginous Quartz, the former mineral amounting to about ¾ of the bulk of the layer, as separated by a magnet from the powder. There are also many minute seams, usually less than an inch long, filled with brown Ochre, sometimes parallel to the lamination and often crossing it obliquely and irregularly.

Fracture uneven. Streak grayish-white. Powder of the darker layers blackish-gray and glittering ; the magnet separates about 60 per cent. of the bulk, in a grayish-black and glittering powder, with a remainder of a brownish-gray and dull.

On account of the presence of the Magnetite, this rock is decidedly magnetic. The material and structure are identical with those of the common pebbles in specimens of certain Quartzytes, but they differ in the absence of Magnetite from the latter and in their more yellowish tints.

Weathered surface is darker than the fresh fracture, and the edges of the ferruginous layers generally assume a yellowish-brown color.

No. 360 (Sp. 923).—*Chloritic Sandstone-Schist.*

Silurian.—Presqu'isle.—West side, North of the Neck.

Light greenish-gray, inclining to apple-green, minutely speckled with white ; dull.

A fine-grained rock, which is a variety of the Kaolinic Sandstone-Schists, belonging to the Silurian. The color is light, and is only very slightly variegated with thin brown lines in some places. It consists of about 7 parts of grayish-green Quartz, in angular granules distinguishable by the lens, and of 3 parts of grayish- to yellowish-white Kaolin, in scattered particles visible to the eye, with a few minute scales apparently of Chlorite and Mica. The structure is decidedly schistose—which is produced by the dissemination of many flat, thin flakes, sometimes ½ inch across, of soft greenish-gray and blackish-green Chloritic Schist, with light greenish-gray streak. A few minute scales of silvery-white Mica are dispersed over the cleavage surfaces and are distinguishable by the eye.

Streak of the rock, greenish-white. The surfaces of the cleavage-planes, and especially of the joints of the rock, are stained or mottled with reddish- and yellowish-brown.

Weathered surface uneven and rough, and of a light reddish-brown color.

MINERALOGICAL NOTES.

MINERALOGICAL NOTES.

THE small variety and imperfect crystallization of the minerals of this region were remarked by Foster and Whitney, in Part II. of their Report, published in the year 1851 ; and brief notes are given in that volume, on pages 95, 18, 82, etc., of the following eighteen minerals: Galena, Sulphuret of Zinc, Iron Pyrites, Sulphuret of Copper, Specular Oxide of Iron, Magnetic Oxide of Iron, Oxide of Manganese, Quartz, Pyroxene, Hornblende, Garnet, Mica, Orthoclase, Talc, Serpentine, Chlorite, Calc-Spar, and Dolomite.

During the period of twenty-one years which has since elapsed, and the extensive opening up of this region by mines and roads, the occurrence of perhaps fifteen more minerals has been discovered ; but several of these are found only in traces or small quantities, and it is difficult to obtain well-crystallized specimens, worthy of the cabinet, of any but two or three. A few hasty notes will now be given of such facts as have come to my notice in the field or in collections, in regard to the following minerals :

Graphite.	Garnet.
Galenite.	Epidote.
Sphalerite.	Muscovite.
Pyrite.	Magnesian Mica.
Chalco-pyrite.	Orthoclase.
Hematite.	Triclinic Feldspars.
Martite.	Tourmaline (?).
Magnetite.	Andalusite.
Pyrolusite.	Staurolite.
Turgite.	Talc.
Göthite.	Serpentine.
Limonite.	Kaolin.
Quartz.	Chlorite.
Pyroxene (?).	Calcite.
Anthophyllite.	Dolomite.
Amphibole.	Siderite.

Graphite (popularly called " Plumbago ") occurs in tiny scales and in films in the carbonaceous slates.   (Nos. 246 to 251.)

Galenite (" Galena ") was observed by Foster and Whitney in small quantity at Presqu'isle.   An argentiferous variety has been since found, in the region north of the Carp River, in quantities sufficient to induce the opening of several mines.   It is, at these localities, associated with Sphalerite, Pyrite, and Chalcopyrite, (and, it was reported at the Holyoke mine, Pyrostilpnite,) in milky Quartz. (Holyoke and Lake Superior Silver Lead Mines, etc.)

Sphalerite (" Zinc Blende," or " Black-Jack ") has been observed at Presqu'isle, the Holyoke Mines, the Sedgwick Mines, etc., always in small quantity and with the association stated under Galenite.

Pyrite (" Iron Pyrites ") is very commonly disseminated through all the rocks, but almost always in tiny irregular particles or in small cubes, rarely $\frac{1}{4}$ of an inch across.   In some cases it has been suspected to be auriferous (Pyritiferous Conglomeritic Talcose Schist, north side of Lake Palmer, S. W. $\frac{1}{4}$ of N. E. $\frac{1}{4}$ of S. 25— T. 47—R. 27).

Chalcopyrite (" Copper Pyrites ") is the only ore of copper (excepting a few traces of Green Carbonate at Presqu'isle, etc.,) which has been noticed in this region, and always at a very few localities (Presqu'isle, Holyoke Mine, Sedgwick Mine, etc.), and in small quantity : usually in tiny particles and strings, associated with Galenite, as stated under that mineral.

Hematite (" Specular Ore ").   I have neither the opportunity nor the necessary suite of specimens for a proper description of the characteristics of this mineral peculiar to this region.   All its common earthy and amorphous forms are easily studied in the vast beds which have been opened ; and I believe small veins have occurred, at the Jackson Mine, and the Iron Mountain Mine, containing small crystals of Specular Ore.   The only specimens of interest to the collector are the following : Black Micaceous-Iron, in seams or sheets, sometimes a foot or more across (Lake Superior Mine, etc.) ; the so-called " Bird's Eye Ore," (No. 6) ; indurated red and yellow Ochre, often in films of coppery color and lustre, lining geodes in Milky Quartz, which form fine specimens at several localities (Iron Mountain Mine, etc.); and Red Chalk, which may be procured in abundance from the decomposed Chloritic Schist at " Kimball's Cut," on the Peninsula Railroad, and in the E. part of S. 18—T. 47—R. 26. An unusual association is the occurrence of much Micaceous-Iron in small masses and seams, along with Quartz, Chlorite, and crystallized Feldspar, in a coarse Dioryte on the east side of lake *Angeline.*

Martite (part of the " Specular Ore "). A pseudomorphous form of Hematite after Magnetite (Dana's System of Mineralogy, page 142), is so commonly distributed in tiny octahedra or triangular scales, rarely $\frac{1}{8}$-$\frac{1}{4}$ inch across, that I have applied the name to one schist (No. 2, Appendix B). It sometimes occurs in Chlorite-Schist, but is usually associated with brownish-red Jasper, and fine specimens consisting of alternations of blackish-blue Martite and bright-red Jasper, with the contrast heightened by the glacial polish, may be easily obtained at the Cleveland Knob, etc. Specimens also are common, containing tiny octahedra of Magnetite, of Martite, and of the one partially altered into the other.

Magnetite (" Magnetic Iron Ore ") is very commonly disseminated through most of the rocks, generally associated with Pyrite in the crystalline rocks, in particles, or in octahedra which are rarely $\frac{1}{8}$ inch in diameter. In the beds of ore the grains are imperfectly crystalline and sometimes loosely adherent, like the " shot ores " of the Adirondack Iron-region of New York ; the magnetic character is sometimes very decided, so that the powder clings to the fragments ; the surface is often iridescent, and good specimens are easily obtainable at the Washington Mine, etc.

Pyrolusite (" Binoxide of Manganese ") of an iron-black or brownish-black color, is abundantly disseminated through some Hematite ores in several deposits (as at N. E. cor. of Sect. 12–T. 47–R. 27), in pulverulent coatings, tiny scales and films, and mamillary masses made up of radiating needles, sometimes 2 or 3 inches in diameter; some of which form fair specimens for the cabinet (Sp. 893 and 894).

It also occurs on a rosy Quartzyte, and is associated with Ochre and a little Mica (Sp. 897), with Magnetite and Anthophyllite (No. 178), or with Turgite (Sp. 895). Streak black and sometimes sub-metallic. Gives evidence of alteration, by affording water, when heated in a closed tube, and may be the mineral from this region reported as Manganite in Dana's localities (System of Mineralogy, page 784). Credner also mentions the occurrence of " streaks of a pure, compact, black Psilomelan, mixed with tiny particles of Hausmannite " (Article, loc. cit., page 543).

Turgite (part of the " Hematite "), of a reddish-black color, has been found to occur (Sp. 895, from N. W. ¼ Sect. 9—T. 49—R. 33), in botryoidal masses associated with reniform coatings of brownish Ochre and brownish-black Pyrolusite. Streak brick-red, sometimes brownish-yellow. When heated before the blowpipe in a closed tube, it decrepitates and yields water.

Göthite (the glittering crusts on the " Hematite ") has been found in abundance (at the well-known locality at the Jackson Mine), in lamelliform crystals of a brownish-black color, usually less than ½ inch in length, arranged in stellated or radiating groups, in drusy cavities of Limonite (or perhaps of Turgite ?) and Hematite. The finest specimen I have seen was a stalactite of Limonite, about one foot long, completely covered with radiating blades of Göthite over one inch in length. It also occurs at the Lake Superior Mine (and probably elsewhere), in seams crossing a Feldspathic Argillyte, etc. (Sp. 1139). Streak brownish-yellow.

Limonite (popularly called " Hematite ") has been found at the Jackson Mine, Lake Superior Mine, Foster Mine, and several others, in considerable quantity, and with all the variety of mamil-lary, botryoidal, and stalactitic forms which are common to this ore. It is associated with Hematite, Göthite, Turgite, Pyrolusite, and many varieties of Ochre, and good specimens may be easily obtained.

Quartz (" Flint," " Chert," etc.) is very commonly distributed, in the ordinary massive forms of milky Quartz, smoky Quartz, etc., in connection with the ores, but good crystals are very rare. Several coarse varieties of Jasper, Chalcedony, and Semi-Opal are easily obtained.

Pyroxene (Augite) may possibly be an accessory constituent of certain rocks. Pyroxenic Diabase is reported to occur, but, so far as my observations have gone, I believe that rock and this mineral to be entirely absent from the Iron-Region.

Anthophyllite is the name first applied by Prof. G. J. Brush to the brownish-gray hydrous micaceous mineral, in tiny scales and blades, which enters largely into the constitution of the schists already described (Nos. 174 to 178). See also Wright's observations, in Appendix C.

Amphibole (popularly called "Hornblende"), although the universal constituent of the Diorytes, in its black and greenish-black variety—Hornblende—almost always occurs in small fibrous poorly crystallized blades. The most coarsely crystallized specimens may be procured from a ridge between Negaunee and Teal Lake, in the swamp near Barlie's Brook (N. E. qr. of S. W. qr. of Sect. 22—T. 47—R. 27), near a waterfall in a swamp (N. E. cor., S. W. qr. of S. W. qr., Sect. 7—T. 47—R. 27), and on "Raspberry Hill" (Sect. 7—T. 47—R. 26). Seams of *Actinolite*, however, occur in one schist (No. 17), and a quartzose vein occurs in Dioryte (on the crest of the hill, north of Lake Fairbanks), which contains an abundance of massive Actinolite, of a coarse columnar structure, in layers 2 or 3 inches thick, associated with a little Chlorite. *Tremolite* is distributed in small short blades through a dolomite (No. 103), and was also observed in that association, in the Menominee region, by Credner (Article, page 527); and this is, I suspect, the "Kyanite" said to occur in a marble at Sect. 36—T. 42—R. 29. *Asbestus* was found by Dr. Houghton at Presqu'isle, and is distributed in considerable quantity through a rock near Lake Gogebic, so as to form an Asbestus-rock, filled with small garnets.

Garnet sometimes occurs in coarse, partially decomposed dodecahedrons, generally less than $\frac{1}{2}$ inch in diameter, in Talcose and Chloritic Schists, at the Washington Mine, at Republic Mountain, Smith Mountain, etc., but good specimens are rare.

13

Epidote may be easily obtained, in small imperfect crystals, from the quartzose veins which traverse the Dioryte on the shore between Light-House Point and Granite Point, between Negaunee and Teal Lake, and elsewhere, and from similar veins in Chloritic and Amphibole-Gneiss.

Muscovite ("Mica") in tiny scales is disseminated through the Granite in small quantity.

Magnesian Mica, a brown, brownish-black, and black variety, is disseminated in tiny scales through the altered forms of Dioryte and Chloritic Gneiss, in association with similar scales of Chlorite. It is generally softened by decomposition, so as to cut like Chlorite. There may possibly be another Mica, represented by the black scales in the same rocks ; and one variety (at the Washington Mine), distributed in isolated scales, has been denominated *Ottrelite* by Prof. G. J. Brush (Vol. I., page 105).

Orthoclase ("Feldspar") is the chief constituent of the Granite, occurring in coarse reddish masses in which the Quartz is sometimes so arranged as to produce a Graphic Granite.

Feldspar, of, I suspect, two triclinic varieties, probably Oligoclase and Albite, is an important constituent of the Diorytes and Gneisses, occurring generally in small irregular thin plates, but sometimes in well-crystallized but tiny prisms (No. 344).

The striation is not usually strongly marked or very common to the facets. The color of the Feldspar in the Diorytes is most commonly greenish-white, while in the Gneisses it generally inclines to grayish-white ; though both colors occur in both these classes of rock. It has been generally subjected to a process of decomposition, by which it assumes a flesh-red, salmon-color, or deep-brownish-red (whose incipient stages, just staining the edges of or fissures in the grains, may be best studied in the coarser Gneisses, No. 258), and which ends in the production of Kaolin (Nos. 227 and 244).

In one Dioryte in which the Feldspar is greenish-white, where the texture is compact and fine-grained (No. 318), veins occur of almost pure Feldspar, which resemble Orthoclase in color and general appearance, but contain many drusy geodes in which characteristic crystals of some triclinic variety may be distinguished. On the North shore of Lake Angeline, Sect. 10—T. 47—R. 27, small veins occur, in a coarse Dioryte, of an aggregate of milky Quartz, bunches of minute scales of Green Chlorite, Micaceous-Iron, and an imperfectly crystallized Feldspar, from which geodes may be obtained sometimes containing fair crystals of the latter. Mention has already been made of a purplish Feldspar, in radiating plates, which occurred, associated with green Quartz, in a seam through Amphibolyte (No. 319).

Between Forestville and Palmer's Saw-Mill is a ledge of Green-stone, by the roadside, traversed by many veins of a Feldspar, from which geodes, containing good crystals, were procured. Similar veins were noticed in the Talcose Schists near Palmer's Saw-Mill, and in those on the Lake Shore near the mouth of Chocolate River, being there associated with Epidote, Calcite, and Quartz.

Tourmaline is said, by Dr. Houghton (Appendix E), to occur at the mouth of Dead River in " beautiful specimens in small quantities."

Andalusite, of a pink color and coarsely-fibrous structure, is disseminated in some abundance through Mica-Schist, often in association with Staurolite. It occurs in imperfect crystals or crystalline masses, whose bright color contrasts well with the dark matrix. Fine specimens, an inch or more in length, are said to occur in the collection at the State University, Ann Arbor, Mich.

Staurolite (" Cross-stone ") is abundantly disseminated through Mica-Schist (No. 301) in blackish-brown, perfect crystals, sometimes in twins, less than an inch in length, often associated with Andalusite.

Talc (" Soapstone ") is disseminated through certain Schists of rather uncommon occurrence (Nos. 53, 54, 74, etc.), generally in association with Chlorite, but always in minute scales or films, of no particular interest as specimens. The only exception, to my knowledge, is on the North side of the West end of Moss Mountain (N. E. qr. of Sect. 11—T. 47—R. 27), where some seams of quite pure Talc occur in Talcose Schist, part of which is indurated into a kind of greenstone.   The *Steatite* which is also said to occur North of Teal Lake is probably a similar indurated Talcose Rock.   Dr. Credner mentions a " Talcose rock, consisting only of fibrous Talc, which forms a kind of soapstone " at the Upper and the Little Be-quenesec Falls (T. 39—R. 30) ; also the occurrence of Laumontite and Quartz in a Talcose Slate at the latter Falls.

Serpentine occurs in tiny films and seams, through an altered Magnesian Dioryte (No. 322), especially at Presqu'isle ; but no good specimens of the pure mineral have been found.

Certain bright green films in this rock were found by T. S. Hunt to contain Chromium, so that Chromite and other allied minerals may yet be found.

Kaolin is very generally distributed in small white masses, having a soapy feel, sometimes in lumps as large as a hen's egg.   It is most abundant in certain Ochre-Schists (No. 244) at the Marquette Mine, etc., imparting to them shiny surfaces and greasy feel, and the association of these layers and seams of aggregated Ochre and Kaolin, with Chloritic Schists at the Lake Superior Mine, suggests that they are probably derived from the decomposition of the latter. It is very commonly distributed in small particles through certain schists (No. 227) and the Silurian Sandstones.   In the latter in-stances the particles often retain a rectangular form, suggesting the fragments of Feldspar from which this mineral has always been derived.

Chlorite is one of the most common minerals, both in the altered Diorytes, and the Gneisses, Schists, etc., already described.   There is no difficulty in obtaining specimens of the pure mineral in bunches made up of tiny scales, associated with Feldspar and Quartz (see Feldspar).   A coarse seam, made up of large blackish-green plates, resembling Chloritoid, was also observed at one locality on the edge of the Granite region, but crystals are very rare and minute.

Calcite (" Calc-Spar ") is mentioned by Foster and Whitney as having been found in good crystals at Presqu'isle and forms abun-dant seams through one rock there (No. 242).

Elsewhere it has been observed only as crusts on calcareous altered Diorytes (near Marquette), on calcareous Chloritic Schist (North shore of Teal Lake), etc.

Dolomite is distributed in flesh-colored rhombs, ¼ to 1 inch in diameter, through some parts of the siliceous Dolomite-Marbles, sometimes contrasting finely with the lighter-colored rock (No. 109).

In other localities small geodes occur, lined with small rhombs of white Dolomite (No. 104).

Siderite ("Spathic Iron") is disseminated in concretionary films through a Limestone already described (No. 101), and also in small bunches in a boulder (No. 189) whose origin is unknown; but not in specimens worthy of notice.

A few specimens, of perhaps other minerals, as yet await identification—one of which bears a resemblance to Vesuvianite (No. 147), while another occurs, in some abundance, near Negaunee, in veins associated with Quartz, Epidote, and crystallized Feldspar.

APPENDIX B.

LITHOLOGY.

BY

T. B. BROOKS AND A. A. JULIEN.

APPENDIX B.

CATALOGUE of the Michigan State Collection of Huronian Rocks and associated ores of the Iron-Region of Lake Superior, numbered 1 to 100.

Duplicate suites have been forwarded to the following institutions and individuals without charge :

University of Michigan, Ann Arbor, Mich.
Michigan State Library, Lansing, Mich.
State Agricultural College, Lansing, Mich.
Hillsdale College, Hillsdale, Mich.
Kalamazoo College, Kalamazoo, Mich.
Adrian College, Adrian, Mich.
Albion College, Albion, Mich.
Olivet College, Olivet, Mich.
Boston Institute of Technology, Boston, Mass.
Harvard University, Cambridge, Mass.
School of Mines, University of Pennsylvania, Philadelphia, Pa.
School of Mines, Columbia College, New York.
Union College, Schenectady, N. Y.
Cornell University, Ithaca, N. Y.
Smithsonian Institute, Washington, D. C.
Sheffield Scientific School, Yale College, New Haven, Conn.
Stevens Institute, Hoboken, N. J.
Washington University, St. Louis, Mo.
The State Cabinet, Madison, Wis.
Royal School of Mines, Stockholm, Sweden.
Royal School of Mines, Freiberg, Saxony.
Museum of Practical Geology, London, England.
United States Military Academy, West Point, N. Y.
Prof. Raphael Pumpelly, Cambridge, Mass.
A. R. Marvin, Esq., Cambridge, Mass.
Alexis A. Julien, Esq., School of Mines, New York.
J. Blodget Britton, Esq., Philadelphia, Pa.
A few suites are still undistributed.

[The following descriptions (except the numbers in Roman numerals of the Huronian formation to which the specimen belongs, the locality, popular or provisional name in brackets, and the approximate specific gravities) are by Mr. Julien ; and the references to specimens by numbers are all to his descriptions contained in Appendix A.   Chap. X., Vol. I., contains analyses of all the ores. Specimens numbered 1, 4, 14, 60, 62, and 82 to 100, both inclusive, are wanting in the suites: these varieties of rock were of least importance for the purposes of this report, and in some instances would have been obtained with great difficulty.   It is believed that Mr. Julien's very minute descriptions, in Appendix A, of specimens from my private collection, identical with those wanting here, will cause their omission not to be seriously felt.—T. B. BROOKS.]

No. 1.—Talcose Quartz-schist.   See No. 150.

No. 2.—Below Formation V.   Martite-Schist, from Clarksburgh. Specific gravity of 5 pieces varied from 4.12 to 4.39; average 4.21. Pseudomorphous after Magnetite.   Rather fine-grained.   Many octahedra, more or less sharply defined.   Slightly magnetic.   Many cavities containing more or less Kaolin.   No distinct lamination.   Resembles No. 239, but differs in its cellular structure and Kaolin.

No. 3.—Below Formation II. or III.   Brownish Chloritic Gneiss, from S. W. ¼ Sect. 30—T. 48—R. 28.   Specific gravity of 5 pieces varied from 2.65 to 2.76; average 2.70.   Feldspar light-brown, and with good cleavage and lustre.   Seams of Chlorite. Lamination not very distinct.   Differs from No. 276 chiefly in the color of Feldspar.

No. 4.—Schalstone.   See No. 338.

No. 5.—Below Formation V.   Fine-grained Hematite-Schist (red specular ore), from West-end Mine, Cascade.   Specific gravity of 8 specimens varied from 4.40 to 4.94 ; average 4.72.   Mostly very fine-grained, with thin bands full of ill-defined octahedra. Slightly magnetic, but more than No. 2.   Structure decidedly schistose, almost slaty.   Little lustre.   A variety of No. 240.

No. 6.—Below Formation V.   Granuliferous Specular-Iron Schist (Bird's-eye ore), from Bagaley Mine, Cascade.   Specific gravity of 6 pieces varied from 3.61 to 3.90; average 3.74.   Chiefly made up of exceedingly minute scales of Micaceous-Iron. Perhaps one-twentieth of its bulk consists of imperfectly crystallized and decomposed Garnets (?), $\frac{1}{32}$ inch in diameter. Allied to No. 237.

No. 7.—Formation IV. Red Feldspathic Gneiss, 100 yards north of West-end Mine, Cascade. Specific gravity of 5 pieces varied from 2.53 to 2.62; average 2.57. Chiefly red cleavable Orthoclase. A very little white Mica. Quartz in parallel flakes. No allies.

No. 8.—Formation V.—Brownish-gray Quartzyte (Lower Quartzyte), Republic Mine. Specific gravity of 5 pieces varied from 2.65 to 2.71; average 2.67. Fine-grained. Quartz, brownish-gray. Many specks of Ochre. Differs from No. 129 only in greater proportion of brownish Ochre.

No. 9.—Formation V.—Mottled Pink Dolomite-Marble (marble), from Chocolate Quarry, L. S. Specific gravity of 4 pieces varied from 2.80 to 3.06; average 2.88. Very fine-grained. Blackish-brown streaks and spots. A Quartz vein. Resembles No. 106, differing in grain.

No. 10.—Formation V.—Mottled Chloritic Schist (clay slate), from Chocolate Quarry, L. S. Specific gravity of 5 pieces varied from 2.73 to 2.81; average 2.77. Blackish-green and light chocolate. Almost slaty. Resembles Nos. 182 and 183 (829), and also No. 192 in its character as a transition from Chloritic Schist to Argillyte.

No. 11.—Formation V.—Salmon-colored Dolomite (marble), Morgan Furnace Quarry. Specific gravity of 8 pieces varied from 2.78 to 2.87; average 2.82. Chiefly made up of the mineral, Dolomite, in large masses, with fine cleavage and lustre. Many fine-grained gray veins. An unusual form of Nos. 108, 109, etc.

No. 12.—Formation V.—Mottled Feldspathic Argillyte (clay slate), from Morgan Furnace Quarry. Specific gravity of 9 pieces from 2.71 to 2.88; average 2.80. Blackish and reddish-brown. Weathers reddish-gray. Like No. 191.

No. 13.—Formation V.—Talcose Siliceous Schist (Novaculite), from Whetstone Quarry, Teal Lake. Specific gravity of 5 pieces varied from 2.71 to 2.78; average 2.73. Ash-gray to brownish-gray on fracture, greenish on cleavage-surface. Like No. 161, but less fissile.

No. 14.—Formation V.—Talco-Siliceous Dolomite, from Lake Fairbanks's Kilns. Like Nos. 110 and 111 (800).

No. 15.—Formation VI.—Magnetic Quartz-Schist, from Republic Mine. Specific gravity of 5 pieces varied from 3.13 to 3.42; average 3.29. Fine-grained. Grayish-black. Quartz, Magnetite, and a chloritic Mica. Resembles the dark layers of Nos. 151 and 153.

No. 16.—Formation VI.—Micaceous-Iron Quartz-Schist, from Cannon, Sect. 28—T. 47—R. 30. Specific gravity of 6 pieces varied from 2.92 to 3.42; average 3.16. Fine-grained. Reddish-gray. Quartz, Micaceous-Iron, and Magnetite. Structure inclining to slaty. Seams covered with Micaceous-Iron. Differs very slightly from Nos. 32 and 33.

No. 17.—Formation VI.—Actinolitic Magnetite-Schist (magnetic ore), from Magnetic Mine, Sect. 20—T. 47—R. 30. Specific gravity of 4 pieces varied from 4.15 to 4.51; average 4.36. Alternate fine-grained and crypto-crystalline laminæ. Thin seams of altered Actinolite. Allied to No. 228, with Actinolite in place of Chlorite.

No. 18.—Formation VII.—Coarse Altered Dioryte, from Republic Mine. Specific gravity of 5 pieces varied from 2.94 to 3.08; average 3.03. Greenish-black, speckled with gray. Semi-porphyritic. Contains a little Chlorite and brown Mica; resembles No. 303.

No. 19.—Formation VIII.—Magnetic Quartz-Schist, from Republic Mine. Specific gravity of 5 pieces varied from 3.46 to 3.57; average 3.51. Fine-grained. Quartz, Magnetite, and perhaps Mica. Almost slaty. Resembles No. 233 in texture and general appearance.

No. 20.—Formation VIII.—Banded Argillyte-Slate (clay slate), from R. R. Cut, E. of Negaunee and Teal Lake. Specific gravity of 5 pieces varied from 2.67 to 2.71; average 2.69. Cleavage across stratification. Like No. 221 (983) in material and texture, and between Nos. 191 and 221 (983) in color.

No. 21.—Formation VIII.—Fine-Grained Greenish Quartzyte, from N. W. end of Lake Fairbanks. Specific gravity of 5 pieces varied from 2.64 to 2.69; average 2.66. Slightly mottled with reddish-brown. Like No. 126, but with grains less distinct.

No. 22.—Formation IX.—Micaceous Altered Dioryte, from Republic Mine. Specific gravity of 5 pieces varied from 2.96 to 3.05 ; average 2.99. Black, speckled with gray. Contains much brownish-gray Mica, especially conspicuous on the weathered surface. Resembles No. 303, but is much more micaceous ; also like No. 18.

No. 23.—Formation X.—Magnetic Quartz-Slate (magnetic schist), from Republic Mine. Specific gravity of 4 pieces varied from 3.73 to 3.86 ; average 3.79. Resembles No. 19. One thin seam occurs, containing many minute Garnets.

No. 24.—Formation X.—Manganiferous Ochrey Hematite. Specific gravity of 5 pieces varied from 3.10 to 3.54 ; average 3.28. Thin seams and bunches of Pyrolusite and Quartz. Tiny bunches of Kaolin.

No. 25.—Formation X.—Disintegrated Ochrey Hematite (Hematite ore), from Rolling Mill Mine, Negaunee. A coarse angular gravel. Minute crystalline scales of Pyrolusite more abundant than in No. 24.

No. 26.—Formation X. Banded Limonitic Quartz-Schist (Foster Rock), from Foster Mine. Specific gravity of 5 pieces varied from 2.80 to 2.99; average 2.88. Grayish-brown Quartzyte with thinner layers of brownish-black Limonite ; allied to No. 156.

No. 27.—Formation X. Brown Anthophyllite-Schist, from Washington Mine. Specific gravity of 5 pieces varied from 3.44 to 3.62 ; average 3.52. Many minute black scales of Magnetite. Banded. Like No. 174.

No. 28.—Formation X. Green Feldspathic Argillyte, from N. W. end of Lake Fairbanks. Specific gravity of 5 pieces varied from 293 to 3.17 ; average 3.08. A crypto-crystalline schist apparently made up of Feldspar, Chlorite, and a little Pyrite. Similar in texture to No. 209, but partly decomposed by weathering.

No. 29.—Formation XI. Black Dioryte-Schist, from Republic Mine. Specific gravity of 5 pieces varied from 2.98 to 3.05 ; average 3.02. No traces of alteration. Decidedly schistose. Allied to Nos. 328 and 329, but their structure is granular, while in this the generally parallel arrangement of the blades of Amphibole produces a fibrous structure.

No. 30.—Formation XI. Coarse Black Dioryte, from Republic Mine. Specific gravity of 4 pieces varied from 2.74 to 3.04 ; average 2.92. Like Nos. 18 and 22. Greenish-black. Few traces of alteration; perhaps a little Chlorite.   Resembles Nos. 303 and 306.

No. 31.—Formation IX.   Black Micaceous Greenstone-Schist, from south of and under Grand Central ore deposit.   Specific gravity of 5 pieces varied from 2.78 to 2.82 ; average 2.79.   Almost aphanitic.   Much Mica in minute scales, which have· a coppery color on the cleavage planes.   A little Chlorite.   Allied to Nos. 335 and 336, but differing especially in finer grain and more irregular structure.

No. 32.—Formation XII.   Micaceous-Iron Quartz-Schist (Jasper), from Republic Mine.   Specific gravity of 4 pieces varied from 3.09 to 3.80; average 3.45.   Very fine-grained.   Grayish-white and smoky Quartz and scales of Micaceous-Iron.   A few thin quartzose layers.   Allied to No. 172, but with coarser and unbroken Quartz-layers.

No. 33.—Formation XII.   Micaceous-Iron Quartz Schist [banded] (Jasper Schist), from Michigamme Mine.   Specific gravity of 5 pieces varied from 3.09 to 3.50 ; average 3.23.   Alternations of layers in which reddish-gray Quartz or Micaceous-Iron predominates.   Exactly like No. 152 to the eye, but the black layers are pseudomorphous after Magnetite.

No. 34.—Formation XII.   Disintegrated Ochrey Hematite (Hematite), from Lake Superior Mine.   A gravel made up of angular fragments of brownish-red Hematite, mostly of the size of peas ; a disintegrated variety of a common earthy Hematite.

No. 35.—Formation XII.   Ochrey Hematite-Schist (Hematite), from Winthrop Mine.   Specific gravity of 4 pieces varied from 2.69 to 3.09 ; average 2.82.   Fracture earthy, and adheres strongly to the tongue.   Cleavage-surfaces shining.   An ordinary variety of Hematite.

No. 36.—Formation XIII.   Micaceous-Iron Quartz-Slate (mixed or 2d class ore), from Republic Mine.   Specific gravity of 5 pieces varied from 3.41 to 3.88 ; average 3.66.   Many scales are triangular.   Like No. 32.

No. 37.—Formation XIII.   Micaceous-Iron Quartz-Schist (2d. class ore), from Lake Superior Mine.   Specific gravity of 5 pieces varied from 3.31 to 3.98 ; average 3.63.   Quartzose layers broken up and irregular.   Large folia of Micaceous-Iron.   Allied to No. 172, but with coarser Quartz-layers.

No. 38.—Formation XIII. Specular-Iron Schist, from Lake Angeline Mine. Specific gravity of 4 pieces varied from 4.47 to 4.96 ; average 4.68. Many minute octahedra. Allied to No. 237.

No. 39.—Formation XIII. Granular Magnetite (magnetic ore), from Republic Mine. Specific gravity of 5 pieces varied from 4.98 to 5.01 ; average 4.99. Grayish-black. Grains nearly as large as mustard-seed. Slightly resembles No. 229, without its structure and fineness of grain.

No. 40.—Formation XIII. Soft Fine-Grained Magnetite (magnetic ore), from Spurr Mountain. Specific gravity of 5 pieces varied from 4.64 to 4.87 ; average 4.74. Brownish-black. Resembles No. 229, but differs in color and structure.

No. 41.—Formation XIII. Hard Fine-Grained Magnetite (magnetic ore), from Michigamme Mine. Specific gravity of 5 pieces varied from 4.72 to 4.97 ; average 4.84. Blackish-brown. Like No. 40.

No. 42.—Formation XIII. Compact Magnetite-Schist (Slate ore), from Edwards Mine. Specific gravity of 4 pieces varied from 4.86 to 4.95 ; average 4.91. Blackish-brown. Much of this ore is crypto-crystalline. A few thin greenish films of Chlorite. Allied to No. 228, but differs chiefly in color and a less slaty structure.

No. 43.—Formation XIII. Chloritic Magnetic Hematite-Schist (Granular green specular ore), from New York Mine. Specific gravity of 4 pieces varied from 4.01 to 4.40 ; average 4.18. Compact like No. 42, and containing more Chlorite. Many minute octahedra. Perhaps schistose. A transition variety between Nos. 228 and 239.

No. 44.—Formation XIII. Kaolinic Hematite-Schist (specular ore), from Cleveland Mine, School-house opening. Specific gravity of 5 pieces varied from 4.54 to 4.69 ; average 4.59. Very fine-grained. Brownish-black, speckled minutely with grayish-white. An ordinary variety, allied to No. 2.

No. 45.—Formation XIII. Specular-Iron Schist (steely specular ore), from Jackson Mine. Specific gravity of 5 pieces varied from 4.87 to 5.23 ; average 5.07. Blackish-brown. Allied to No. 237.

No. 46.—Formation XIII. Micaceous-Iron Schist (specular slate ore), from Republic Mine. Specific gravity of 4 pieces varied from 5.09 to 5.56 ; average 5.24. Structure inclining to slaty. Slightly magnetic. An ordinary variety.

No. 47.—Specular-Iron Schist (specular slate ore), from Jackson Mine. Specific gravity of 4 pieces varied from 5.11 to 5.14; average 5.12. Very fissile, this cleavage crossing the stratification at a high angle. Allied to No. 237.

No. 48.—Granular Specular-Iron Schist (specular slate ore), from Lake Superior Mine. Specific gravity of 5 pieces varied from 4.79 to 5.31; average 5.04. Thin folia approaching Micaceous-Iron. Many tiny granules of red Ochre disseminated throughout, perhaps derived from Martite. Allied to No. 237, but differs in the granules and higher lustre.

No. 49.—Micaceous-Iron Schist (slate ore), from Champion Mine, No. 4 shaft. Specific gravity of 8 pieces varied from 4.42 to 5.00; average 4.70. Tiny scales. Slightly magnetic. Like No. 46.

No. 50.—Formation XIV. Gray Ferruginous Quartzyte (Upper Quartzite), from Republic Mine. Specific gravity of 5 pieces varied from 2.74 to 3.03; average 2.82. Many minute scales of Micaceous-Iron. Differs from No. 21, chiefly in the black scales.

No. 51.—Micaceous Conglomerate-Schist (conglomerate), from Washington Mine. Specific gravity of 5 pieces varied from 2.66 to 2.70; average 2.69. Many films of brownish-gray Mica enveloping nodules of Quartz. Resembles No. 122, but differs in the Mica and its less abundance.

No. 52.—Arenaceous Magnetic Quartz-Schist, from Michigamme Mine. Specific gravity of 4 pieces varied from 2.89 to 3.08; average 2.98. Minute granules of white Quartz and Magnetite. Loosely aggregated bunches of the former. The arenaceous Quartz is like that of No. 358.

No. 53.—Formation XIII. Grayish-green Talc-Schist, from Republic Mine. Specific gravity of 5 pieces varied from 3.00 to 3.30; average 3.09. Chiefly made up of Talc, in minute scales. Differs from No. 226, chiefly in deeper color and greater compactness.

No. 54.—Formation XIII. Brownish magnetic Talc-Schist, from Old Washington Mine. Specific gravity of 5 pieces varied from 2.75 to 2.84; average 2.78. Talc in corrugated folia. A few crystals of Magnetite, and slightly magnetic. Almost slaty. Resembles No. 81, but differs in color and greater coarseness.

No. 55.—Formation XIII. Gray Feldspathic Argillyte, from

Barnum Mine, Hanging Wall. Specific gravity of 5 pieces varied from 2.76 to 2.89; average 2.83. Chiefly Feldspar, less Mica, and a little Magnetite and Pyrite. Slightly magnetic. Somewhat resembles No. 196, but differs in its fibrous films and its Magnetite.

No. 56.—Formation XV. Micaceous Feldspathic Argillyte, from Champion branch R. R. Specific gravity of 4 pieces varied from 2.82 to 2.89; average 2.85. Grayish-black. Much black Mica, in minute scales; partly in brownish-gray films. Resembles Nos. 210 and 213, but without their slaty structure.

No. 57.—Formation XVI. Limonitic Quartz-Schist (Hematite), from South of Champion Kilns. Specific gravity of 5 pieces varied from 2.70 to 3.00; average 2.84. Smoky-gray and yellowish-brown ochrey bands. Compare No. 157.

No. 58.—Formation XVII. Grayish-green Anthophyllite-Schist, from R. R. Cut, Bi-ji-ki River. Specific gravity of 5 pieces varied from 3.04 to 3.34; average 3.15. Contains thin layers coarsely crystallized. Compare No. 178 (1116).

No. 59.—Formation XVII. Anthophyllitic Magnetite-Schist, from Bi-ji-ki River. Specific gravity of 9 pieces varied from 3.16 to 3.60; average 3.39. Black scales of Magnetite. A little Pyrite. Slightly magnetic, and the magnet separates about 40 per cent. from the powdered rock. Allied to No. 178 (1155), but with a much greater proportion of Magnetite.

No. 60.—Dioryte-Greenstone (concretionary), Ely's Point, Marquette.

No. 61.—Formation XIX. Staurolitiferous Mica-Schist (also containing Andalusite), from Island in Michigamme Lake. Like No. 301. Specific gravity of 5 pieces varied from 2.58 to 2.79; average 2.70.

No. 62.—Green Siliceous Schist, like No. 158.

No. 63.—Porphyritic Chlorite-Schist, like No. 186.

No. 64.—Quartzose Carbonaceous Slate (Plumbago), from L'Anse Range, Sect. 9—T. 49—R. 33. Specific gravity of 4 pieces varied from 2.10 to 2.17; average 2.12. Like No. 248.

No. 65.—Pyritiferous Talcose Gneiss, from Falls of Sturgeon River, Sect. 8—T. 39—R. 29. Specific gravity of 4 pieces varied from 2.67 to 2.76; average 2.71. Much grayish-green Talc, in thin seams. A few cubes of Pyrite. Resembles No. 298, but more bunchy in structure.

14

No. 66.—Greenish-gray Fine-Grained Dolomite-Marble, from Sect. 11—T. 39—R. 29. Specific gravity of 5 pieces varied from 2.79 to 2.84; average 2.81. Almost crypto-crystalline in texture. Like No. 105, but a little finer.

No. 67.—Purple Ochrey Hematite (Hematite), Breen Mine Ore. Specific gravity of 5 pieces varied from 3.16 to 3.22; average 3.18. A few indistinct fucoidal impressions. Color reddish-brown, inclining to purple. A common variety, but of unusual color.

No. 68.—Hematite-Schist, from Sect. 11—T. 39—R. 29. Specific gravity of 7 pieces varied from 3.30 to 3.88; average 3.56. Blackish-blue, and almost without lustre. A dull, less fissile variety of No. 237.

No. 69.—Porphyritic Speckled Dioryte, from Sturgeon Falls, Menominee River. Specific gravity of 9 pieces varied from 2.92 to 3.03; average 2.98. Fibrous blades of brownish-green Amphibole, about ⅛ inch long, and white compact Feldspar; making a fine contrast. Has no allies.

No. 70.—Chloritic Aphanyte-Schist, from M. and O. Road (Gorge). Specific gravity of 9 pieces varied from 2.94 to 3.07; average 2.98. Perhaps derived from the alteration of a Dioryte. Thin seams of brown Mica. Resembles No. 339, but is more decidedly chloritic.

No. 71.—Quartzose Chloritic Dioryte (Conglomeritic Diorite), from 20th mile-post, M. H. & O. Road. Specific gravity of 5 pieces varied from 2.90 to 2.93, average 2.91. Imperfect crystals of greenish-black Amphibole, with a high lustre. Much Chlorite in scales and films. Slightly resembles Nos. 305 and 308.

No. 72.—Speckled Dioryte, from Marquette Greenstone Quarry. Specific gravity of 5 pieces varied from 2.70 to 3.00; average 2.87. Finer-grained than No. 75, and with more alteration in its two constituents. Resembles No. 309.

No. 73.—Chlorite-Potstone Schist, from Marquette Greenstone Quarry. Specific gravity of 5 pieces varied from 2.53 to 2.68; average 2.60. Much Calcite disseminated, especially in seams and bunches. An intermediate variety between Nos. 340 and 341, consisting chiefly of the fine-grained material of the former, enveloped in broad films of Chlorite.

No. 74.—White Talcose Slate, from Grace Furnace, Marquette. Specific gravity of 5 pieces varied from 2.60 to 2.64; average 2.62.

Very fissile. Thin flakes of Quartz, separated by films of whitish Talc. No allies.

No. 75.—Blackish-green Dioryte, from Light-House Point Quarry, S. E. side. Specific gravity of 8 pieces varied from 2.96 to 3.08 ; average 3.03. A little Epidote in thin seams. Feldspar greenish-gray, partly altered to a reddish-orange. Somewhat resembles No. 303.

No. 76.—Quartzose Chlorite-Schist, from Light-House Point Quarry, N. W. side, Marquette. Specific gravity of 5 pieces varied from 2.92 to 3.03 ; average 2.96. Greenish-black Chlorite in continuous films. Almost a slaty structure. Seams of Quartz and of Calcite. Only slightly resembles No. 182.

No. 77.—Porphyritic Mottled Dioryte, from Pic-Nic Rocks, Marquette. Specific gravity of 10 specimens varied from 2.82 to 3.00 ; average 2.90. Constituent minerals unchanged on the weathered surface. Same as No. 317.

No. 78.—Magnesian Altered Dioryte (Serpentine), from Presqu'-isle, Lake Superior, N. E. corner. Specific gravity of 8 pieces varied from 2.80 to 2.92 ; average 2.86. Many facets of altered Amphibole conspicuous. Resembles No. 321, but is a little less altered.

No. 79.—("Trap"), from Washington Mine. Specific gravity of 5 pieces varied from 2.85 to 3.01 ; average 2.93. Much Pyrite. May be a variety of the Aphanyte, Nos. 354 and 355, but much coarser.

No. 80.—Reddish Chloritic Gneiss. Weathers to yellowish-gray, slightly greenish and reddish. Resembles No. 276.

No. 81.—Bluish-black Argillyte-Slate (clay slate), from Huron Bay.

No. 82.—Trappean Dioryte. (Nos. 347, 348, and 349.)

No. 83.—Green Porphyry. (No. 351.)

No. 84.—Jasper-Schist. (Nos. 166 and 167.)

No. 85.—Jasper-Breccia. (Nos. 124 and 125.)

No. 86.—Talcy Chloritic Gneiss. (Nos. 298 and 299.)

No. 87.—Hornblende-Gneiss. (Nos. 261 and 262.)

No. 88.—Hornblende-Schist. (No. 271.)

No. 89.—Pseudomorphous Chlorite-Schist. (Nos. 179, 180, and 181.)

No. 90.—Black Gneiss. (No. 257.)

No. 91.—Chloritic Argillyte. (No. 219.)

No. 92.—Chloritic Dioryte.　(No. 324.)

No. 93.—Epidotic Hornblende-Gneiss.　(No. 268.)

No. 94.—Black Dioryte-Aphanyte (" Trap ").　(Nos. 354, 355, and 356.)

No. 95.—Coarse Red Granite.　(No. 252.)

No. 96.—Ferruginous Granite.　(No. 253.)

No. 97.—Ferruginous Crystalline Limestone.　(No. 101.)

No. 98.—Chloritic Dioryte-Wacké.　(No. 325.)

No. 99.—Brown Wacké.　(No. 352.)

No. 100.—Coarse Green Amphibolyte.　(No. 319.)

APPENDIX C.

LITHOLOGY.

BY

CHAS. E. WRIGHT.

APPENDIX C.

Specimen No. 1001 (Freiberg determination). — Dark-green Diorite, compact and fine-grained, containing considerable chlorite or decomposed hornblende. The feldspar shows under the microscope the striation of the twin crystals. On a fresh fracture may be readily seen several small white spots, owing probably to the decomposition of a lime feldspar. It contains a very little magnetic ore and pyrites as accessory minerals. Hardness = 4. Streak powder very pale green. Spec. gr. = 2.78.—Formation XI.—Location, Pioneer Quarry, Jackson Mine.—Provisional name employed in body of Report, Chloritic Schist.

Sp. No. 1002 (Freiberg determination).—Grayish-green Diorite, fine-grained, and containing less chlorite than No. 1001, but has more cleavage, which is very distinct in two directions. The hornblende in a section of the rock under the microscope appears of a leek-green color, and possesses the dichromatic property only in a slight degree. The feldspar is partially decomposed. Some of the feldspar crystals are tinged with red. The specimen contains a little iron pyrites and magnetic ore. Hardness = 4.—Streak powder light-green or yellow.—Sp. gr. = 2.68.—Formation XI.—Location, Pioneer Quarry, Jackson Mine.—Provisional name in body of Report, Dioritic Schist.

Sp. No. 1003 (Freiberg determination).—Compact Diorite, very similar to No. 1002. Color grayish-green. The crystals are more distinct than in No. 1002. The hornblende is slightly dichromatic. The feldspar is somewhat decomposed. On a fresh fracture can be seen several yellow spots of ochreous iron ore. Magnetic iron ore and chlorite are contained as accessories. Hardness = 5. Streak powder very pale green. Spec. gr. = 2.82.—Formation XI.—Location, South of West part of Jackson Mine.—Provisional name in Report, Hornblendic Diorite.

Sp. No. 1004.—Dark-green Diorite. Very fine-grained and compact. In a section under the microscope can be seen crystals of feldspar and hornblende. Some of the feldspar crystals show the striation plainly and are probably labradorite. Chlorite and magnetic ore are contained as accessories. Hardness = 4.5. Streak powder pale green. Spec. gr. = 2.85.—Formation XI.—Location, South of West part of Jackson Mine.—Provisional name in Report, Hornblendic Diorite.

Sp. No. 1005.—Dark-green Chloritic Diorite Schist. The texture is so fine that the single ingredients cannot be seen even with a loupe. A section under the microscope shows an apparent semi-fluid structure, with a broken and deranged appearance. With a power of 100 diameters no crystals can be seen. Certain portions of the light-green amphibolitic mineral not only possess the property of polarizing the light, but are also dichromatic. It contains a little magnetic ore and pyrites. Hardness = 3.5. Streak powder pale green. Spec. gr. = 2.68.—Formation XI.—Location, South-west part of Jackson Mine.—Provisional name used in Report, Chloritic Schist.

Sp. No. 1006.—Fine-grained Dioritic Schist. Partially decomposed and contains considerable chlorite and clay. Hardness = 3. Streak powder light-green. Spec. gr. = 2.82.—Formation XI.—Location, South-west part of Jackson Mine.—Provisional name in body of Report, Chloritic Schist.

Sp. No. 1007.—Grayish-green Diorite. On a fresh fracture the cleavage planes of the hornblende may be seen. The grains or crystals of the feldspar are too small to be recognized even with a good loupe. Examined under microscope striated feldspar can be seen. The hornblende possesses the dichromatic property very distinctly. The rock contains a few crystals of actinolite and grains of magnetic ore. Hardness = 5. Streak powder pale yellow. Spec. gr. = 3.—Formation XI.—Location, N. E. corner Sect. 1—T. 47—R. 27, or N. W. corner Sect. 6—T. 47—R. 26.—Provisional name used in Report, Diorite.

Sp. No. 1008.—Dark-green Diorite. The cleavage planes of the hornblende can be seen with the unaided eye. On a weathered surface the feldspar is very much decomposed and worn away, leaving the crystals of the hornblende very prominent. Under the microscope it may be readily seen that the percentage of the amphibole exceeds that of the feldspar. Needles of actinolite are disseminated through the rock. It contains a few crystals of magnetic ore and pyrites. Hardness = 4.5. Streak powder greenish-white. Spec. gr. = 2.91.—Formation XI.—Location, N. E. corner Sect. 1—T. 47—R. 27, or N. W. corner Sect. 6—T. 47—R. 26.—Provisional name used in Report, Diorite.

Sp. 1009.—Fine-Grained Diorite. Color grayish-green. This is a tough rock, in which the single minerals are not visible to the naked eye. A weathered surface shows but little decomposition of the feldspar. With the microscope the amphibole and feldspar appear to be about equally divided. The accessory minerals are pyrites and magnetic ore. Hardness = 5. Streak powder nearly

white.   Spec. gr. = 2.90.—Formation XI.—Location, N. E. corner
Sect. 1—T. 47—R. 27, or N. W. corner Sect. 6—T. 47—R. 26.—
Provisional name used in Report, Diorite.

Sp. No. 1010.—Same as 1009, except specific gravity, which is
2.77.—Formation XI.—Location N.W. ¼ of N.W. ¼ Sect. 7—T.
47—R. 26.—Provisional name used in Report, Diorite.

Sp. No. 1011.—Aphanite or very fine-grained Diorite.   The
texture resembles a compact, dark-colored limestone.   Under the
microscope a power of 100 diameters is hardly sufficient to resolve
the apparently homogeneous ground mass, but with a power of 400
diameters the amphibole is seen to consist of hornblende in broken
crystals, and small needles of actinolite, that are closely interwoven
through the entire rock, giving it a grayish-green color.   Hardness = 5.   Streak nearly white.   Spec. gr. = 2.90.—Formation XI.
—Location, N. W. ¼ of N. W. ¼ of Sect. 7—T. 47—R. 26.—
Provisional name used in Report, Diorite (compact).

Sp. No. 1012.—Grayish Diorite.   Having an open texture with
dark-green spots, resembling very much a Diabase.   Under the
microscope can be seen crystals of a double striated feldspar, very
similar to labradorite; also sections of crystals corresponding to
augite.   This would seem to confirm the supposition of its being a
Diabase: the unmistakable dichroism of the hornblende deter-
mines it as a Diorite.   It is possible that a Diabase may be found
either above or below this.   As accessories may be considered (augite, labradorite) magnetic ore and pyrites.   Hardness = 5.   Streak
nearly white.   Spec. gr. = 3.00.—Formation XI.—Location, N.W.
¼ of N. W. ¼ Sect. 7—T. 47—R. 26.—Provisional name used in
Report, Diorite.

Sp. No. 1013.—Dark-green Diorite.   The cleavage planes of the
hornblende are quite distinct.   Under the microscope the hornblende and feldspar appear to be about equally divided.   The crystals of hornblende are checked or striated parallel to the principal
axis.   Dr. Zirkel, in his work on Basaltic Rock, 1870, considers
this one of the best characteristics for hornblende in distinguishing
it from augite.   Striated crystals of hornblende appear to possess a

stronger dichromatic power than plain ones. The feldspar shows no striation. It contains a very little pyrites. Hardness = 5.5. Streak powder pale green. Spec. gr. = 2.91.—Formation XI.—Location, N. W. ¼ of N. W. ¼ Sect. 7—T. 47—R. 26.—Provisional name used in Report, Diorite.

Sp. No. 1014.—Light-green Diorite. Under the microscope the crystals of hornblende and feldspar are very indistinct. The hornblende is very light-colored and is but slightly dichromatic. It contains as accessories chlorite and magnetic ore. Hardness = 5.5. Streak powder nearly white. Spec. gr. = 2.81.—Formation IX.—Location, N.W.¼ of N. W. ¼ of Sect. 7—T. 47—R. 26.—Provisional name used in Report, Diorite.

Sp. No. 1015.—Chloritic Schist. This is a very dark-green colored specimen, composed principally of chlorite, feldspar and hornblende. With the microscope can be detected a few grains of quartz, and leaves of mica. Hardness = 4. Streak pale-green. Spec. gr. = 2.68.—Formation XI.—Location, Pioneer Quarry, E. of Negaunee, Sect. 6—T. 47—R. 26.—Provisional name used in Report, Chloritic Schist.

Sp. No. 1016.—Grayish-green Diorite or Dioritic Schist. Under the microscope it appears very similar to No. 1004. Hardness = 4.5. Streak powder pale-green. Spec. gr. = 2.82.—Formation XI.—Location, Pioneer Quarry, E. of Negaunee, Sect. 6—T. 47—R. 26.—Provisional name used in Report, Diorite.

Sp. No. 1017.—Aphanite. Color dark-green. Somewhat decomposed. Under the microscope the amphibole is seen to consist of actinolite. It contains considerable magnetic ore and a small percentage of mica. There are several narrow seams in the section filled with actinolite and feldspar. Hardness = 5. Streak powder yellow to brown. Spec. gr. = 3.15.—Formation XI.—Location from South of New England Mine, N. E. ¼ Sect. 20—T. 47—R. 27.—Provisional name used in Report, Compact Diorite.

Sp. No. 1018.—Diorite with Mica. Very dark-green specimen. The rock shows but little signs of decomposition. The cleavage planes of the hornblende are very distinct. Under the microscope it can be seen that the percentage of the hornblende exceeds that of the feldspar. The hornblende is strongly dichromatic. The mica is of a brownish-yellow color and is dichromatic. As accessories may be counted magnetic ore and pyrites. Hardness = 5.5. Streak powder light-green. Spec. gr. = 3.09.—Location, S. E. ¼ Sect. 15—T. 47—R. 28.—Provisional name used in Report, Hornblendic Diorite.

Sp. No. 1019.—Gneiss with Micaceous Diorite. Color dark gray. Contains orthoclase and a white feldspar resembling albite. The amphibole under the microscope has a deep-green color and the mica a yellowish-brown; both are dichromatic. There is a very little quartz and decomposed iron ore in the section. Hardness = 5. Streak gray. Spec. gr. = 2.74.—Location, N. W. ¼ of Sect. 15—T. 47—R. 28.—Provisional name used in Report, Dioritic Schist.

Sp. No. 1020.—Gneiss and Amphibole Rock. Color a dark green. It shows no signs of decomposition. Under the microscope it can be seen that the percentage of the amphibole (hornblende and actinolite) exceeds that of all the other minerals. The feldspar shows no striation. The amphibole is strongly dichromatic. The mica is very distinct. It contains magnetic ore and pyrites. Hardness = 5.5. Streak powder pale green. Spec. gr. = 3.00.—Location, N. E. of Old Michigan Mine, near N. W. corner Sect. 18—T. 47—R. 28.—Provisional name used in Report, Hornblendic Diorite.

Sp. No. 1021.—Gneiss with Hornblende Rock. Resembles No. 1020. Under the microscope the mica appears to be finely divided and evenly distributed. The hornblende possesses the dichromatic property in a remarkable degree, changing from a deep green to pale yellow. The hornblende, quartz and mica are contained nearly in the same proportion. It contains, as an accessory, magnetic ore. Hardness = 6. Streak powder pale green. Spec. gr. = 3.03.—Formation IX.—Location, Washington Mine.—Provisional name used in Report, Diorite (dark green).

Sp. No. 1022.—Hornblendic Gneiss with Mica, very similar to 1021, only the mica is more grouped together and in large leaves. It contains small crystals of magnetic ore, that are clustered together. Hardness = 5.5. Streak nearly colorless. Spec. gr. = 3.04.— Formation XI.—Location, Southward of Old Washington Mine.— Provisional name used in Report, Chloritic Schist.

Sp. No. 1023.—Changed Gneiss. A gray rock, containing a little chlorite. The actinolite has changed to a pale yellow color, but is still dichromatic. The magnetic ore does not appear to have decomposed, as the white ground mass surrounding the grains of ore is not stained or tinted. Hardness = 4. Streak powder gray. Spec. gr. = 2.83.—Location, near N. and S. Centre line Sect. 1—T. 47—R. 29.—Provisional name used in Report, Dioritic Schist (spotted).

Sp. No. 1024.—Diorite. Compact and fine-grained. Somewhat decomposed. The two varieties of amphibole (hornblende and actinolite) are very evenly distributed through the section. The needles or spikes of the actinolite are very small. There are several crystals of calcite which in the polarized light appear very similar to a triclinic feldspar. Hardness = 4. Streak powder white. Spec. gr. = 2.63.—Location, E. side of Sect. 13—T. 47—R. 28. —Provisional name used in Report, Diorite (conglomeritic).

Sp. No. 1025.—Calcareous Diabase or Diorite. The crystals of calcite are quite large and easily distinguished. On a fresh fracture can be seen a black mineral, which is about the hardness of calcite (3) and resembles hornblende or augite. It possesses no visible cleavage and is probably a decomposition. Under the microscope the calcite, as in 1024, resembles labradorite. The black mineral in the section has a pale green color. With the prisms turned at right angles, the black mineral gives a dark field. What is interesting is, that the mineral is slightly dichromatic. On a weathered surface the calcite is decomposed and washed out, leaving the rock very porous. Hardness = 5.5. Streak powder gray. Spec. gr. = 2.70.—Location, N. E. ¼ of N. E. ¼ of Sect. 14—T. 47—R. 28.—Provisional name used in Report, Dioritic Rock (amygdaloidal).

Sp. No. 1026.—Fine-grained Chloritic Schist.   Contains considerable mica.   On a fresh fracture the glistening specks of mica can be readily distinguished from the dark green chlorite.   Under the microscope the small grains of quartz are rendered very distinct. It contains a few crystals of magnetic ore, also needles of actinolite. Hardness = 3.   Streak powder light green.   Spec. gr. = 2.93.— Formation XI.—Location, Lot 4—Sect. 20—T. 28—R. 30.—Provisional name used in Report, Chloritic Schist.

Sp. No. 1027.—Dark-gray Anthophyllite Rock, or Quartzite containing anthophyllite.   It has a distinct parallel cleavage.   The anthophyllite is unevenly distributed through the section in seams, and is nondichromatic, which distinguishes it from actinolite.   The quartz consists of small grains ($\frac{1}{20}$ millm.).   It contains minute crystals of magnetic ore (less than $\frac{1}{100}$ millm. in diameter).   Hardness = 4–7.   Streak powder white.   Spec. gr. = 3.21.—Formation XII.—Location, Lot 5—Sect. 20—T. 48—R. 30.—Provisional name used in Report, Anthophyllitic Schist.

Sp. No. 1028.—Fine-grained Chloritic Schist.   Color dark-green, similar in appearance to 1026.   In a section can be seen considerable Amphibole.   It contains less Mica than 1026.   Hardness = 4.   Streak light-green.   Spec. gr. = 2.84.—Location, Lot 5 —Sect. 21—T. 48—R. 30.—Provisional name in Report, Chloritic Schist.

Sp. No. 1029.—Light-gray Quartzite or Granulite-like rock.   The grains of quartz are small.   The gray color is caused by hornblende, which, in a section under the microscope, resembles fine moss. This is probably a metamorphic rock.   Hardness = 7.   Spec. gr. = 2.67.—Formation L.—Location between Sects. 20 and 21—T. 48— R. 30.—Provisional name used in Report, Quartzose Gneiss.

Sp. No. 1030.—Fine-grained Gray Chloritic Schist.   The grains of quartz are small.   The chlorite is very evenly distributed through the section.   It contains a few broken crystals of hornblende. Hardness = 6.   Streak gray.   Spec. gr. = 2.64.—Formation XIX.— Location, Lot 7—Sect. 30—T. 48—R. 30.—Provisional name used in the Report, Quartzose Mica Schist.

Sp. No. 1031.—Coarse-grained Hornblende Gangue Rock. The cleavage planes of the hornblende can be easily recognized with the naked eye. By using only the upper prism and revolving it, some of the hornblende crystals change from white to yellow. It contains considerable chlorite, also a few leaves of mica and several minute crystals of magnetic ore, that average less than $\frac{1}{100}$ of a millm. in diameter. Hardness = 4. Streak powder greenish-black. Spec. gr. = 3.10.—Formation XIX.—Location, Lot 7—Sect. 30—T. 48—R. 30.—Provisional name used in Report, Mica Schist (with seams of black hornblende).

Sp. No. 1032.—Anthophyllitic Schist and Magnetic Ore. The rock on a fresh fracture has a dark-gray color, with several yellow spots. The acicular crystals of anthophyllite are woven together, forming a reticulated mass. Some of the grains or crystals of the magnetic ore are nearly a millimeter in diameter, while others in the section can scarcely be seen with a power of 100 diameters. Hardness = 6. Streak brown. Spec. gr. = 3.27.—Formation XVII.—Location, Lot 3—Sect. 30—T. 48—R. 30.—Provisional name used in Report, Anthophyllitic Schist.

Sp. No. 1033.—Anthophyllitic Schist and Magnetic Iron Ore. Very similar to 1032. The anthophyllite is more or less colored yellow. Hardness = 6. Streak powder brown. Spec. gr. = 3.33. —Formation XI.—Location, Lot 3—Sect. 30—T. 48—R. 30.—Provisional name used in Report, Quartzose Anthophyllitic Schist.

Sp. No. 1034.—Magnetic Ore, with Quartz, Actinolite and Chlorite. The specimen is very friable. Some portions of it consist nearly of pure silica that resemble a freestone, and is cut in different directions by thin seams filled with magnetic ore. The actinolite has a brown color and the chlorite in the section a deep green. The magnetic ore constitutes nearly one-half the entire rock. Hardness = 5—7. Streak black. Spec. gr. = 3.34.—Formation XIII. —Location, Lot 4—Sect. 20—T. 48—R. 30.—Provisional name used in Report, Quartzose Magnetic Schist (banded).

Sp. No. 1035.—Specular Iron Ore and Quartz.—Formation XII.— Lot 4—Sect. 20—T. 48—R. 30.—Provisional name in Report, Specular Quartz Schist.

Sp. No. 1036.—Compact Chloritic Argillaceous Schist. Color black. The texture is so fine that the single ingredients cannot be seen even with a loupe. Cut with a knife, it leaves a black shining surface. Before the blowpipe in the oxydation flame a small chip of it changes to a grayish-white, which is probably due to a small percentage of carbon. Hardness = 3.5. Streak powder dark-gray. Spec. gr. = 2.73.—Formation XV.—Location near centre Sect. 27 —T. 48—R. 30.—Provisional name used in Report, Argillite (carbonaceous).

Sp. No. 1037.—Dark-gray Anthophyllitic Schist. Containing magnetic and an ochreous brown iron ore. In a thin section under the microscope, the anthophyllite has a brown color, and certain portions of it are gray. Hardness = 4. Streak grayish. Spec. gr. = 3.16.—Formation XVII.—Location near centre N. W. ¼ Sect. 25—R. 30.—Provisional name used in Report, Anthophyllitic Schist.

Sp. No. 1038.—Grayish-green Chloritic Schist. Compact and fine-grained. Under the microscope can be seen several parallel seams of quartz, also a few crystals of hornblende. Hardness = 5. Streak powder gray. Spec. gr. = 2.67.—Formation VIII (?).— Location, S. W. ¼ of S. W. ¼ of Sect. 34—T. 48—R. 28.—Provisional name in Report, Dioritic Schist (feldspathic).

Sp. No. 1039.—Fine-grained Argillaceous Schist. Color greenish. It has a slaty structure and a very distinct parallel cleavage. In a thin section a few fragments of hornblende can be seen. It contains very evenly distributed considerable chlorite. Hardness = 3. Streak pale yellow. Spec. gr. = 2.85.—Formation VII.— Location, N. E. ¼ of N. E. ¼ of Sect. 4—T. 47—R. 28.—Provisional name used in Report, Clay Slate (greenish).

Sp. No. 1040.—Jaspery-brown Iron Ore. The specimen has a banded structure. The brown iron varies in color from a brownish-red to a dirty yellow (ochreous). The grains of quartz under the microscope are very small ($\frac{1}{20}$ millim.). A section taken across the lamination resembles silicified wood. Hardness = 5-7. Streak yellow. Spec. gr. = 3.15.—Formation VI.—Location, N. E. ¼ of

N. E. ¼ of Sect. 4—T. 47—R. 28.—Provisional name used in Report, Limonitic Quartz Schist.

Sp. No. 1041.—Light-gray Quartzite. In a section under the microscope with a power of 100 diameters can be seen several acicular crystals, resembling actinolite. The gray color of the specimen is due to this actinolite-like mineral. It contains an occasional crystal of garnet. Hardness=6.5. Spec. gr.=2.66.—Formation V.—Location, S. E. ¼ of N. E. ¼ of Sect. 4—T. 47—R. 28.—Provisional name in Report, Gray Quartzite.

Sp. No. 1042.—Dark-gray Quartzite. With the microscope can be seen a little hornblende and chlorite. The grains of quartz are smaller than in 1041. Hardness=7. Spec. gr.=2.74.—Formation V.—Location, S. E. ¼ of N. E. ¼ of Sect. 4—T. 47—R. 28.—Provisional name used in Report, Feldspathic Diorite Rock (compact).

Sp. No. 1043.—Decomposed Diorite and Magnetic Ore. The specimen has a grayish-green color. It contains a little chlorite and clay. On a fresh fracture the crystals or grains of magnetic ore can be easily distinguished. Under the microscope the rock appears to have a semifluid structure. The crystals of feldspar are quite large, some of them are bent, while others are broken. Fragments of hornblende are scattered through the section. Hardness=3. Streak powder green to black. Spec. gr.=3.12.—Formation XIII.—Location, Washington Mine.—Provisional name used in Report, Steatitic Schist (with grains of Magnetite).

Sp. No. 1044.—Coarse Granular Magnetic Ore. The crystals of magnetite can be seen with a good loupe. It contains a little quartz and chlorite. Hardness=5.5. Streak black. Spec. gr.=4.28.—Formation XII.—Location, Washington Mine.—Provisional name used in Report, Magnetic Iron Ore.

Sp. No. 1045.—Micaceous Specular Iron Ore and Quartz. The parallel layers of ore and quartz are uneven, thereby giving to the specimen a wavy or corrugated structure, resembling some varieties of gneiss. It contains several small crystals of garnet and

15

magnetic ore. Hardness=6.5. Streak red. Spec. gr.=3.86.—Formation XII.—Location, S. W. of Old Washington Mine.—Provisional name, Specular Quartz Schist.

Sp. No. 1047.—Brownish-gray Diorite. The surface of a fresh fracture appears to be spotted. Some of the grains of feldspar are colored a pale red. The amphibole is a dark-green. In the section can be seen small crystals of magnetic ore. It contains a very little chlorite. Hardness=5. Streak yellowish-brown. Spec. gr.= 2.79.—Formation XIII.—Location, Washington Mine.—Provisional name, Chloritic Rock.

Sp. No. 1048.—Dark-green or bluish-gray Actinolite Rock, with garnets. On a fresh fracture the red garnets set in the dark-green actinolite give the surface a very pretty appearance. With the microscope can be seen several small grains of quartz; also particles of specular and magnetic iron-ore. Hardness=5.5. Streak brownish-red. Spec. gr.=3.21.—Formation XII.—Location, Washington Mine.—Provisional name used in Report, Hematitic Quartzose Schist (garnets).

Sp. No. 1049.—Diorite. The cleavage planes of the hornblende can be readily distinguished. The feldspar is somewhat decomposed. In a section under the microscope can be seen clusters of magnetic or specular iron-ore crystals; also a few grains of quartz. Hardness=5.5. Streak powder grayish. Spec. gr.=3.18.—Formation XIII.—Location, Washington Mine.—Provisional name in Report, Hornblendic Rock.

Sp. No. 1050.—Fine-grained Specular Iron Ore. The specimen has a bright glistening appearance and is inclined to a micaceous structure. It is somewhat friable. Contains magnetic ore and quartz. Hardness=3. Streak brownish-red. Spec. gr.=4.51. —Formation XIII.—Location, Washington Mine.—Provisional name, Specular Slate Ore.

Sp. No. 1051. (Missing).—Formation XIII.—Location, Washington Mine.—Provisional name used in Report, Talcose Schist (micaceous).

Sp. No. 1052.—Dark-green Chloritic Schist. It contains a large percentage of quartz. The grains of quartz are very small. In a section can be seen several crystals and particles of specular ore ; also a few crystals of garnet. Hardness=4. Streak brownish-red. Spec. gr.=2.87.—Location, Washington Mine.—Provisional name, Quartzose Schist (with argillite).

Sp. No. 1053.—Chloritic Argillaceous Brown Iron Ore. This is probably a decomposed Diorite. Hardness=2. Streak brownish-yellow. Spec. gr.=2.77.—Formation XIII.—Location, Washington Mine.—Provisional name, Chloritic dyke material.

Sp. No. 1054.—Magnetic Ore. The grains or crystals of the ore can be seen with the naked eye. Hardness=5–6. Streak black. Spec. gr.=4.83.—Formation XIII.—Location, Washington Mine.—Provisional name used in Report, Granular Magnetic Ore.

Sp. No. 1055.—Decomposed Dioritic Schist. Contains chlorite, talc, clay, and magnetic iron ore. Under the microscope a section shows an apparent semifluid structure, and while in this state it is very evident that a flowing movement has taken place. Shred-like or skeleton crystals of hornblende are scattered through the entire section. There cannot be seen even an outline of a feldspar crystal ; only fragments remain, that may be recognized in the polarized light. The grains of magnetic and specular ore are grouped together. It contains a few slender crystals of epidote. Hardness =4.5. Streak brown. Spec. gr.=3.13.—Location, Washington Mine.—Provisional name in Report, Chloritic Schist.

Sp. No. 1056.—Dark-gray Quartzite. Contains magnetic ore, pyrites, hornblende, and chlorite. The grains of quartz are small. The pentagonal dodecahedron crystals of pyrites are unevenly distributed. The crystals of magnetic ore are very minute, none of them exceeding $\frac{1}{20}$ of a millm. in diameter. The percentage of hornblende and chlorite is small. Hardness=6.5. Streak green to black. Spec. gr.=2.66–3.30.—Formation XIII.—Location, Washington Mine.—Provisional name in Report, Quartzite (pyritiferous dyke material).

Sp. No. 1057.—Anthophyllite Schist. Contains magnetic iron ore and quartz. A section under the microscope shows a reticulated structure. Certain portions of the anthophyllite are colored brownish-yellow. Hardness=5. Streak pale yellow to black. Spec. gr.=3.52.—Formation X.—Location, Washington Mine.— Provisional name used in Report, Micaceous Ferruginous Schist.

Sp. No. 1058.— Anthophyllite Schist and Quartz. The ingredients are unevenly distributed. There are several red seams in the rock composed of quartz, anthophyllite and hematite ore. In a section can be seen crystals of garnet and magnetic ore. Hardness=5–7. Streak reddish. Spec. gr.=3.00.—Formation X.— Location, Washington Mine.—Provisional name used in Report, Micaceous Ferruginous Schist.

Sp. No. 1059.—Black Magnetic Iron Ore. Contains silica and a little chlorite, also a trace of manganese. Granular and easily friable. Hardness=5.5. Streak black. Spec. gr.=4.70.—Formation XIII.—Location, N. W. ¼ of S. W. ¼ of Sect. 24—T. 48—R. 31. —Provisional name in Report, Granular Magnetic Ore.

Sp. No. 1060.— Specular Ore. The specimen possesses two interesting characteristics, that is, portions of the specular are crystallized in octahedrons, which are slightly magnetic. Hardness=6. Streak brownish-red. Spec. gr.=4.92.—Formation XIII.—Location, New York Mine.—Provisional name in Report, Octahedral Specular Ore (Martite).

Sp. No. 1061.—Anthophyllite and Magnetic Ore Schist. This is a very fine-grained slaty-looking specimen. In a section under the microscope the ingredients appear to be about equally divided. Hardness=6. Streak powder black. Spec. gr.=4.46.—Formation X.—Location, South of the New England Mine.—Provisional name used in the Report, Banded Magnetic Schist.

Sp. No. 1062.—Actinolite Schist. Very fine-grained and has a blackish-green color. Some portions of the rock are partially decomposed. Contains a little magnetic ore. Hardness=5. Streak dirty green. Spec. gr. $=3.14$.—Formation XI.—Location, South of New England Mine.—Provisional name used in Report, Chloritic Rock.

Sp. No. 1063.—Actinolite and Hornblende Schist. Very similar to 1062. It has a brownish-green color and is more decomposed than specimen 1062. Contains a little pyrites. Hardness$=3.5$. Streak yellowish-green. Spec. gr. $=3.05$.—Formation XI.—Location, South of New England Mine.—Provisional name in Report, Chloritic Rock.

Sp. No. 1064.—Quartz and Specular Ore. This is a very fine-grained, reddish-bluish-gray specimen, filled with small cavities, that are beautifully studded with crystals of quartz, garnet, and specular ore. The percentage of quartz and specular ore appears to be about the same. Hardness$=6$. Streak red. Spec. gr. $=3.80$. —Formation XII.—Location, New England Mine.—Provisional name used in Report, Hematitic Quartzose Schist.

Sp. No. 1065.—(Missing). Formation XII.—Location, New England Mine.—Provisional name used in Report, Ferruginous Quartz Schist.

Sp. No. 1066.—Same as Specimen No. 1064.—Formation XII. —Location, New England Mine.—Provisional name used in Report, Quartzose Red Hematite Schist.

Sp. No. 1067.—Decomposed Specular Ore. Contains clay. Hardness$=2$–5.5. Streak blood-red. Spec. gr. $=4.34$.—Formation —.—Location, New England Mine.—Provisional name used in Report, earthy Hematite.

Sp. No. 1068.—Argillaceous Chloritic Schist. Very compact and has a dark-gray color. With a good loupe can be seen on a fresh fracture small crystals of iron pyrites. Under the microscope, using polarized light, can be seen a few fragments of hornblende. Hardness$=4$. Spec. gr. $=2.95$.—Formation XII.—Location, New England Mine.—Provisional name, Chloritic Schist.

Sp. No. 1069.—Hematite Ore and Quartz. The specimen is somewhat decomposed and contains parallel seams of ochreous iron ore. There can be plainly seen white specks of a hydrous silicate of alumina—" Kaolinite." Hardness=2–6.5. Streak red to yellow. Spec. gr.=3.20.—Formation XII.—Location, New England Mine.—Provisional name used in Report, Quartzose Limonitic Schist.

Sp. No. 1070.—Hematite Ore. Somewhat decomposed. Contains fine grains of quartz and a little clay. Hardness=4. Streak yellowish-red. Spec. gr.=3.24.—Formation XIII.—Location, New England Mine.—Provisional name, Hematitic Chloritic Schist.

Sp. No. 1071.—Specular Ore, containing grains of magnetic ore. It has a bluish-black color and submetallic lustre. It contains a little silica. Hardness=6. Streak brownish-red. Spec. gr.= 4.46.—Formation XIII.—Location, New England Mine.—Provisional name used in Report, Jaspery Specular Ore.

Sp. No. 1072.—Argillaceous Schist. Very fine texture, of a light-greenish color. It contains a little specular ore and chlorite. Hardness=3. Streak powder pinkish-gray. Spec. gr.=3.08. —Formation XIII.—Location, New England Mine.—Provisional name used in Report, Clay Slate (greenish).

Sp. No. 1073.—Specular Schist. Contains a very little magnetic ore and silica. Hardness=5. Streak brownish-red. Spec. gr.= 4.—Formation XIII.—Location, New England Mine.—Provisional name used in Report, Jaspery Specular Ore.

Sp. No. 1074.—Manganiferous Iron Ore. This is a brownish-black ore and has the appearance as if it had been burnt. It contains small specks of Kaolin. Streak brownish-red. Spec. gr.= 4.00.—Formation X.—Location, Iron Mountain Mine.—Provisional name used in Report, Manganiferous Siliceous Ore.

Sp. No. 1075.—Jaspery Specular Schist. This ore is slightly banded. Hardness=6. Streak red. Spec. gr.=3.83.—Formation X.—Location, Iron Mountain Mine.—Provisional name used in Report, Quartzose Iron Schist.

Sp. No. 1076.—Same as 1075.—Formation X.—Location, East end of Ogden Mine.—Provisional name used in Report, Quartzose Iron Schist.

Sp. No. 1077. (Missing).—Formation X.—Location, Foster Mine. —Provisional name, Soft Hematite (porous, bronzy).

Sp. No. 1078.—Hornstone.—Formation X.—Location, Foster Mine.—Provisional name used in Major Brooks's Report, Cherty Quartz Schist.

APPENDIX D.

ORE DEPOSITS.

APPENDIX D.

RELATES to the discovery of ore by the United States Linear Surveyors. (See Vol. I., Part I., Chapter I.)

1. *Specimens of Iron Ore collected.*—" Catalogue of specimens collected by William A. Burt, Deputy Surveyor, while surveying Township lines, under Dr. Houghton's contract, dated June 25th, 1844, for surveying with reference to mines and minerals."

East boundary of Township 47 North, Range 27 West.

No. of Specimen.	Sect.	
55	12	Compact quartz rock ; No. 2, quartz, with Spathose Iron.
56	12	No. 1, Brown Hematite, steel-gray ; No. 2, Taconic steel slate.
57	12	Brown Hematite, steel-gray.
58	12	Quartz, with Spathose Iron.
59	1	Quartz, with Spathose Iron.
60	13	No. 1, Fine, large, granulated, sub-crystalline Spathose Iron ; No. 2, same with Quartz ; No. 3, Spathose, earthy, sub-laminated Iron.
61	24	Nos. 1 and 2, Spathose Iron ; No. 3, Hydrated Carbonate of Iron, with milky Quartz and specks of Mica.
62	13	Spathose Iron, brown, amorphous, sub-laminated.
63	25	Near a pond ; 2 specimens Spathose Iron, granular, sub-crystalline.
64	25	Near a pond ; Spathose Iron, granular, sub-crystalline.
66	1	Spathose, steel-gray, Iron ore.

In running north on the east line of Sect. 13—T. 47—R. 27, Mr.

Burt's returns are thus : " In some places on N. ½, the needle would not take any direction, but would dip to the bottom of the box ; also at the end of the line. N.B.—Two good solar compasses were used on the town line, and the variations of the needles determined by both. When the variations were about 45° or 50°, the needle appeared to be weak, linked, and nearly destitute of magnetism. Spaltoric and Hæmaltic Iron ore abound on this line."

(Signed). WM. A. BURT, D. S.,

for DOUGLAS HOUGHTON, D. S.

(From official U. S. Land Office records).

2. *Extract from Judge Burt's Diary and Jacob Houghton's Statement.* —In his official diary of the year 1844, William A. Burt says : " East boundary of Township 47 North, Range 27 West. This line is very extraordinary, on account of the great variations of the needle, and the circumstances attending the survey of it. Commenced in the morning, the 19th of September ; weather clear ; the variation high and fluctuating, on the first mile, section one. On sections 12 and 13, variations of all kinds, from south 87 degrees east, to north 87 degrees west. In some places the north end of the needle would dip to the bottom of the box, and would not settle anywhere. In other places it would have variations 40, 50, and 60 degrees east, then west variation alternating in the distance of a few chains. Camped on a small stream in section 13.

" September 20.—Raining. Staked the line on south half of section 13, the needle being useless.

" September 21.—Snow fell in the forepart of the day, from three to six inches deep. Mr. Ives came to us ; had been left lame near corner of Towns. 47 and 48, Ranges 26 and 27."

In this connection, Mr. Jacob Houghton says : " On the evening of the 15th of September, we reached the lake and established the north-east corner of Town. 47 north, Range 25 west, between the Chocolate and Carp Rivers. We thence ran west the township line, between Towns. 47 and 48, and camped at the town corner on the east side of Teal Lake, on the 18th of September.

" On the morning of the 19th we started, running the line south, between Ranges 26 and 27. So soon as we reached the hill to the south of the Lake, the compass-man began to notice the fluctuation in the variation of the magnetic needle. We were, of course, using the Solar Compass, of which Mr. Burt was the inventor, and I shall never forget the excitement of the old gentleman when viewing the changes of the variation—the needle not actually traversing alike in any two places. He kept changing his position to take observations, all the time saying, ' How would they survey this country without my compass ? What could be done here without my compass ? ' It was the full and complete realization of what he had foreseen when struggling through the first stages of his invention. At length the compass-man called for all to ' come and see a variation that will beat them all.' As we looked at the instrument, to our astonishment the north end of the needle was traversing a few degrees to the south of west. Mr. Burt called out, ' Boys, look around and see what you can find ! ' We all left the line, some going to the east, and some to the west, and all of us returning with specimens of Iron ore, mostly gathered from outcrops. This was along the first mile from Teal Lake. We carried out all the specimens we could conveniently."

We give here also a statement made by Mr. William A. Burt, a year later, to wit in 1846. (See Jackson's Report, 1849, Part III., page 852, Ex. Doc.)

" It may be reasonably inferred that not more than one-seventh of the number of Iron ore beds were seen during the survey of the Township lines ; and if this district of Townships be subdivided with care in reference to mines and minerals, six times as many more will probably be found. If this view of the Iron region of the Northern Peninsula of Michigan be correct, it far excels any other portion of the United States in the abundance and good qualities of its Iron ores."

3. *Description of certain Ore Deposits.*—" In June of the following year, Dr. Houghton and Mr. Burt, with their party, were engaged in sub-dividing the Township above mentioned (T. 47, R. 26), when the former made a personal examination in reference to Iron ore, especially at the corners of sections 29, 30, 31, and 32.

" These rocks (metamorphic group) are throughout pervaded by the argillaceous, red and micaceous oxides of Iron, sometimes intimately disseminated, and sometimes in beds or veins. These are frequently of so great extent as almost to entitle them to be considered as *rocks*. The largest extent of Iron ore noticed in Township 47, Range 26, is near the corner of sections 29, 30, 31, and 32. There are here two large beds or hills of ore, made up almost entirely of granulated, magnetic, or specular Iron, with small quantities of spathose and micaceous Iron. The more northerly of these hills extends in a direction nearly east and west, for at least one-fourth of a mile, and has a breadth of little less than 1,000 feet ; the whole of which forms a single mass of ore, with occasional thin strata of imperfect chert and jasper.

" At its southerly outcrop the ore is exposed in a low cliff, above which the hill rises to the height of 20 to 30 feet. The ore here exhibits a stratified or laminated structure, and breaks readily into sub-rhomboidal fragments, in such manner as will greatly facilitate the operations of quarrying or mining the ore. This bed of Iron will compare favorably, both for extent and quality, with any known in our country." (See Jackson's Report, Ex. Doc., 1849, Part III., page 835).

APPENDIX E.

LITHOLOGY.

APPENDIX E.

Remarks on Rocks between Chocolate River and Granite Point, embracing Marquette Harbor, from unpublished MSS. left by Dr. Douglas Houghton, now in the University of Michigan. (The figure, parentheses and foot-notes are by T. B. Brooks.)

CHOCOLATE RIVER is the boundary between the United States and Indian lands. * * * (See Map I.) It may also be said to be the boundary of Geological Districts, for the westerly curves of the shore come upon the *metamorphic* group at the point where that group of rocks first appears upon the Lake. It is thus the boundary between these rocks,—*formerly considered primary*,—and the sand-rocks (Silurian) already described.

    *   *   *   *   *   *

The Metamorphic Region (Laurentian and Huronian) presents numerous abrupt and conical peaks which have frequent faces of bare rock that is perceptible even at a distance, while the sand-rock region presents " even, unbroken ridges."

Metamorphic Rocks between Chocolate and Presqu'isle.

The Talcose slate and quartz rocks are plainly and regularly stratified, dipping North about 10°, West about 80°.

The Serpentine * rock (our Diorite) is less perfectly stratified, and in fact its stratification may be considered as somewhat doubtful. The rock itself has much the appearance of greenstone, being essentially composed of feldspar and hornblende so intimately blended as not unfrequently to appear homogeneous.

There is associated with the rock sufficient trace of serpentine to give it character. This rock, taken separately, would be regarded as injected greenstone trap, and the only objection I can conceive to

---

* Serpentine was a provisional name with Dr. Houghton.

16

considering it as such, is the fact that it uniformly occurs, dipping *in mass*, in the same direction and angle as that of the talcose slates and quartz rocks; or, in other words, that it simply fills a space between those rocks and never cuts across them, and further, that it has produced no perceptible change in the rocks with which it has been brought in contact.

It is allowed that neither of these circumstances is regarded as conclusive upon the subject, but they have led me to infer that the deposition or formation of the serpentine rocks was coeval with that of the slates with which it occurs.*

The slates seem to have been considerably disturbed at many points, subsequent to deposition, and while yet in an unsolidified state, or when softened by the action of secondary causes; for the talcose slate is not unfrequently much contorted, and in one instance it was noticed to be so much so as to be doubled back on itself. The talcose slate when not disturbed has almost invariably a jointed structure; joints usually dip south about 40°.

It has, frequently intervening, thin beds of milky and greasy quartz, with small imperfect crystals of quartz occupying little druses. Associated with these thin beds or strata of quartz, is a mineral that closely resembles hematitic iron ore, appearing in thin veins or a sub-pipeform structure.†

Beds of a coarse novaculite occur in the talcy quartz rocks just west from the Chocolate River.

The quartz rock alternates with the talcose slates, forming the bulk of the whole mass. (See Fig. 18.) It is usually granular, though sometimes compact, with a conchoidal fracture. It readily separates into blocks in the line of the cleavage, that is, in the line of its dip; which like the slate is N. 10°, W. 80°, the beds varying from a few inches to several feet in thickness. No minerals were noticed in the quartz rock, excepting small quantities of the hematite, before described, and sulphuret of iron.

The *serpentine rock*, as has already been stated, alternates with the quartz and talcose slate rocks. It has much the appearance of

---

* I conceive that it would be difficult at this time to write a better general description of these rocks of the same length than is here given.

† The Eureka Mine is in this formation.

Fig. 18.

GEOLOGICAL SECTION. CHOCOLATE FLUX QUARRY, NEAR MARQUETTE, L. S.

(Illustrating Dr. Houghton's notes). Total length represented, 575 steps.

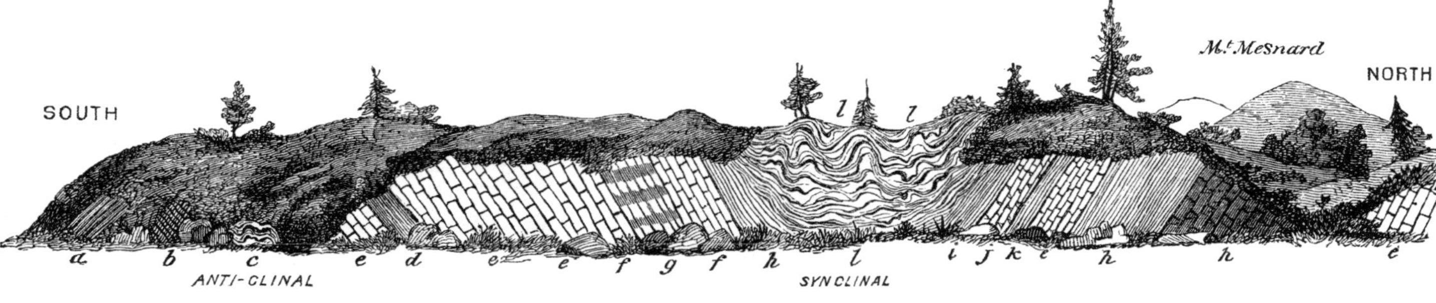

a. Talco-argillaceous schist ; holds epidote, feldspar, calcite and quartz. b. Diorite with slate layers. c. Talcy argillaceous slate—" bird's-eye "—contorted. d. Red quartzite, laminated with white quartz, and having intercalated layers of schist. e. Red quartzite. f. White quartzite. g. Siliceous and quartzite layers. h. Talco-argillaceous slate. i. Brick-red talcose argillaceous slate filled with siliceous fragments which project from the weathered surface. j. Talcy quartzite. k. Calcareous quartzite, used as flux. l. Brown argillite, associated with reddish and mottled, coarse and fine-grained, sometimes banded and generally siliceous, and often talcy and feldspathic limestone—*much contorted.* This series of rocks are believed to be the equivalent of the Lower or Teal Lake Quartzite, No. V. See Specimens 9 and 10, State Collection ; also see Julien's descriptions, Specimens 106 to 113, Appendix A.

a compact trap greenstone. It occupies comparatively a small space of the whole amount of the rock upon the coast. Sulphuret of iron and hematitic iron were noticed in small quantities in the serpentine rock, and milky and imperfect common quartz occur more frequently.

(The non-conformable junction between the quartz schist and the sandstone just east of the Carp, which is given in Dana's Geology, is figured and accurately described.)

(Dr. H. says the very lowest portion is sub-conglomeritic, but the upper part is similar to the ordinary rock of the coast. Both conglomerate and sandrocks are of a deep-red color. He had before divided the sandstones into an upper white and lower red series.)

Granite was seen on point south of mouth of Dead River.* It is composed of quartz, feldspar and hornblende ; that at the north of the river is finer grained, of a light-gray color, and contains beautiful specimens of tourmaline in small quantities. The rock at 1st Rapids, in Dead River, is described as of similar character as that at mouth of stream, but less *hornblende*. It is stratified, dipping N. 80° W., and it must probably be regarded as a metamorphic rock altered to a gneiss.

The two islands off Presqu'isle are of granite, like the above.

Presqu'isle.†—At the N.E. point of the island is a cliff of trap rocks 20 to 60 feet high, ¼ mile long ; upon this rests the sandrock, which in turn rests on a coarse conglomerate made up of large and small pebbles of primary rock. In one place the conglomerate was 20 feet and the sandrock over it 30 feet thick. This sandrock is of a deep-red color, and is the same in character as the lower group.

The bedding has been much disturbed, the mass raising considerably as it approaches the trap, and at points the disturbance has been so great as to destroy all appearance of stratification. So great has been the action of the elevating power, and so intense the heat of the protruded mass, near the points of junction of the trap, conglomerate and sandstone, that not only all stratification is lost,

---

* This is the first point west from the Sault where the "true primary" has been observed on the coast.

† This locality was afterwards described by Foster and Whitney. See their Report. Also by Dr. Rominger.

but the character of the rocks is completely changed, and they pass by insensible degrees into trap, it being difficult to determine when the sandstone and conglomerate end and the trap begins.

Portions of the sandrock and conglomerate bear the marks of *fusion* so strongly as to leave no doubt in the minds of an observer. Both sandrock and conglomerate have been shattered in every possible direction, and the veins or fissures thus formed have been filled with impure quartz, and less frequently with calcareous spar, the most minute ramifications down to ⅛ of an inch in thickness, being filled, and occasionally veins may be seen from 1 to 2 inches thick.

(Dr. H. compares the process to the injection of a blood-vessel.)   *   *   *   *

The conglomerate and sandstone, but more particularly the latter, are frequently vesicular, the vesicles being numerous but small; they were no doubt the result of the passage of gaseous vapors during the time these rocks were in a state of semi-fusion, or softness. So perfect is the reticulated structure, that it sometimes closely resembles fine reticulated earthy pumice of recent volcanoes.

The present condition of the sandstone and conglomerate is such as to lead to the inference that the *uplift* of the strata took place after the perfect induration.

The trap appears to be fused hornblende rock of a dark, almost black or green color, nearly homogeneous and not columnar, is exceedingly hard and tough, and when struck with a hammer gives a clear, ringing sound.   (See Spec. 78, State Collection.)

Occupying an intermediate space between the conglomerate and trap proper, is an irregular mass of rocks, of a coarse but homogeneous texture, traversed in all directions by veins, which veins are filled by injected matter of a dark, almost black color. It is exceedingly difficult to determine to which of the rocks this belongs, but a minute examination has satisfied me that it is a mixture of trap with conglomerate.

We find associated with the trap milky and common quartz, in small crystals, sulphuret of iron, calcareous spar, imperfect serpentine and asbestos, but none of these minerals in great quantities. They usually occur in what may be called the joints of the rocks.   *   *   *   *

It is in the upper part of the fused rock—when it is passing into sandstone, or just within the lower edge of the sandstone—that the principal minerals occur, but at these points the sandrock has so far lost its character as scarcely to be recognized as such ; for it appears as a dark-green, nearly black rock, breaking, or rather separating, into small irregular masses, in such a manner that a fair fracture can scarcely be obtained.

In this, as also in the lower or conglomerate portion of the sandrock, thin veins of galena, sulphuret of iron, with a small portion of the green carbonate of copper, occur, connected with gangues which are either quartz or calcareous, or both united. The minerals are sometimes all associated in the same vein. One vein is parallel with the bedding of the rock, and appears like a bed, but the sandrock is so much shattered that it is impossible to determine its original relation with any degree of certainty. The vein alluded to pursues an irregular and tortuous course, dipping at a high angle and thinning out to mere threads and strings, and again swelling to a width of several inches ; once it was seen 12 inches. Again, the mineral is in distinct *nests*, separate from the veins.

(Dr. H. remarks that he made a careful study of this vein, so as to be able to dispel the illusion held by Indians and traders that there was gold and silver here, this being a favorite landing in passing along the lake-shore in canoes and small boats. These views were not published, owing to Dr. Houghton's death, and not heeded. Mining was afterwards begun here, and ended disastrously.)

APPENDIX F.

IRON-ORE DOCK.

(SEE PLATE.)

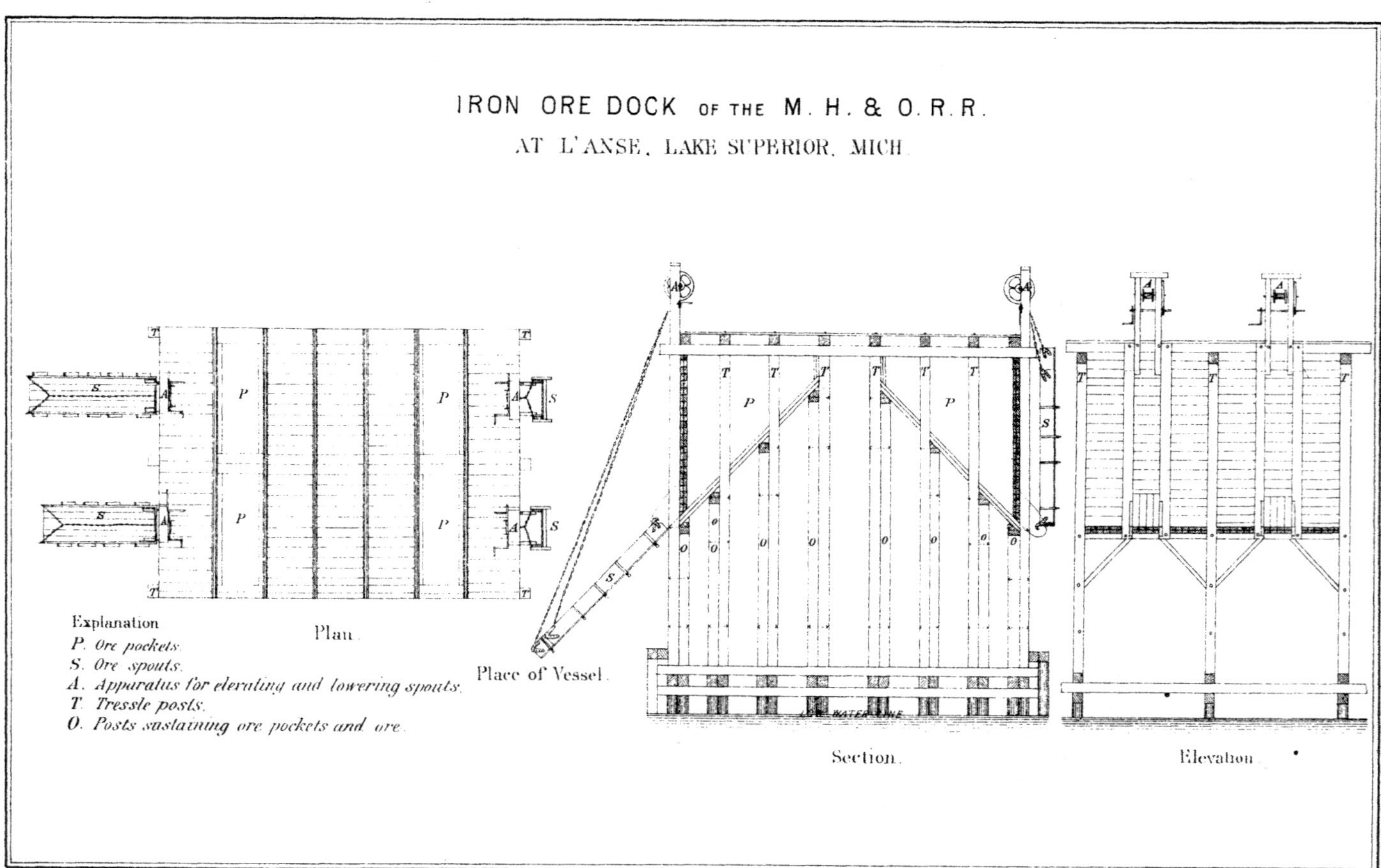

IRON ORE DOCK OF THE M.H.&O.R.R.
AT L'ANSE, LAKE SUPERIOR, MICH.
Plan.
Place of Vessel.
Section.
Elevation.
WATER LINE
Explanation
P. Ore pockets.
S. Ore spouts.
A. Apparatus for elevating and lowering spouts.
T. Tressle posts.
O. Posts sustaining ore pockets and ore.
Pl. XX

APPENDIX F.

MARQUETTE, HOUGHTON AND ONTONAGON RAILROAD.

L'ANSE, MICH., *January 31st*, 1873.

MAJOR T. B. BROOKS:

DEAR SIR: In conformity with instructions received from Jacob Houghton, Esq., chief engineer, I herewith submit plans and description of the Marquette, Houghton and Ontonagon Railroad Iron-Ore Dock, at this terminus of the road.

The ore dock is 546 feet long, 36 feet wide, by 38 feet high, and is composed of 43 bents, with clear spans of 12 feet. The foundation is of piles—one pile for each post, driven with a 2,000 lb. hammer, falling 35 feet.

The piles are cut off 3 feet above water and capped; above the caps are placed the streak-sills, and on these rest the main bents. The main posts, sills, caps, pocket-posts, pocket-post caps, streak-sills, and side-stringers are 12 × 12 inch timber. The track-stringers are 12 × 14 inch timber. The pocket-posts are not framed with the main bents, but simply rest on the main sills, and are bolted to main posts. The ore dock has 80 vessel pockets, 40 on each side, and at the end are 4 steamboat pockets.

Each pocket will hold about 75 tons of ore. The dock is of sufficient capacity to load four vessels and one steamboat at the same time. For convenience of loading, the vessel pockets are divided into sets of 20; these are again divided into sets of 2. The height of each set above low water is as follows: 20 ft., 19 ft., 20 ft., 21 ft., 22 ft., 23 ft., 21 ft., 20 ft., 19 ft., and 20 ft. The ore is delivered on board the vessels from the pockets by means of spouts. These are of varying length, and as follows: the 1st, 3d, 5th, 7th, 10th, 13th, 15th, 17th, and 19th are 16 feet long; the 9th and 12th are 12 feet long, and the 2d, 4th, 6th, 8th, 11th, 14th, 16th, 18th, and 20th are 18 ft. long.

The steamboat pockets are 12 feet above water, with short

spouts 9 feet long, which deliver the ore into hand-carts, and in them it is wheeled on board the steamer.

The above arrangement of pockets and spouts has been found by experience to be the best adapted for the expeditious loading of vessels.

The spouts are of 2-inch pine plank, lined with $\frac{1}{4}$-inch tank-iron, and are hinged at the mouth of the pockets. They are raised or lowered by a crab-wrench, placed as shown on the plans.

The outside tracks on the dock are used for discharging the ore into the pockets; the centre track is for empty cars, which are transferred by means of a transfer table, placed between bents Nos. 41 and 42.

The pockets are lined with one course of 3-inch pine plank and one course of 3-inch hardwood plank. The mouths have an additional lining of $\frac{1}{4}$-inch tank-iron.

The timber used in the construction of the ore dock is white and Norway pine. The smaller details of construction are shown by the accompanying plans, which represent: a front elevation, with spouts removed; a section, with side planking removed, showing angle of inclination, and a plan of top of dock.

Respectfully yours,

C. H. Palmer, Jr.,
Assist. Engineer.

Note.—Chapter I., Vol. I., contains a description of a dock owned by the same company, with view showing vessels loading.

APPENDIX G.

CENSUS STATISTICS.

APPENDIX G.

United States Census Statistics for the Upper Peninsula of Michigan--Census of 1870.

POPULATION BY COUNTIES.

(Chapter IX., Vol. I., gives the nationality at several Marquette mines.)

Chippewa.

	POPULATION					Dwellings.	Families.	Voters.
	Total.	Native.	Foreign.	White.	Colored.			
Sault Ste Marie............	1213	932	281	610	*3	226	223	§207
Sugar Island..............	238	126	112	162	†76	48	48	44
Warren	238	139	99	178	‡2	46	48	45
Total.................	1689	1197	492	950	739	320	319	296

* Also 600 Indians. † All Indians. ‡ Also 58 Indians. § Does not include U. S. soldiers.

Delta.

	POPULATION					Dwellings.	Families.	Voters.
	Total.	Native.	Foreign.	White.	Colored.			
Centreville................	86	43	43	86	....	10	12	8
Delton....................	833	406	427	828	*5	113	115	137
Escanaba	1370	774	596	1356	†4	205	220	224
Masonville	152	62	90	152	....	19	19	19
St. Martin's Island........	101	78	23	101	....	....	....	....
Total.................	2542	1363	1179	2523	19	347	366	388

* All Indians. † Also 10 Indians.

Houghton.

	POPULATION.					Dwellings.	Families.	Voters.
	Total.	Native.	Foreign.	White.	Colored.			
Adams.....................	670	253	417	670	....	125	117	97
Baraga	160	100	60	155	*5	23	23	33
Calumet..................	3182	1131	2051	3175	†2	394	518	394
Franklin.................	2163	1052	1111	2145	*18	465	399	283
Hancock..................	2700	1113	1587	2693	‖6	400	433	493
Huron....................	769	373	396	769	....	157	139	93
L'Anse...................	33	23	10	33	....	14	10	11
Portage.............	1540	841	699	1520	‡12	245	276	263
Quincy...................	1117	432	685	1117	....	201	216	120
Schoolcraft.	669	225	444	629	§4	120	121	62
Webster	876	467	409	872	4	216	177	95
Total.................	13,879	6010	7869	13,778	101	2360	2429	1944

* All Indians.   † Also 5 Indians.   ‡ Also 8 Indians.   § Also 36 Indians.   ‖ Also 1 Indian.

Keweenaw.

	Total.	Native.	Foreign.	White.	Colored.	Dwellings.	Families.	Voters.
Clifton	615	285	330	615	....	165	114	105
Copper Harbor............	359	173	186	358	†1	81	49	114
Eagle Harbor.............	778	374	404	778	....	215	150	118
Grant	152	83	69	152	....	158	25	27
Houghton.................	1325	665	660	1321	*2	260	235	268
Sherman..................	929	449	480	929	....	162	156	171
Sibley	28	30	17	47	....	69	10	12
Total.................	4205	2059	2146	4200	5	1110	739	885

* Also 2 Indians.   † An Indian.

Marquette.

	Total.	Native.	Foreign.	White.	Colored.	Dwellings.	Families.	Voters.
Chocolay..................	260	95	165	260	....	47	47	40
Ishpeming................	6103	1757	4346	6094	*1	893	988	606
Marquette................	4617	2186	2431	4497	†58	768	846	985
Munissing................	799	305	494	797	‡2	127	127	145
Negaunee.................	3254	1450	1804	3552	2	517	573	586
Total.................	15,033	5793	9240	14,900	133	2352	2581	2362

* Also 8 Indians.   † Also 62 Indians.   ‡ Both Indians.

VILLAGES.

Marquette 4,000
Negaunee 2,559

Mackinac.

| | POPULATION. | | | | | Dwellings. | Families. | Voters. |
	Total.	Native.	Foreign.	White.	Colored.			
Holmes.................	938	722	216	837	*2	....	....	129
Moran..................	373	312	61	315	†4	....	....	4
St. Ignace	405	349	56	254	‡19	....	....	38
Total.................	1716	1383	333	1406	310	....	....	171

* Also 99 Indians.   † Also 54 Indians.   ‡ Also 132 Indians.

Menominee.

	Total.	Native.	Foreign.	White.	Colored.	Dwellings.	Families.	Voters.
Cedarville	194	109	85	192	*2	23	23	41
Menominee	1597	809	788	1585	†9	224	246	343
Total	1791	918	873	1777	14	247	269	384

* Both Indians.   † Also 3 Indians.

Ontonagon.

	Total.	Native.	Foreign.	White.	Colored.	Dwellings.	Families.	Voters.
Algonquin.................	54	32	22	54	....	8	8	7
Carp Lake.................	25	17	8	23	*2	5	5	6
Greenland.................	548	295	253	548	....	98	99	78
Ontonagon.................	739	512	227	711	†13	141	142	148
Rockland	1479	858	621	1477	*2	265	267	177
Total.................	2845	1714	1131	2813	32	517	521	416

* All Indians.   † Also 15 Indians.

POPULATION OF SCHOOLCRAFT COUNTY.

Whites, 797 ; Indians, 2.

Grand Total for the Upper Peninsula...............	44,499	20,437	23,263	42,347	1353	7253	7224	5096

ACREAGE, VALUATION AND TAXES.

COUNTIES.	No. of Towns and Wards.	No. of Acres of Land Assessed in 1871.	Aggregate of Real and Personal Estate as equalized by State Board of Equalization for 1871.	Total of Taxes Apportioned for 1871.
Marquette	9	424,383 00	$3,990,000 00	$4,794 53
Menominee	2	....	1,570,000 00	1,886 52
Keweenaw	7	238,306 43	1,570,000 00	1,886 54
Ontonagon	5	244,959 60	1,310,000 00	1,573 74
Schoolcraft	3	....	520,000 00	624 85
Chippewa	3	135,904 81	450,000 00	540 68
Delta	4	132,939 00	450,000 00	540 68
Houghton	11	303,422 47	2,100,000 00	2,523 50
Mackinac	3	73,957 21	450,000 00	540 68

APPENDIX H.

MAGNETIC ANALYSIS.

APPENDIX H.

Magnetic Analysis.

TABLE of percentage of powder of various Lake Superior ores lifted by the magnet, with color of same. The chemical analysis of the same specimens is given in Chapter X., Vol. I. The mixed red and black oxides here given are described under Iron Ores in Chapter III., Vol. I., and their magnetic properties in Chapter VIII., Vol. I.

Number of Analysis.	Name of Mine.	Kind of Ore.	Percentage lifted by the Magnet.	Percentage *not* lifted by the Magnet.	Color of Powder.
225	Michigamme	Magnetic	96.42	3.58	Grayish Black.
226	Spurr Mountain	Magnetic	94.91	5.09	do. do.
227	Champion " Slate "	Specular	5.10	94.90	Steel Gray.
228	Champion " Black "	Magnetic	96.90	3.10	Steely Black.
229	Jackson "Old Pioneer"	Specular	.78	99.22	Purplish Brown.
230	Jackson " Slate "	Specular	.29	99.71	Purple.
231	Jackson Hematite	Hematite	.09	99.91	Light Brown.
232	Magnetic	Magnetic	95.91	4.09	Grayish Black.
233	Republic " Specular "	Specular	.04	99.95	Steely Gray.
234	Republic " Magnetic "	Magnetic	85.37	14.63	do. Black.
235	Kloman	Specular	2.79	97.21	do. Gray.
236	New York " R.R. Pit "	Specular	6.20	93.80	Brownish Purple.
237	N. York " Taylor's Pit "	Specular	15.09	84.91	Purple.
238	N. York Beardslie's Pit	Specular	39.76	60.24	Purplish Black.
239	New England	Hematite	.32	99.68	Raw Umber.
240	Winthrop	Hematite	.19	99.81	Dark Purple.
241	Rolling Mill	Hematite	1.41	98.59	Purplish Brown.
242	Williams	Hematite	2.28	97.72	Purple.
243	Himrod	Hematite	.07	99.93	Purplish Brown.
244 to 248	Menominee ⎫	Specular	7.58	92.41	Purplish Silver Gray.
249 to 253	Iron Region ⎭	Specular	1.21	98.79	do. do. do.

APPENDIX I.

MINING LAWS.

APPENDIX I.

Synopsis of the Mining Laws of Michigan.—One of the first questions asked by a capitalist proposing to invest money in a mining enterprise, is in relation to the laws under which the property is held. These, both State and Federal, vary widely in different portions of the United States, and still more from the elaborate and extensive mining codes of Europe.

The greater part of the mining property of the Upper Peninsula is owned by persons residing beyond the limits of the State, and in some instances by citizens of other countries. The Michigan laws, contained in many volumes, are often not accessible to such persons ; so for their benefit, as well as for any others who desire to inform themselves quickly regarding the leading features and requirements of the laws of Michigan relating to mining and manufacturing companies, the following synopsis was prepared by Mr. C. D. Lawton, and has also been overlooked by Messrs. Daniel H. Ball, and James M. Wilkinson, of Marquette.

As several of the provisions of the earlier laws were afterwards amended, the synopsis must be read through to get at the present law.

Synopsis of the Laws in reference to the formation of Corporations for mining, smelting, or manufacturing iron, copper, etc. Approved February 5th, 1853. (See Laws of 1853, p. 53.)

SECTION 1. Provides that all corporations organized under this act shall be capable of suing and being sued in any court in this State ; may have a seal and may alter it at pleasure. The majority of the stockholders of each shall elect the officers, prescribe their duties, etc., and determine the by-laws.

SEC. 2. Provides that the number of persons forming the corporation shall not be less than three, that the articles of agreement shall be in writing, that they, their successors and assigns, shall constitute a body corporate under the name assumed by the company ; also that no two companies shall have the same name.

Sec. 3. Provides that before any company organized under this act can commence business, the articles must be filed at length in the office of the Secretary of State, and in the office of the clerk of the county in which the company propose to operate. (See 19 Mich., p. 194; also 12 Mich., p. 395.)

Sec. 4. The articles of every such association shall be signed by the persons associating in the first instance, and acknowledged before some person authorized by the laws of this State to take acknowledgments of deeds, and shall state—

First. Distinctly and definitely the purpose for which the same is formed;

Second. The amount of their capital stock, and the number of shares;

Third. The amount of capital stock actually paid in;

Fourth. The names of the stockholders, their respective residences, and the number of shares held by each person;

Fifth. The place in this State where their office for the transaction of business is located, and the county or counties in which their business is to be carried on;

Sixth. The term of its existence, not to exceed thirty years.

Sec. 5. Every corporation shall, annually, in the month of July, make a report, signed by a majority of the board of directors, containing—

First. The amount of capital actually paid in;

Second. The amount invested in real estate;

Third. The amount of their personal estate;

Fourth. The amount of their debts and credits, as near as may be;

Fifth. The name of each stockholder, and the number of shares held by him at the date of such report; and every such report shall be verified, on oath, by the officers signing the same; which report shall be filed in the office of the Secretary of State, and with the clerk of the county where the mine is situated, in said month of July; and if any person shall, as to any material facts, knowingly (and *willfully*) swear or affirm falsely, he shall be deemed guilty of perjury and be punished accordingly; and every company organized for mining or smelting purposes shall within the said month of July, file a copy of said report with the clerk of the county where the mine of the company is located ; and if the directors of any mining company shall, intentionally, neglect or refuse to make such report and file the same and a copy thereof, as hereinbefore provided, each of such directors shall be deemed guilty of a misdemeanor, and upon conviction thereof shall be punished by a fine not exceeding one thousand dollars.

SEC. 6. The amount of the capital stock in every such corporation shall be fixed and limited by the stockholders in their articles of association, and shall, in no case, be less than ten thousand dollars, nor more than five hundred thousand dollars, and shall be divided into shares of twenty-five dollars each. The capital stock may be increased, and the number of shares, at any meeting of the stockholders called for that purpose : *Provided,* That the amount so increased shall not, with the existing capital, exceed five hundred thousand dollars. (See Sec. 6 of an act supplementary to this act, approved February 6th, 1855.)

SEC. 7. Provides that it shall not be lawful to use the funds of the corporation for any other purpose than those set forth in the articles of association.

SEC. 8. Provides that any two members may call the first meeting, by giving 15 days' notice through some newspaper, of time and place of meeting. (All stockholders may appear without notice and act.)

SEC. 9. Provides that there shall be at least 3 directors and not more than 9, one of whom must be a resident of this State ; that they shall hold office for one year, or until their successors are chosen.

SEC. 10. Provides that the officers shall be chosen from among the directors.

SEC. 11. Provides that the directors may call in the capital stock from time to time ; if any stockholder neglects to pay his installment, after due notice his stock may be sold at public auction.

SEC. 12. Provides that a majority of the directors constitute a quorum, and at a meeting of the stockholders, the majority of the stock shall be capable of transacting business; stockholders may vote by proxy.

SEC. 13. Provides that if an election of directors does not take place at the annual meeting, an election may be held any time thereafter by giving 30 days' notice.

SEC. 14. Provides that the books shall be open to the inspection of the stockholders, and that as often as once a year a statement of the company's affairs shall be laid before the stockholders.

SEC. 15. Provides for the holding of real and personal estate, and that all companies engaged in the mining or manufacturing of iron or copper shall not hold to exceed 10,000 acres of land.

SEC. 16. Provides that the stock shall be deemed personal property, to be transferred on the books only as the directors determine; that the corporation shall have a lien on the stock of the members for debts due the company. (See 17 Mich. Reports, p. 141.)

SEC. 17. Provides that each stockholder shall be individually liable for all labor performed for the company, and such liability may be enforced after an execution against the company shall be returned unsatisfied, or any time after an adjudication in bankruptcy; and further, that any stockholder who shall be compelled to pay such claim shall have right to call upon all stockholders to contribute their part of the sum so paid, and may sue them jointly or severally.

SEC. 18. Provides that every mining corporation shall in the month of July of each year make a report of the amount mined, to be filed with the county clerk and auditor-general.

SEC. 19. Provides for a similar report for any corporation organized for manufacturing purposes.

Sec. 20. Provides for the imposition of specific taxes on mining products, and is superseded by the act of 1872, March 29.

Sec. 21. Provides that the property of the company, not including capital stock, shall be subject to the usual taxation.

Sec. 22. Provides that any legal process may be served, provided the officers of the company cannot be found in the county, by posting it conspicuously at the company's place of business.

Sec. 23. Provides for the personal liability of each of the directors, in case of non-compliance with Sections 3, 5, 18, and 19. (See 19 Mich. Reports, p. 187).

Sec. 24. Provides that in case any corporation shall become insolvent by reason of the violation of the provisions of this act, the directors assenting to such violation shall be liable for all debts contracted thereafter.

Sec. 25. Provides that the Legislature, for just cause, may rescind the charter of any corporation, and may amend or repeal this act.

Sec. 26. Provides that this act shall be subject to the provisions of the act of 1846, chap. 55, title 10, so far as applicable to companies formed under this act. (Sections 27, 28, 29, relate to Salt Companies.)

AN ACT supplementary to the foregoing.   Approved February 6th, 1855.   (Laws of 1855, page 26.)

Section 1. Provides that any company organizing under the preceding act, may have an office anywhere in the United States, and hold its business meetings thereat, such office to be designated in the articles of association, which articles must also designate an office within this State.

Sec. 2. Provides that the first meeting may be held within this State, or at the business office without the State, in which latter case, 15 days' previous notice must be given in some newspaper in Detroit, and also in the county in which said office is located.

SEC. 3. Provides for the manner of sale of all stock forfeited by reason of the non-payment of assessments ; such stock belonging to residents of the Upper Peninsula, shall be sold at the county seat in which the mine is located, 30 days' previous notice being given in some newspaper published on the Upper Peninsula, and such stock belonging to residents of the Lower Peninsula, shall be sold at the office of the company, if the company have an office in the Lower Peninsula, and if none, then in the city of Detroit, 30 days' notice being given in the county where the sale is to be made.

SEC. 4. Provides that all meetings and corporate acts, had by any company organized under the preceding act, had beyond the limits of this State, and within the United States, shall be held valid, in the same manner as if had within the State.

SEC. 5. Provides that any corporation doing business under special charter, may dissolve and reorganize under the previous act. The reorganization to be made within 60 days from date of disso-lution of special charter.   All demands against the company under the special charter shall remain in force under the new organization.

SEC. 6. Provides that any company organized under the previ-ous act may at any time increase its capital stock to not to exceed $1,000,000, by a vote of two-thirds of the stockholders, and the shares to $50 each, the number not to exceed 20,000. A company may also diminish its capital stock, and the number of shares, and price per share in same ratio.   (See Act of February 9th, 1857.)

SEC. 7. Provides for the immediate effect of the supplemental act.

AN ACT to authorize Mining Companies to subscribe and take stock in Plank Roads or Railroads, and to regulate Taxation thereon. Approved February 8th, 1855. Amended and approved March 14th, 1863.

SECTION 1. Provides that any mining company in the Upper Peninsula of Michigan, duly organized, may take stock in any company organized for the purpose of improving or constructing canals, harbors, plank roads, or railroads, when with a view strictly of facilitating transportation to the mines, and the amount of capital so paid out shall be considered as part of the capital of the road, harbor, or canal company, and as such be taxed, being deducted from capital of the mining company.

SEC. 2. Provides that the president and secretary of the mining company shall, before the first day of May of each year, return to the State Treasurer the amount which the company has so subscribed, and other particulars relating thereto.

———

AN ACT to confer certain powers on Mining Companies.   Approved Feb. 13th, 1855.

SECTION I. Provides that it shall be lawful for any mining company, duly organized under the laws of this State, to establish its business office anywhere in the United States, provided it also maintain a business office within this State, and that any process served upon the agent in charge of this office shall be binding on the company.   The location of such office shall be fixed by the stockholders and certified to the Secretary of State.

SEC. 2. Provides that offices which have been heretofore established without the State shall remain until otherwise changed by the company, provided that within six months hereof an office be located within the State, and a return of the fact made to the Secretary of State.

SEC. 3. Provides that all meetings and corporate acts of any incorporated mining company heretofore had without the State and within the United States, shall have the same legality as if had in this State.

SEC. 4. Provides that in lieu of specific tax on corporate stock of chartered mining companies shall be subject to a specific tax, in manner set forth in Section 20 of an act to authorize the formation of corporations for mining, etc., approved February 5th, 1853. (Amended, 1872.)

AN ACT to authorize Mining Corporations to increase the number of shares.   Approved
   February 9th, 1857.

SECTION 1. Provides that all mining companies heretofore organized shall have power to increase the number of shares to not
to exceed 20,000 shares.

SEC. 2. Provides that no such increase of number of shares shall
take effect, until the company shall properly file with the Secretary
of State the resolution of the board of directors in regard to the
same.

———

AN ACT to authorize the consolidation of Mining Companies.   Approved February 17th,
   1857.   [See Act of 1871.]

SECTION 1. Provides that all mining companies organized under
the act of 1853, may consolidate with other such corporations, and
in such case the company purchasing shall become vested with all
the corporate rights and franchises, in addition, of the company
thus absorbed.

SEC. 2. Provides that no such consolidation of mining companies
shall take place without the prior consent of the majority of the
stockholders of both companies.

SEC. 3. Provides that after consolidation any such company shall
have power to call in and cancel its prior certificates of stock, and
to reissue new certificates, and cancel the certificates of any stockholder who shall neglect, after due notice, to return his certificates.

SEC. 4. Provides that any corporation thus assuming the franchises and property of another, assumes also its liabilities.

SEC. 5. Provides that in the reissue of stock, there shall be no
increase of stock beyond the joint capital stock of the companies
thus consolidating.

———

AN ACT supplementary to the Mining Act of 1853.   Approved March 14th, 1865.

SECTION 1. Provides that it shall be lawful for any corporation organized under the act of 1853 to conduct its operations anywhere within the United States.

SEC. 2. Provides that any corporation organized under the original act, must first cause the articles of association to be filed with the Secretary of State, and with the clerk of the county in which the office of the company in this State is situated.

SEC. 3. Provides that any such corporation, conducting any of its operations without the limits of this State, shall be subject to the laws of this State, so far as applicable.

AN ACT supplementary to the act of 1853, to authorize the formation of Mining and Smelting Companies. Approved March 27th, 1867.

SECTION 1. Provides that no meeting of the stockholders of any company organized under the provisions of the act of 1853, for the purpose of mining or smelting in the Upper Peninsula, shall be legal unless due notice be given of the time, place, and objects of the same, to be previously published, two weeks from an annual and four weeks from a special meeting, in some newspaper in the county in which the business is carried on, or, if no newspaper is published in such county, then in some paper published nearest to the mine or place where the business is carried on : a copy of such notice shall be sent 20 days prior to the meeting to each of the stockholders, unless personal service be made, and certified thereto, upon each and every stockholder. (See Act 6 of Laws of 1872.)

SEC. 2. Provides that no sale, division, or mortgage of any of the property or franchises of any such corporation shall be made, except it be authorized by a three-fifths vote of the entire interest of the stock of the company, at a meeting called in accordance with the provisions of Section 1.

SEC. 3. Provides that any person wishing to perpetuate the evidence of any proceedings, taken under the preceding sections, may—

First. Procure an affidavit of the serving of the proper notices.

Second. Procure an affidavit of publication of notice of meeting.

Third. Procure a certified transcript of the proceedings of such meeting.

Fourth. Secure the record thereof in the Register's office of the proper county, such evidence to remain *prima facie* evidence of the facts.

SEC. 4. Provides that any meeting called as here set forth may adjourn to any time not exceeding sixty days, to any specified place.

SEC. 5. Provides that all acts or parts thereof contravening the provisions of this act are hereby repealed.

AN ACT to authorize the consolidation of Mining Companies. Approved January 27th, 1871.

SECTION 1. Provides that mining corporations may by a vote of three-fifths of the entire capital of each, actually present or legally represented at a meeting called for the purpose, agree to consolidate, and upon the terms of such consolidation. The number of shares and capital stock of the consolidated corporation shall not be greater than the aggregate stock and shares of the companies thus consolidated. No company shall thus consolidate whose capital paid in or whose expenditures for land and improvements are less than $100,000 : before the completion of such consolidation, the several corporations shall file in the office of the Secretary of State the verified certificates of the proper officers of each company, showing the amount of capital stock paid in, the amount expended for lands and improvements thereon. The lands of such corporations shall be known as mineral lands, and shall be in every case adjacent to each other. The capital of no consolidated corporation shall be divided into a greater number of shares than 80,000, and the amount of stock called in shall in no case exceed the aggregate of the unpaid stock of the several corporations at the time of consolidation, and that the par value of the shares shall be fixed at the meeting at which the consolidation is effected, and shall not exceed $25, nor be less than $10, and each certificate of stock issued shall upon its face state the par value thereof and the amount of assessment to which it is liable.

SEC. 2. Provides that the consolidated corporation shall enjoy the aggregate franchises, rights and estates pertaining to the several corporations, and be subject to the liabilities existing against each, and the several corporations shall exist for the purpose of prosecuting or defending any legal proceedings then pending or subsequently instituted against or by either of them.

SEC. 3. Provides that the officers of the several corporations shall continue to exercise all their powers until the new corporation shall be organized, and thereafter shall continue for the purpose of perfecting said union.

SEC. 4. Provides that any mining company consolidated under this act shall have power to call in and cancel the stock of the several companies, and to issue new certificates of stock in the consolidated corporation to the stockholders in such proportions as each shall be entitled to, and to cancel the certificates of any stockholder who shall not return them after the publishing for 90 days of the notice of the resolution in some daily newspaper in Detroit, also in some paper published in the Upper Peninsula, also in some paper published in the place where the principal business office is located.

SEC. 5. Provides for the repeal of all acts inconsistent with the provisions of this act.

———

AN ACT to authorize Corporations of other States to engage in Mining, Smelting, or Refining Ores within this State. Approved April 15th, 1871.

SECTION 1. Provides that corporations formed under laws of other States, for the purpose of mining, etc., ores, may engage in such business in this State, and acquire all necessary property, but shall not hold to exceed 6,000 acres of land at one time.

SEC. 2. Provides that said corporations shall be subject to the same requirements as if organized in this State.

18

SEC. 3. Provides that, except for State taxes and fines, any amount due for labor shall have a first lien over all other claims, on any property within this State belonging to such corporation, in same manner as if the corporation was organized in this State.

SEC. 4. Provides that any corporation doing business in this State shall keep an office, and officer in charge of it, in the county where its business is carried on, and the service of any legal process against such company may be made on such officer. If such officer cannot be found at such place of business, then process may be served by posting a copy thereof in a conspicuous place in such office.

AN ACT amendatory of the foregoing so far as relates to the Imposition of Taxes on Mining and Smelting Corporations. Approved March 29th, 1872.

SECTION 1. Provides that all companies possessed of corporate powers, engaged in mining copper in this State, shall pay to the State a specific tax of 75 cents for each ton of copper obtained, and every such organization engaged in iron mining shall pay a tax of one cent for each gross ton of ore obtained, and every such organization engaged in coal mining shall pay a tax of one-half cent per gross ton. Such taxes to be paid in July, at the office of the State Treasurer, or at such place in Detroit as he may designate. Except for specific taxes upon capital or joint stock, the taxes here designated shall be in lieu of all State tax. Of specific taxes received, whether part due or to accrue from corporate companies engaged in mining in the Upper Peninsula, one-half shall be placed to credit of general fund and one-half to the credit of the counties from which it is received, and be paid to such counties in like manner as other funds, and be used for county purposes.

Nothing herein shall be construed to exempt from State taxation any property not invested in mining or manufacturing as contemplated in this act.

AN ACT to authorize the Auditor-General to assess, by estimated specific Taxes, upon Corporations which might neglect or refuse to make a Report as required by law, and to collect the same. Approved March 29th, 1872.

SECTION 1. Provides that the Auditor-General shall estimate and charge the amount of specific tax due from any corporation neglecting to return the same, as heretofore provided, from the best information he can obtain, and shall forthwith sign a written statement of the amount so estimated, and send by mail, or otherwise, to any officer or director of the corporation.

SEC. 2. Provides that in case any such corporation neglecting to pay the tax so estimated, after not less than 40 days from receiving such notice, and no appeal shall have been taken, the Auditor-General shall issue his warrant to the sheriff of the county in which the principal office in this State is situated, commanding him to forthwith levy and collect the same, with ten per cent. additional for his own fees, by distress and sale of any property of such company found in this State, and make returns to the State Treasurer within ten days thereafter.

SEC. 3. Provides that the sheriff shall give the usual public notice of sale, by conspicuously posting such notice in three public places ten days previously, within the township, city, or village where the sale is to occur, and that the sale shall be by public auction.

SEC. 4. Provides that if the property so distrained cannot be sold for want of bidders, or is insufficient, the sheriff shall return such fact to the Auditor-General, and the company, still neglecting to pay the tax during 30 days thereafter, shall forfeit its charter and franchises.

SEC. 5. Provides that within 30 days, and not thereafter, from receiving notice of the Auditor-General's estimate, the corporation may appeal therefrom to the circuit court of the county of Ingham, under conditions set forth in this section, and upon a full compliance with which the court shall proceed to the trial of the case, and questions of law therein arising may be carried to the supreme court. In this trial the estimate of the Auditor-General shall be *prima facie* evidence of the amount of specific tax due from the corporation. And if, after filing their appeal, the company fail to notice it for trial during the next two successive terms of the court, said appeal shall upon motion of the Attorney-General be dismissed, and the Auditor-General shall immediately issue his warrant for the taxes, as before set forth in Sec. 2, and no further appeal shall be taken.

SEC. 6. Provides that the Auditor-General, immediately after the first of May, 1872, shall estimate and collect the specific tax, as provided in Sec. 5, from all companies which have heretofore neglected to report the same, and the proceedings shall be the same.

SEC. 7. Provides that the term corporation, as used in this act, shall include all companies having power of corporate bodies.

METALLURGICAL QUALITIES.

APPENDIX J.

I REGRET exceedingly that the following communication from Mr. Tuttle was not received in time for me to have made some of the corrections suggested by him on the Statistical Sheets XII. and XIII. of the Atlas. I can now do no better than to insert his letter, and trust he will excuse such use made of a communication not intended for publication. I state at the bottom of the table of "Metallurgical Qualities of certain L. S. Ores," on Sheet XIII., that it is "quite incomplete," and there give a reason. For any inaccuracies in the statements I am not responsible, as it is carefully compiled from information furnished by consumers. I made every effort to obtain a valuable paper on this subject from practical men who had had large experience in the use of these ores in Ohio and Pennsylvania, but did not succeed for want of money.

CLEVELAND, O., March 14th, 1873.

MAJOR T. B. BROOKS, C. E.,
>> *Museum of Practical Geology,*
>> *Jermyn Street, London.*

DEAR SIR : Yours of 7th inst. received, with the advance sheets of statistics, for which I am obliged. I will make some corrections and suggestions. In the list of Blast Furnaces, Sheet XIII., Neshommock Iron Co. should be *Neshannock ;* Harbaugh, *Mathois* & Owens, should be *Matthias;* Andrews & Hitchcock Hubbard, the word Hubbard is their *location*, and should be in smaller letters In the caption to this list of furnaces, please add Ohio after Cleveland.

On the same Sheet, the "Metallurgical Qualities," as reported by consumers, is *not worth anything*. A *few*, perhaps four to six of them, are substantially correct, the others are not ; as for instance,

" Lafayette Iron Co., Brazil," are under the class of *Washington* ores, whereas we never knew of their having a ton of it; and others are under classes of ores of which they have had but a small proportion of their mixture, say $\frac{1}{4}$ or less. Take the first name on the list, Rawle Noble & Co., who undertake to say $\frac{1}{3}$ Jackson ore with $\frac{2}{3}$ Rossie, Ontario & Champlain made an iron " also for steel," which is absurd. The *bonâ fide* results are, that good assorted red specular alone and also with good magnetic makes good Bessemer steel iron wherever the fuel and flux are also good. Red specular alone is red-short; the granular portion from the magnetic mines is neutral or cold-short slightly ; the specular portion of the magnetic mines is red-short, but not quite as red-short as the old red specular ; a mixture of old red specular and magnetic makes a *better* iron than *either alone*.

I would advise to omit the " Metallurgical Qualities " table entirely, as it will only mislead all who do not know that it is erroneous.

On the other Sheet, in the " Diagram showing the production and percentage of Iron Ore, etc.," against the end of the line which shows the production of 1st-class red specular ore is placed 58 per cent., which belongs opposite the end of the next line above, which is the line of percentage of yield. This *line of percentage of yield*, in order to *fairly* represent the facts, ought to be accompanied by the words, " average of all grades," say as follows : " Average estimated yield of iron from each year's total shipments of all grades of ore." The facts being that the percentage (average) has been let down *more* by the introduction of so many leaner ores than by the letting down of the standard of the mines which first constituted the total amount. The customers of the Lake Superior Iron Co. *say* to us that they cannot see but that ore was as good during 1872 as it had been *any* previous year. This was *not* true, however, of every one of the old mines.

The *left* end of the line of the percentage of yield has no indication of what degree the line starts at.

With these suggestions, I do not see but you have got the tables as near right as they can well be. They afford a large amount of information, and are the results of a vast amount of labor.

As to *Lake freights*, I think the following will be as near as a brief statement can be made : Lake freights, Marquette to Cleveland, have ranged from $2 to $6.50 ; average, about $3.20. Lake freights, Escanaba to Cleveland, have ranged from $1.50 to $5.00 ; average about $2.20.

Shall be pleased to hear from you at any time and do anything I can to aid your work.

Respectfully Yours,

H. B. TUTTLE.

APPENDIX K.

CONTORTIONS OF LAMINÆ.

APPENDIX K.

THE lamination, plication and faulting of the banded ore and jasper ("mixed," or 2d class ore) possess so much interest in connection with the identification of the iron ranges, the location of great folds, and illustrate so beautifully in miniature what seems to have occurred on a grand scale in the whole series of rocks in which they are found, and are withal so beautiful in their contrast of colors and infinity of curves, that a series of carefully drawn sketches will here begin, tracing the contorting and faulting effects from simple parallel straight laminations, as shown in Figure 19, to the true breccia of Fig. 29. The possible bearing of these facts on the origin of some breccias has already received notice in Vol. I., Chap. III., page 89. All the illustrations were obtained from the mixed ore, Formation XII., of the Republic Mountain, except Figures 26 and 27, which are from the Laurentian gneisses of the Gogebic district; in all but these last the dark color represents jasper and the white specular ore. The linear scale varies from $\frac{1}{5}$ to $\frac{1}{20}$ of the original.

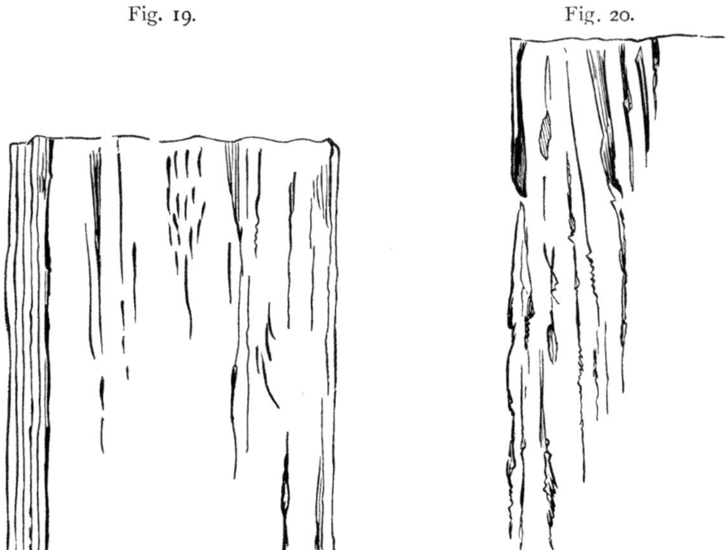

Fig. 19.   Fig. 20.

Figs. 19 and 20 represent uncontorted laminæ, the pure ore greatly predominating; in the latter figure are slight indications of subsequent motion.

In Fig. 21 the laminæ, although still comparatively regular as to their general course, show minor kinks and zig-zags in some of the jasper-laminæ.

Fig. 21.

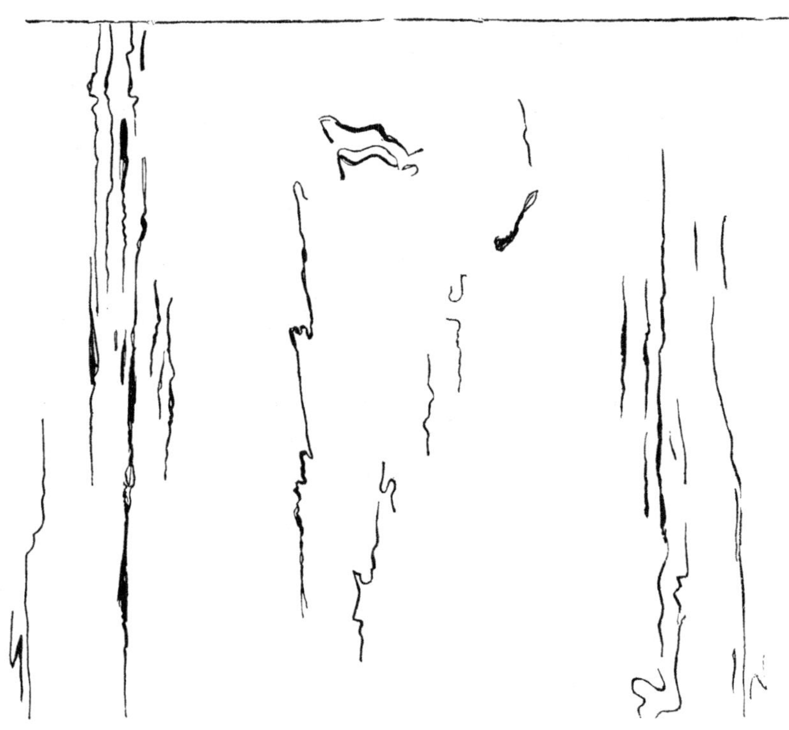

Fig. 22 shows the next stage of progress of bending the layers, together with some variation in their size; a tiny local fault can also be seen.

In Figs. 23 and 24 the process of contorting is carried to such length as to nearly obliterate parallelisms and comparatively uniform size of the laminæ. At *a* in Fig. 23 is a thin lamina of quartz, presenting numerous folds not to be observed in the contiguous and thicker laminæ *c* and *b*. This interesting sketch (scale of one-eighth) was made at 4,600 feet S. E. and 3,700 feet S. W. of the origin of ordinates, Survey of Republic Mountain, Map No. VI.

Fig. 22.

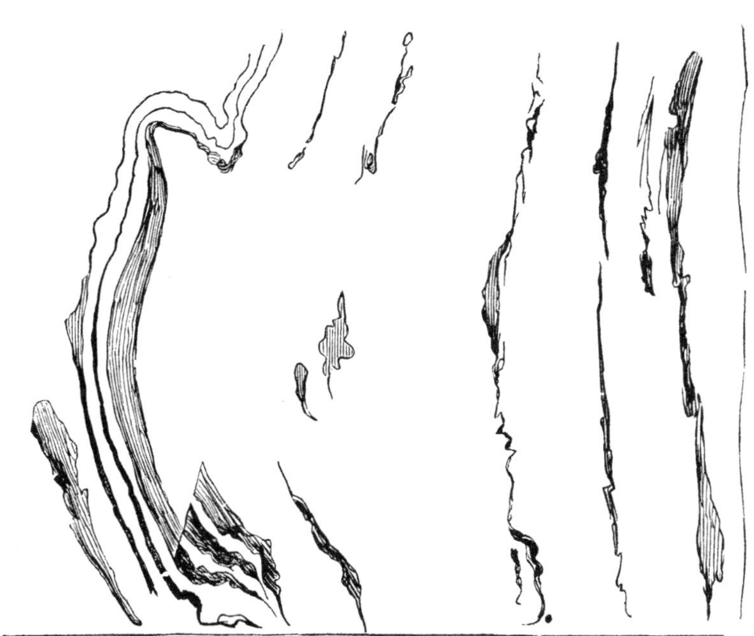

Fig. 23.

Fig. 24.

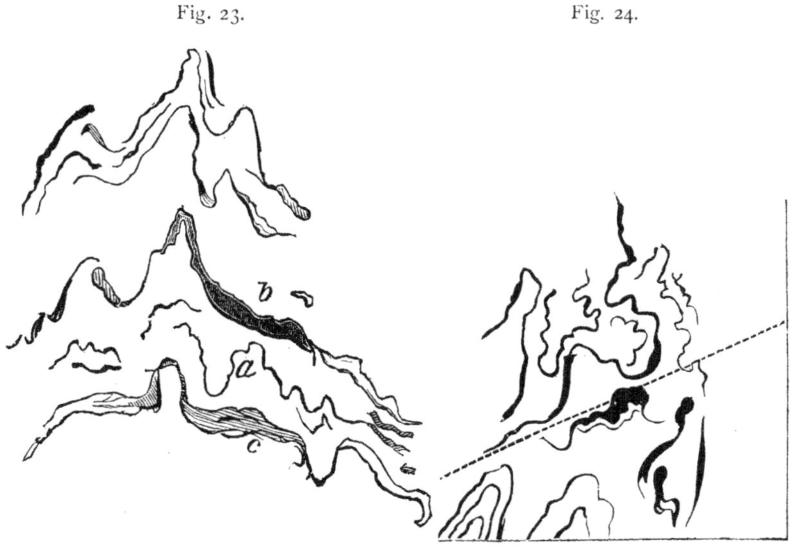

The thick black lamina of Fig. 24 introduces another phase of the metamorphism, which is the semi-faulting shown in Fig. 25, where comparatively regular jasper-laminæ have by a sheering motion been more or less completely separated into lenticular, prismatic and cylinder-shaped masses. If we suppose a similar motion to have taken place on a plane parallel with the surface of the paper, it is evident that the result would be rude spheres and angular breccia-like fragments. Those familiar with the "pinch and shoot" structure of the deposits of magnetic ores of New Jersey and New York (which can also be seen in some of the more extensively

Fig. 25.

worked Marquette mines), must acknowledge that Fig. 25 presents precisely similar phenomena in miniature. The resemblance of this figure to some plans of Swedish iron mines in my possession is very striking.

Fig. 26, sketched in the Laurentian rocks west of Lake Gogebic, presents some interesting minute vein and faulting phenomena.

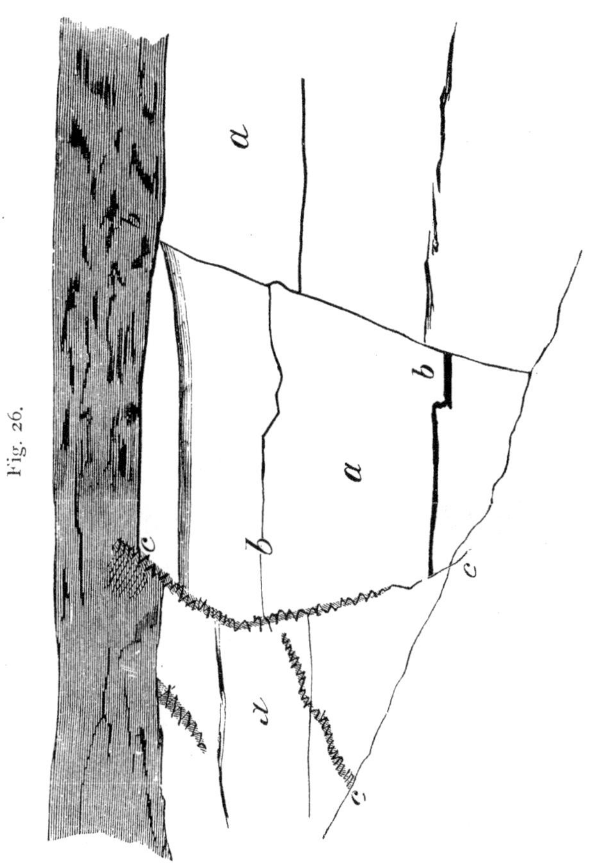

The rock *a* is a hornblendic gneiss ; *b* is made up of thick and thin laminæ of rosy-white orthoclase and coarse-grained quartz ; *c* is still coarser, and of the same composition.

19

Fig. 27 is from the same region as 26, but in it predominates a mineral resembling both chlorite and mica. The dark-colored layers are magnetic iron-ore, which is rare in the Laurentian. This figure shows very beautiful contortions, and a.double system of subsequent faulting. *a, a*, are bunches of segregated gangue. The sketch is one-eighteenth of the original.

Fig. 27.

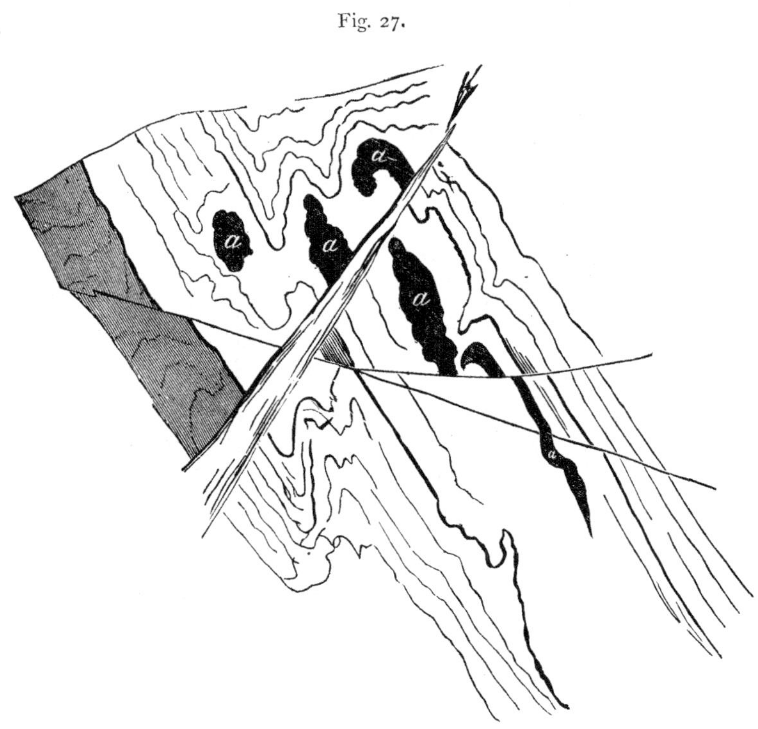

These figures prove conclusively that the same causes were at work in the older rocks, but nothing analogous, so far as I know, has been observed in rocks younger than the Huronian, on the Upper Peninsula.

Fig. 28 was sketched at Republic Mountain, and shows, in order of time—1. Laminæ of jasper, with longitudinal shading. 2. The same laminæ bent, with convexity downward. 3. A vertical vein of quartz, curiously forked in its lower part, cutting both ore and

Fig. 28.

jasper. 4. A horizontal fault, by which the upper half has moved to the right. It may here be observed that quartz veins, except very minute ones, are rare.

Fig. 29, one-tenth of the size of the original, represents (dark) jasper and (white) specular ore, which originally may be supposed to have been arranged in regular alternating parallel layers, but which, owing to subsequent motions and metamorphoses, illustra-

Fig. 29.

ted by this series, is converted into the breccia presented by the figure. This may be regarded as the utmost limit reached by nature in her efforts to obliterate and destroy lamination by means which appear to have been chiefly mechanical.

INDEX.

Printed in Dunstable, United Kingdom